Conversation Analysis and Second Language Pedagogy

Conversation and speaking skills are the key building blocks for much of language learning.

This text increases teachers' awareness about spoken language and suggests ways of applying that knowledge to teaching second language interaction skills based on insights from conversation analysis (CA). Summarizing CA concepts and findings in a heuristic model of interactional practices, it lays out the range of practices that language learners need to master to become interactionally competent.

Conversation Analysis and Second Language Pedagogy

- reviews key CA concepts and findings
- directly connects findings from CA with
- presents a model of interactional prac   ᵢs
- includes numerous transcripts of
- invites readers to complete   ᵢfy and extend their understandings
- features a useful collection of practic   ᵢties.

The time is ripe for a book that blends conversa   analysis and applied linguistics. This text takes that important step, extending the reaches of these once separate academic fields. Assuming neither background knowledge of conversation analysis nor its connection to second language teaching, it is designed for courses in TESOL and applied linguistics and as a resource for experienced teachers, material developers, and language assessment specialists seeking to update their knowledge and hone their craft.

Jean Wong is Associate Professor, The College of New Jersey, Department of Special Education, Language, and Literacy.

Hansun Zhang Waring is Lecturer in Linguistics and Education, Teachers College, Columbia University.

ESL & Applied Linguistics Professional Series
Eli Hinkel, Series Editor

Visit **www.routledge.com/education** for additional information on titles in the ESL & Applied Linguistics Professional Series

Conversation Analysis and Second Language Pedagogy

A Guide for ESL/EFL Teachers

Jean Wong
The College of New Jersey

Hansun Zhang Waring
Teachers College, Columbia University

Routledge
Taylor & Francis Group

NEW YORK AND LONDON

First published 2010
by Routledge
270 Madison Avenue, New York, NY 10016

Simultaneously published in the UK
by Routledge
2 Park Square, Milton Park, Abingdon, Oxon OX14 4RN

Routledge is an imprint of the Taylor & Francis Group, an informa business

© 2010 Taylor & Francis

Typeset in Galliard by RefineCatch Limited, Bungay, Suffolk

Library of Congress Cataloging-in-Publication Data
Wong, Jean.
  Conversation analysis and second language pedagogy : a guide for
  ESL/EFL teachers / Jean Wong, Hansun Zhang Waring.
     p. cm.
  Includes bibliographical references and index.
  1. Second language acquisition.   2. Language and languages.
  3. Language and education.   4. English language—Study and
  teaching—Foreign speakers.   I. Waring, Hansun Zhang.   II. Title.
  P118.2.W66 2010
  428.3'4—dc22   2009044607

ISBN10: 0–415–80636–4 (hbk)
ISBN10: 0–415–80637–2 (pbk)
ISBN10: 0–203–85234–6 (ebk)

ISBN13: 978–0–415–80636–7 (hbk)
ISBN13: 978–0–415–80637–4 (pbk)
ISBN13: 978–0–203–85234–7 (ebk)

JW: For Monica, Nate, and my parents

HW: For Michael and Zoe

Contents

8   Conversation Analysis and Instructional Practices   251

Preface

We met in 2002 at the International Conference of Conversation Analysis in Copenhagen, Denmark. By that time, Jean had already been pursuing the connection between conversation analysis (CA) and language teaching for almost 20 years. As a relative newcomer to CA, Hansun had become thoroughly enamored with its precision, rigor, and immeasurable insights. As language instructors and teacher educators, we were both excited by what CA offers and eager to share with teachers around the world the goldmine of CA findings on language and social interaction. This book is a result of our deep passion for and joint venture in bridging the gap between CA and language teacher education.

Since the mid-1990s, there has been a burgeoning interest in CA, leading to the publication of numerous volumes on the subject. None has, however, tackled the direct application of CA in second language pedagogy. The time is ripe for a book that blends conversation analysis and applied linguistics. It is the next step that extends the reaches of these once separate academic fields, complementing the current tracking of CA for SLA (second language acquisition). We take that next step in writing this volume. Our overall aim is to strengthen teachers' knowledge of language use and to suggest ways of applying that knowledge to teaching second language interaction skills. By encapsulating CA concepts and findings in a heuristic model of interactional practices, we lay out the range of practices for language learners to master in becoming interactionally competent.

Organization of the Book

This book lays out the specific ways in which conversation analysis contributes to enhancing teachers' pedagogical knowledge and instructional practices. To that end, the bulk of the book introduces conversation as a system in its full details. Aside from describing the various interactional practices, each chapter directly engages the reader in considering their pedagogical implication. As the relevance of CA to language teaching is not limited to understanding conversation as a system, we also devote a chapter to CA and instructional practices.

Our book offers these unique features:

- strong synthesis of classic and current conversation analytic work on a wide range of interactional practices
- innovative bridging of conversation analysis and second language pedagogy
- numerous transcripts of actual talk
- lucid and lively presentation
- useful collection of practical teaching activities.

Chapter 1 introduces conversation analysis as a powerful tool to illuminate the structures of conversation and as an exceptional resource for second language pedagogy. A heuristic model of interactional practices is debuted that specifies interactional competence as turn-taking practices, sequencing practices, overall structuring practices, and repair practices.

Chapters 2–7 address each of these practices. Chapter 2 introduces turn-taking practices since the turn is the basic building block of conversation.

Chapters 3 and 4 tackle the next step after getting a turn—doing something with that turn. This is where sequencing practices such as requesting, complimenting, story-telling, and topic management come in. Sequencing practices are divided into basic sequences (Chapter 3) and larger sequences such as topic management and story-telling (Chapter 4).

Chapters 5 and 6 address how sequences can be grouped to play important structuring roles in a conversation. In these chapters we turn to overall structuring practices such as conversation openings and closings. Conversation openings are presented in Chapter 5 and closings are presented in Chapter 6.

Repair, the last component of our model of interactional practices, is taken up in Chapter 7. This chapter details the repair practices that maintain the mutual understanding among participants.

Chapter 8 is devoted to reviewing CA findings on instructional practices in language classrooms and tutorial settings. We focus on new insights from CA concerning routine classroom practices such as pedagogical repair, task design, and the management of participation.

- Each chapter includes pre- and post-reading questions designed to engage and stimulate the readers' thinking of the interactional practices and their connection to language instruction.
- Important concepts are highlighted in boxes and reinforced in the "Key Concepts" section at the end of each chapter.
- Readers are invited to complete a variety of tasks to solidify and extend their understandings: articulating intuitions, evaluating ESL/EFL textbook dialogs, analyzing transcripts, observing own or others' practices, and considering pedagogical ramifications.
- Anecdotes based on our experiences as language learners, language teachers, and teacher trainers are interspersed throughout each chapter to enliven the presentation.
- The application of CA to language instruction is made most salient in the teaching sections near the end of Chapters 2–8. This includes

awareness-raising activities and practicing activities that can be directly used in the ESL/EFL classrooms as well as recommendations for modifying teachers' instructional practices.

• Each chapter ends with a list of suggested readings that allow the reader to further explore the topics presented.

This book is geared towards current and prospective second or foreign language teachers, material developers, and other language professionals. It assumes an audience with neither background knowledge of conversation analysis nor its connection to second language teaching. It may be used as a core or supplementary text in upper-undergraduate and graduate-level courses in TESOL and applied linguistics such as conversation analysis, discourse analysis, sociolinguistics, language pedagogy, or curriculum design. It can also serve as a useful resource for experienced teachers, material developers, and language assessment specialists in updating their knowledge and honing their craft.

So, as we joined each other in exploring the myriad connections between CA and applied linguistics, the two worlds that are very dear to us, we now invite you to come along in this undertaking. We hope the ensuing pages will resonate as much for you as they do for us.

Acknowledgments

This book would not have been possible without the support, advice, and expertise of Eli Hinkel. Her vision, enthusiasm, and detailed comments have helped to shape the book in important ways. We owe her a tremendous debt. We are also fortunate to be surrounded by supportive colleagues, students, and friends. We thank Anne-Marie Barraja-Rohan, Leslie Beebe, Catherine Boxer, Don Carroll, Ashley Cooper, Sarah Creider, Drew Fagan, Naomi Geyer, Greta Gorsuch, Junko Mori, Junko Takahashi, and Verena Verspohl for taking the time to provide careful, detailed, and incisive readings of various chapters of the manuscript. We also thank Monica Link and Craig Gochanour for technical assistance as well as discussions about our model figure. Craig provided us with the visual representation of our heuristic model that is used in the book. We are grateful for the two anonymous reviewers for Routledge who offered excellent suggestions. A very special thank you to students of A&HL 4105 Conversation Analysis (Fall 2008) and A&HT 5377 Speaking Practicum (Summer 2009) at Teachers College, Columbia University, as well as students of ESLM 577 Sociolinguistics (Fall 2008) at The College of New Jersey. Many of their ideas, stories, and critiques have made their way into this book. We are deeply indebted to Naomi Silverman, Senior Editor at Routledge, for her encouragement and support from start to finish. Thank you for having confidence in us. Finally, Meeta Pendharkar as well as the copy editors and production editors at Routledge are owed much gratitude for their efforts in seeing this manuscript through to its publication.

Jean: I thank The College of New Jersey for support of scholarly research grants (SOSA) and a sabbatical leave that made writing this book possible. Co-authoring the book with Hansun Waring was a great pleasure. Her charm, humor, and diligence helped us get through the book. This was our first experience Skyping a book. In connecting with the distant past, I owe much gratitude to Manny Schegloff, who took me on as his student and advisee, beginning at the master's level, even though I was not officially in his department at UCLA. Manny was always encouraging of my interests in connecting CA and applied linguistics. I also remain deeply indebted to Marianne Celce-Murcia and Evelyn Hatch. Their support and mentoring have helped to shape me as an educator and scholar in very significant ways. My teaching debut began when I was 7 years old: I used to teach my mother English (phonics) while she stood ironing other people's shirts in a "Chinese" laundry. "Teach me English," she would say. Little did I know that she would set me on a path for life. Thank you, Mama! And both my parents taught me the value of education. May they rest in peace! Special love and thanks to my daughter Monica and son Nate. Knowing that they were rooting for me ("work hard!", "keep pushing!") was a motivating force. I also had discussions with Monica about the heuristic model figure used in this book; her comments contributed to the final version of the model that we adopted. Over the years, I have also benefited from discussions that I have had about conversation analysis and second language pedagogy with Moya Brennan, Don Carroll, and David Olsher. David and I delivered several joint presentations, and his input has helped to deepen my understanding of conversation analysis and language teaching. I thank Hansun's husband Michael Waring for reading parts of our manuscript and offering his useful comments. I also thank him for doing over-time with childcare and household chores, early-morning and evening shifts after work and "free" weekends for Hansun and me to work! I am also grateful to my sister Susie, Florence, Harry, Karen, Linda, Monica (Shuping), Moya, Serena, Verena, and Yu Shih Yu, who have been supporters in various ways and constant companions through thick and thin. And thanks to Craig for his support and technical skills (design of the model figure used in the book). Last but not least, Charles Chu, my former Chinese professor at Connecticut College, has left me with the impression in indelible ink that learning knows no bounds. The journey continues.

Hansun: I would like to thank Jean for inviting me to join her in pursuing this book project. It was an honor to be asked. I have laughed, learned, and grown so much through this collaboration. I would also like to thank my teachers: Leslie Beebe for showing me the wonders of language, James Purpura for putting me onto the path of CA, and Manny Schegloff and Gene Lerner for the much-needed "boot camp" experience at the Conversation Analysis Advanced Studies Institute (CA ASI 2004) that makes me the analyst I am today. Grandma taught me how to read and write, long before school did. I now read, write, and teach for a living. The news of our book contract came around the same time as the arrival of my daughter Zoe. I would not have made it through the writing days without the unspeakable joy she brings. Zoe took her first steps in the street of New York City a month ago, as I took mine in completing our first book. Thanks also to my parents, who have always taken an interest in my achievements, and to my sister-in-law Patty for taking Zoe out for walks so I could have a few extra hours to Skype with Jean. And finally, to my husband Michael: thank you for always being on my side through life's many projects. I would soon miss having dinner delivered to my desk every night.

Transcription Key

(see Schegloff, 2007 for detailed explanations)

.	(period) falling intonation
?	(question mark) rising intonation
,	(comma) continuing intonation
-	(hyphen) abrupt cut-off
::	(colon(s)) prolonging of sound
<u>word</u>	(underlining) stress
<u>word</u>	the more underlining, the greater the stress
WORD	(all caps) loud speech
°word°	(degree symbols) quiet speech
↑word	(upward arrow) raised pitch
↓word	(downward arrow) lowered pitch
>word<	(more than and less than) quicker speech
<word>	(less than and more than) slowed speech
<	(less than) jump start or rushed start
hh	(series of h's) aspiration or laughter
.hh	(h's preceded by dot) inhalation
(hh)	(h's in parentheses) aspiration or laughter inside word boundaries
[word]	(set of lined-up brackets) beginning and ending of
[word]	simultaneous or overlapping speech
=	(equal sign) latch or continuing speech with no break in between
(0.4)	(number in parentheses) length of a silence in tenths of a second
(.)	(period in parentheses) micro-pause: 0.2 second or less
( )	(empty parentheses) inaudible talk
(word)	(word or phrase in parentheses) transcriptionist doubt
((gazes))	(double parentheses) non-speech activity or transcriptionist comment
$word$	(dollar signs) smiley voice

Chapter 1

Interactional Practices and the Teaching of Conversation

Pre-reading Questions

1. How important are conversational skills in relation to other skills needed in language learning?
2. Think of someone easy to talk with and list 3–5 qualities of his/her way of speaking.
3. Think of someone difficult to communicate with and list 3–5 qualities of his/her way of speaking.
4. If you were asked to teach a conversation class, what would you include in your lesson plans?
5. Imagine that an alien from outer space will be living with you. Give this alien a name. As an extremely considerate, sensitive, and culturally attuned host, think about this alien's total well-being and answer these questions:

    (a) What will you tell the alien about how to interact in English?
    (b) What will you say about the ways in which speakers take turns?
    (c) What will you say about the ways in which speakers open and close conversations?
    (d) What kinds of sample utterances would you give, if any?
    (e) What will you tell the alien about our ways of correcting the talk that we produce in conversation?
    (f) What other aspects of talking and participating in a conversation would you teach your warm and fuzzy friend?
    (g) How will you know whether your alien is ready to interact with other human beings?

Chapter Overview

The importance of conversation as the foundation of all language learning cannot be overstated. As Clark (1996) writes, "face-to-face conversation is the cradle of language use" (p. 9). This chapter begins with a discussion of what is still lacking in the teaching of conversation and introduces conversation analysis (CA) as a unique and innovative tool for achieving this goal. Against the backdrop of communicative competence and interactional competence, a heuristic model of interactional practices is proposed. The model lays out a range of practices for language learners to master in becoming interactionally competent. The chapter ends with an outline of the various chapters that comprise the rest of this volume.

Teaching Conversation

Learning to engage in ordinary conversation is one of the most difficult tasks for second language learners. As Hatch (1978) suggests, one learns how to "do" conversation, and out of conversation syntactic structures develop. In other words, conversation is the medium through which we do language learning. Clearly, then, knowing how to teach conversation is of critical importance for language teachers; this knowledge begins with a solid understanding of what constitutes conversation or **talk-in-interaction**.

> **Talk-in-interaction** refers to differing kinds of talk and their accompanying body language that occur in daily life across settings from casual to institutional contexts. One can have casual conversations in work settings, and vice versa.

Over the past three decades, discourse analysts have made great contributions to our understanding of interaction (e.g., Celce-Murcia & Olshtain, 2000; Hatch, 1992; McCarthy, 1991). In fact, resource books for teachers often emphasize that learners need instruction on features of conversation, and applied linguists have worked to describe those features in relation to pedagogy (Lazaraton, 2001). Thornbury and Slade (2006), for example, discuss the vocabulary, grammar, and discourse features of conversation. However, the descriptions of language or discourse may not yet sufficiently reflect language use. Consider the following from a widely used teacher-training textbook:

> In most oral language, our discourse is marked by exchanges with another person or several persons in which a few sentences spoken by one participant are followed and built upon by sentences spoken by another.
>
> (Brown, 2007, p. 224)

Although the examples that Brown provides in his teacher-training book (not shown here) illustrate that people don't actually talk by stringing sentences together, the general characterization of "sentences spoken" can be misleading (Schegloff, 1979a). As leading conversation analysts Sacks, Schegloff, and Jefferson (1974) have shown early on, the "sentence" is *not* the basic unit of conversation (cf. "real grammar" in Biber & Conrad, 2009; for a much broader definition of grammar, also see Purpura, 2004). Accurate understandings of how conversation works take hours of investigations into minute details of recorded interactions, a hallmark of conversation analysis (CA).

The suggestion that ESL/EFL textbook writers use authentic spoken language data for the design of language instructional materials is gaining increasing prominence (Burns, 1998; Carter & McCarthy, 1997; McCarthy, 1991; Scotton & Bernsten, 1988; Thornbury, 2005). Nonetheless, as Burns (1998) notes, even though communicative language teaching (CLT) has been promoted for a number of years now, there is always room for improvement in terms of instructional materials and teaching techniques. Applied linguists have recognized the contribution of CA over the years with an increasing interest in a merger between the two disciplines (Bowles & Seedhouse, 2007; Richards & Seedhouse, 2005; Schegloff, Koshik, Jacoby, & Olsher, 2002; Seedhouse, 2005a). The nod to CA, however, often lacks sufficient details to be of direct pedagogical usefulness for language teachers. For instance, the importance of turn-taking is frequently mentioned in various teacher training books, but instructors are given minimal, if any, information regarding how the turn-taking system operates. Just as a novelist has the ability to help readers zoom in on an aspect of daily life that they might not have noticed or thought about as important, a CA outlook on talk-in-interaction can help ESL/EFL teachers reach a similar kind of heightened awareness and understanding of oral language.

This book brings the core findings of conversation analysis to language teachers. It provides a comprehensive and systematic introduction to the basic features of conversation. It is designed to invigorate teachers' interest in the structures of interaction. Teachers can translate this awareness into pedagogy, using the suggested teaching activities provided in subsequent chapters as a guide. Our goal is to equip language teachers with a new kind of tool kit for teaching conversation.

> **Author's story (JW):** When I was training to become an ESL teacher at UCLA in the early 1980s, I first learned of conversation analysis (CA) in a discourse analysis course. The professor said, "There's a guy named Schegloff in the sociology department here who does this stuff called CA, which examines the details of conversation." I thought, "Gee, if I'm going to teach English, I should know how conversation works just as I should know how grammar works." So I sashayed across the campus to Schegloff's office. That was how I got into CA.

Conversation Analysis

Each of us engages in talk-in-interaction on a daily basis. Ordinary conversation is the most basic mode of interaction or "primordial site of sociality" (Schegloff, 1986, p. 112). It is the means by which we handle our daily lives and get things done, from mundane matters such as chatting with a friend to critical ones such as planning a wedding, a divorce, a business partnership, and so on.

Conversation analysis is a unique way of analyzing language and social interaction. It originated in sociology in the 1960s with the work of Harvey Sacks, Emanuel Schegloff, and Gail Jefferson. During the course of its forty-year history, CA has spread rapidly beyond the walls of sociology, shaping the work of scholars and practitioners in a variety of disciplines, including but not limited to: applied linguistics, anthropology, psychology, and communication studies.

One of CA's fundamental concerns is: what do people do in order to have a conversation? What are the commonsense practices by which we engage in conversation? Remember the times when someone was angry with you and gave the cold shoulder, not answering your *hello* or *how are you*? No matter how hard you tried, the other party did not say a word. If you think about those cold-shouldered moments in social interaction, you realize that it takes two people to do the talk. What does it mean to keep a conversation going? From a CA perspective, having a conversation is the product of much joint effort (Schegloff, 1997a).

CA researchers analyze actual instances of talk, ranging from casual conversation between friends, acquaintances, co-workers or strangers to talk in more formal settings such as classrooms, doctor–patient consultations, courtroom proceedings, radio talk programs, interviews, and so on. The latter falls within the domain of institutional talk (Drew & Heritage, 1992). Thus, an umbrella term for CA's research object is talk-in-interaction. In what follows, we introduce the principles of CA in three broad categories: (1) collecting data; (2) transcribing data; (3) analyzing data.

Collecting Data

CA requires **naturally occurring data** that has been recorded and transcribed.

> **Naturally occurring data** refers to actual occurrences of talk not gathered from interviewing techniques, observational methods, native intuitions, or experimental methodologies.

Artificial or contrived conversations in experimental settings (e.g., asking two strangers to talk and record their conversation) should not be taken as the representative of what goes on in naturally occurring talk.

The naturally occurring data must be audio- or video-recorded for the following reasons (Pomerantz and Fehr, 1997, p. 70):

(1) certain features are not recoverable in any other way;
(2) playing and replaying facilitates transcribing and developing an analysis;
(3) recording makes it possible to check a particular analysis against the materials;
(4) recording makes it possible to return to an interaction with new analytic interest.

Transcribing Data

The recorded data must be finely transcribed, using CA's transcription system (see complete key at the beginning of this volume). The symbols indicate speakers' pauses, sound stretches, stress, pitch, pace, volume, or the like, as illustrated in Figure 1.1.

Transcriptions are exacting in these minute ways because it is participants who are so exacting in talk-in-interaction. Inbreaths, outbreaths, silence, sound stretches, cut-offs, pitch rises and falls, and so on, are not extraneous elements of ordinary talk. For example, silence carries interactional meaning. If you wait too long before answering someone's invitation, the inviter may think you are not interested.

Analysts transcribe the talk as they hear it, not making any corrections or changes in relation to what speakers actually say (e.g., *gonna* for *going to*). For the sake of visual clarity, we have in subsequent chapters standardized some unconventional spellings in CA transcripts that readers might find distracting, such as *sistuh* for *sister*, *bedder* for *better*, *wz/wuz* for *was*, *t'* for *to*, *thet* for *that*, *yer* for *you're*, etc.

Aside from the above, we have left intact more commonly used spellings of spoken forms such as *gonna, wanna, gotta, cuz, y'know*, etc. Increasingly, we see these spelling forms in newspaper articles, advertising, and daily correspondence at least in American English, for example, an issue of *New York Times Sunday Magazine* had "fuhgitduhaboutit" ("forget about it") on its cover.

Unfortunately, what learners hear outside the classroom may not match the language taught inside the classroom. For instance, if students only learn to articulate greetings such as *How are you?* by fully pronouncing each word, they

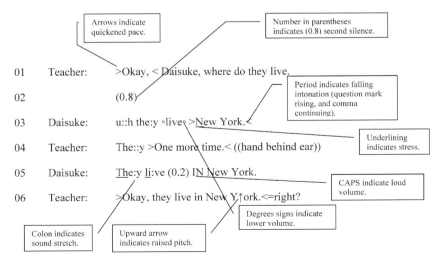

Figure 1.1 Transcription Illustrations.

may not have a clue when they hear *Hawaryuh?*, which many proficient speakers use frequently in face-to-face interaction, on the telephone, on the radio, on the television, and so on. The question of whether to excise all unconventional spellings from language instruction is more complex than meets the eye. Writing the utterance as it is heard helps one to access the very pronunciations that many proficient speakers use on a daily basis. This is the equivalent of using "invented spelling" as a resource for developing literacy skills in first language acquisition (Gambrell, Morrow, & Pressley, 2007).

Reading a CA transcript takes some getting accustomed to. To facilitate the reading of subsequent chapters, we suggest first studying the transcription symbols. They will become increasingly recognizable as one sees them repeated in data extracts. Depending on the level of their students, teachers may decide on whether to use CA transcriptions in their language classes. In fact, CA-type spellings will help learners access the actual sounds of oral language.

Analyzing Data

CA analysts approach the data from an **emic perspective** (Pike, 1967).

Emic perspective is a way of looking at language and social interaction from an "insider's" perspective, i.e., stepping inside the shoes of participants to understand their talk and actions.

What distinguishes CA from other emic approaches (e.g., ethnography of speaking) is that, for CA, the insider's perspective is not obtained by interviewing the speakers, but by uncovering how the participants treat each other's talk in the details of interaction. More specifically, CA's emic procedures are unique in five ways:

(1) unmotivated looking;
(2) repeated listening and viewing;
(3) answering "why that now?";
(4) case-by-case analysis;
(5) deviant case analysis.

First, the analysis begins with unmotivated looking (Psathas, 1995), which involves initially examining the data without a set of hypotheses. In other words, an analyst remains open and curious about any potential discoveries. Unmotivated looking does not exclude having a general area of interest such as turn-taking at the outset of a project. Second, the analysis involves repeated listening and viewing to make initial observations. Third, making observations means writing everything that comes to mind when examining a piece of data in answering the question "Why that now?" (Schegloff & Sacks, 1973, p. 299). That is, why a particular utterance is said in this particular way at this particular moment. Asking this question may seem contradictory to the principle of unmotivated looking, except that it is a question that participants themselves ask. For example, if we hear *It's cold in here*, we need to figure out why someone is saying this at this particular moment: is it a statement, a complaint, or a request? In CA analysis, we would look at whether it is treated by the participants themselves as a statement, a complaint, or a request by examining the details of the interaction, i.e., how the current turn is constructed and what the co-participant makes of it. Fourth, when something of interest emerges that may be a regular interactional practice, the analyst examines other transcripts from other participants, i.e., developing an analysis or building an argument on a case-by-case basis. Finally, cases that do not fit into the general argument are not discarded as outliers but treated with special care (i.e., deviant case analysis) (ten Have, 2007), which may yield three outcomes: (1) the deviant case becomes a basis for reworking the existing argument; (2) the deviant case turns out to fit into the existing argument upon closer analysis; (3) the deviant case is an instance of a different interactional practice.

Interactional Competence and Interactional Practices

As Hymes (1974) writes, "[a] child from whom any and all of the grammatical sentences of a language might come with equal likelihood would be of course a social monster" (p. 75). Essential to one's language development is the ability to communicate functionally and interactively, i.e., communicative competence, the development of which is the goal of **communicative language teaching** (CLT) (Canale & Swain, 1980; Celce-Murcia, 2001).

> **Communicative language teaching (CLT)** is an approach to the teaching of a second or foreign language that emphasizes communication as both the goal and means of learning a language. Within this approach, learners regularly work in pairs and groups, authentic materials and tasks are used, and skills are integrated from the beginning.

In Celce-Murcia's (2007) revised model of communicative competence, she emphasizes the vital but often neglected role of **interactional competence** (see Kasper, 2006a; Young & Miller, 2004; Young, 2008).

> **Interactional competence (IC)** is the ability to use the various interactional resources, such as doing turn-taking or dealing with problems of understanding.

Language learners need to develop interactional competence in conjunction with other components of communicative competence. Conversation analysis offers a wealth of knowledge that can make our understanding of interactional competence more specific, more systematic, and more pedagogically sound. Conversation analysis delivers the stuff that interactional competence is made of, i.e., **interactional practices**.

> **Interactional practices (IP)** are the systematic verbal and nonverbal methods participants use to engage in social interaction.

Just as applied linguists have spoken of language as a system (e.g., phonology, morphology, syntax, semantics, and discourse), various interactional practices combine to form conversation as a system:

(1) Turn-taking practices: Ways of constructing a turn and allocating a turn.
(2) Sequencing practices: Ways of initiating and responding to talk while performing actions such as requesting, inviting, story-telling, or topic initiation.
(3) Overall structuring practices: Ways of organizing a conversation as a whole as in openings and closings.
(4) Repair practices: Ways of addressing problems in speaking, hearing, or understanding of the talk.

These practices can be heuristically represented in a Model of Interactional Practices, as shown in Figure 1.2 below.

Turn-taking practices lie at the base because the turn is the most elementary unit of conversation; two or more turns are connected in sequencing practices to accomplish social actions such as complimenting, complaining, or story-telling; sequences can then be brought together in overall structuring practices to organize a conversation, as in openings and closings; repair practices filter throughout the entire system by targeting problems of speaking, hearing, or understanding of the talk. That you are able to have a conversation with

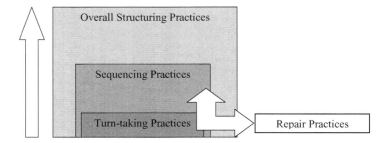

Figure 1.2 Model of Interactional Practices.

someone in the first place is evidence that you know about these interactional practices, although perhaps not at a conscious level, at least not until attention has been directed to them.

Turn-taking Practices

Without turns, there is no social interaction. This is why turn-taking practices appear at the base of our model. A turn is the basic unit of conversation. A fundamental question in conversation is: How do we figure out when to begin talking and when to stop? Do we announce each time we are about to start and stop, for example, saying, "It's my turn now," or "I'm finished, and it's your turn"? Do we speak in the order of our height, weight, age, or time of arrival into the conversation? Why don't we all talk at the same time and crash into each other all the time? How come there usually isn't a long gap of silence between one turn and another? It's almost as if some invisible traffic system were in place, giving us signals for when to go, when to stop, or when it's okay to cruise through the conversation but with caution. Important findings from conversation analysis can help teachers to unveil this traffic system so that they may in turn help second language learners to map out these invisible rules of behavior. (We don't want our second language learners driven nuts!)

Proficient speakers don't need to know these traffic rules, just as they don't need to know grammar to produce perfectly grammatical sentences. But for a second language learner, not knowing the turn-taking system might mean never getting a chance to speak or, at the other end of the spectrum, coming across as an insensitive bully! Knowing how to participate in turn-taking is the single most elemental "driving force" in learning how to "do" conversation. It is the axle in the wheel of social interaction, the main supporting shaft that undergirds interactional competence.

Author's story (HW): As a nonnative speaker of English who came to the United States years ago, I quickly discovered that American education is a system where talk matters, and silence is not golden. Yet, for a very long time, I had trouble getting a word in edgewise. My "ah-hah" moment only arrived upon reading CA's classic turn-taking article. I learned that every turn has its possible completion, there is a way to predict that completion, and there is a very narrow window around that completion where the next person can start speaking. I now sit in weekly faculty meetings projecting my colleagues' turn completion points. The knowledge of turn-taking has not only made me a better listener, but I get to contribute as well!

Sequencing Practices

Getting a turn to talk does not mean people know what to do with that turn, that is, how to use the turn to get things done. Sequencing practices refer to participants' ways of connecting two or more turns, for example, in making and responding to a request, telling a story, or managing a topic. A cursory glance through ESL/EFL textbooks reveals units on giving advice, expressing agreement/disagreement or the like, and applied linguists have come a long way in advocating for authentic materials in language teaching (e.g., Boxer & Pickering, 1995). Despite all good intentions, textbook dialogs are not always an accurate representation of what people say (Wong, 2002, 2007). Part of the problem is that teachers sometimes rely on their intuitions of, for example, how to do an invitation to teach language learners about invitations. However, our intuitions often turn out to be incomplete or even misleading (Bernsten, 2002; Wolfson, 1989). As a result, even with the goal of teaching real language, instructors often do not know how to make that real language teachable because they do not have sufficient understanding of the interactional practices.

Author's story (HW): Before coming to the United States, as an English major in a Chinese university, I took a course called "American Culture." I learned that the appropriate response to compliments is "Thank you." That, of course, is not always true, and it has perhaps made many learners of English sound unduly presumptuous. The rules of compliment responses turn out to be far from simplistic. Anita Pomerantz (1978) found that Americans are in fact torn between expressing self-deprecation and showing agreement. As such, the actual response often involves downgrading the compliment.

Overall Structuring Practices

Overall structuring practices refer to ways of organizing a conversation as a whole, as in openings and closings. Openings and closings are two kinds of segments found in all conversations. These segments are composed of sequences of two or more turns. For example, a telephone closing is regularly composed of a preclosing sequence (e.g., an exchange of *okay, alright,* or the like) and another sequence where speakers exchange *goodbye,* as shown in the example below (Schegloff & Sacks, 1973):

01	A:	O.K.
02	B:	O.K.
03	A:	Bye bye.
04	B:	Bye.

Proficient speakers of a language breeze through these sequences with the greatest of ease. In fact, we probably know some tricks to extend a conversation that is about to close. The phrase *by the way* is one such ploy. When this phrase is used at the end of a conversation, the closing stands vulnerable to opening up, perhaps for longer than someone might wish. Or, if a conversation were to close too abruptly, we might think there is something amiss. Nonetheless, ESL/EFL learners do not necessarily know how to get out of a conversation or how to extend it in a second language. They may not understand that closing a conversation is not always as simple as just saying *goodbye*.

> **Author's story (HW):** In an adult ESL class that I videotaped, a student had just finished giving her presentation in the front of the classroom. Before returning to her seat, she said "bye" to her classmates and they reciprocated with "bye." Since she was only returning to her seat, clearly it was unnecessary and inappropriate to say *goodbye*.

Repair Practices

Repair practices are the various ways of addressing problems in speaking, hearing or understanding of the talk (Schegloff, Jefferson, & Sacks, 1977). The notion of repair includes but is not limited to error correction. The organization of repair is a complex system for doing "maintenance work" that avoids or averts miscommunication. Repair helps us clarify what we say, check our understanding of what another has said, correct something we just said, and so on.

For example, speakers can use *what?* because they did not hear clearly or did not understand what another has just said. As proficient speakers, we usually know how to interpret whether *what?* is targeting a problem of hearing or understanding. However, learners of a second language are not necessarily attuned to these subtleties.

> **Author's story (JW):** Once when my seven-year-old daughter Monica was speaking on the telephone with her grandmother, who was originally from China. I heard Monica repeating *What?* several times, and her grandmother's replies became increasingly louder. Finally, Monica lifted the phone receiver away from her ear and said in exasperation, "Popo [i.e., 'grandmother'], I can hear you. I just can't understand you!"

In sum, conversation analysis has the potential to play a key role in second language teaching (Barraja-Rohan & Pritchard, 1997; Houck & Tatsuki, forthcoming). While trained language teachers are armed with sophisticated knowledge of grammar, phonology, or sociolinguistics, the same level of sophistication is often lacking in their understanding of interactional practices.

Despite the emphasis on speaking as the most difficult and important skill in language learning, existing descriptions of what actually goes into the teaching of speaking can still be impoverished or partial either because they do not reflect the way people talk, or because they do not provide enough details that inform teachers about how spoken language works. Conversation analysis provides a "one of a kind" look into what makes conversation happen. It is a goldmine that we shall tap into in ensuing chapters, making what is otherwise intuitive and elusive explicit, teachable, and enriching for second language teachers and their learners.

Chapter Summary

An important goal of second language teaching is to develop learners' communicative competence, in which interactional competence figures prominently. Conversation analysis is a powerful tool for revealing the various interactional practices that constitute interactional competence: turn-taking, sequencing, overall structuring, and repair. Turn-taking practices are ways of constructing a turn and allocating a turn. Sequencing practices allow us to implement actions with the turns. Overall structuring practices organize a conversation into segments such as openings and closings. Repair practices ensure that participants understand one another. The sum total of these practices is represented in a heuristic model of interactional practices, which are introduced in detail in subsequent chapters. The final chapter focuses on CA insights into instructional practices in the classroom or tutorial settings. Understanding these practices is foundational to enhancing teachers' pedagogical knowledge of teaching conversation.

Key Concepts

- **Communicative language teaching (CLT)**: An approach to the teaching of a second or foreign language that emphasizes communication as both the goal and means of learning a language. Within this approach, learners regularly work in pairs and groups, authentic materials and tasks are used, and skills are integrated from the beginning.
- **Emic perspective**: A way of looking at language and social interaction from an "insider's" perspective, i.e., stepping inside the shoes of participants to understand their talk and actions.
- **Interactional competence (IC)**: The ability to use the various interactional resources, such as doing turn-taking or dealing with problems of understanding.
- **Interactional practices (IP)**: The systematic verbal or nonverbal methods participants use to engage in social interaction.
- **Naturally occurring data**: Actual occurrences of talk not gathered from interviewing techniques, observational methods, native intuitions, or experimental methodologies.

- **Talk-in-interaction:** Differing kinds of talk and their accompanying body language that occur in daily life across settings from casual to institutional contexts. One can have casual conversations in work settings, and vice versa.

Post-reading Questions

1. Having read the chapter, what, if anything, would you change about the way you would teach your resident alien (in the pre-reading question at the beginning of this chapter) so that this new arrival is able to participate in social interaction with ease and not stick out like a novice?
2. Do you have any anecdotes about language learners' misuse, misinterpretation, or misunderstanding of language that resemble the authors' stories in this chapter?
3. What are the features of conversation analysis as a methodology?
4. Why is conversation analysis useful as a resource in second language teaching?
5. What is interactional competence? How is it related to interactional practices?
6. What are the four sets of interactional practices? Give an example of each.
7. Having read the chapter, what questions or ideas do you have regarding the teaching of conversation to second language learners?

Suggested Readings

Barraja-Rohan, A.-M., & Pritchard, C.R. (1997). *Beyond talk: A course in communication and conversation for intermediate adult learners of English*. Melbourne, Australia: Western Melbourne Institute of TAFE (now Victoria University of Technology). http://eslandcateaching.wordpress.com/

Celce-Murcia, M. (2007). Rethinking the role of communicative competence in language teaching. In E. Alcon Soler & M. P. Safont Jorda (Eds.), *The intercultural language use and language learning* (pp. 41–58). Dordrecht: Springer.

Houck, N., & Tatsuki, D. (Eds.) (forthcoming). *Pragmatics from theory to practice*, (Volumes 1 and 2). Alexandria, VA: TESOL Publications.

Kasper, G. (2006). Beyond repair: Conversation analysis as an approach to SLA. *AILA Review, 19*, 83–99.

ten Have, P. (2007). *Doing conversation analysis: A practical guide* (2nd edition). London: Sage.

Young, R. (2008). *Language and interaction: An advanced resource book*. New York: Routledge.

Chapter 2

Turn-taking Practices and Language Teaching

Pre-reading Questions

1. As part of teaching conversation to second language learners, is it necessary to focus on turn-taking practices? Why or why not?
2. If you were to teach turn-taking, what are the three things you would include in your lesson plans?
3. Do you know anyone whose turn-taking behavior frustrates you? If yes, how so?

Chapter Overview

This chapter provides an overview of the turn-taking system. The ability to engage in turn-taking is an essential component of interactional competence. It is an important aspect of conversation techniques, enabling one to start and remain involved in a conversation. It is not by coincidence that turn-taking lies at the center of our model of interactional practices. It is indeed the vehicle for the other practices. Of the many aspects of spoken English, turn-taking is perhaps the least tackled in pedagogical materials and classroom instruction, mostly because it is the least understood. To begin addressing this gap, we introduce a conversation-analytic account of how turn-taking is managed, detailing a wide range of practices for turn construction and turn allocation. Transcripts of naturally occurring talk showcasing real-life turn-taking are used for illustration. Pedagogical relevance of the various turn-taking practices is considered throughout the chapter. We conclude by suggesting ways of teaching turn-taking in conversation.

Turn-taking Practices

As discussed in Chapter 1, **turn-taking** is a key component of interactional practices.

> **Turn-taking practices** refer to way of constructing a turn and allocating a turn.

Without turns, there is no interaction. Learning how to manage turn-taking is the very basis for learning how to communicate in a second language. Our international students frequently remark on the difficulty of knowing when to jump into a conversation. Many opportunities of participation and, by extension, learning are lost because of this difficulty. Moreover, specific practices of turn-taking may vary from culture to culture, and understanding these differences can help learners avoid cross-cultural mishaps. The varying perceptions of silence, for example, lie at the heart of turn-taking. The tendency to minimize silence in conversation is not necessarily shared by all, and those who have developed a comfortable tolerance for silence may never get a word in edgewise. Despite the importance of turn-taking, pedagogical materials that specifically target this skill are difficult to find (Barraja-Rohan & Pritchard, 1997).

> **Author's story (HW):** One of our students in applied linguistics writes this about turn-taking in an online discussion: "I've really struggled with how to teach it. Maybe one of the reasons this is so hard is that I don't quite understand how it works."

The above comment speaks to both the need for teachers to understand the system of turn-taking as well as the need for available resources for teaching turn-taking.

Fortunately, the organization of turn-taking has been well documented in a series of conversation analytic studies, including Sacks et al.'s (1974) groundbreaking paper. According to Sacks et al. (1974), turn-taking in English features one party [speaking] at a time and the minimization of gaps and silences. These two "achievements" are made possible by a system that comprises (1) a turn-constructional component and (2) a turn allocation component (Sacks et al., 1974). The basic unit of a turn is a turn-constructional unit (TCU), and as each TCU unfolds, it comes to a possible completion point (PCP), which may become a place for speaker transition. In what follows, we consider the various practices involved in turn construction and turn allocation.

Turn Construction

Task 1

List three ways in which you know when someone's turn is coming to an end and it is your turn to talk.

1. _____

2. _____

3. _____

We do not speak in sentences. In fact, that President Obama used all complete sentences in a "*60 Minutes*" interview was headlined "*Complete Sentences Stun Nation*" in a 2008 *Huffington Post* article. Speaking in complete sentences is certainly not considered conversation. Conversation has its own grammar (Biber & Conrad, 2009; Schegloff, 1979a). For language teachers, in order to teach conversation, it is essential to understand its basic units, just as one needs to understand the basic constituents of a sentence. We begin by introducing the basic unit of a turn and its variations.

Turn-Constructional Unit (TCU)

The basic unit of a turn is the **turn-constructional unit (TCU)**. These units can be lexical, phrasal, clausal, or sentential (see examples below).

Turn-constructional unit (TCU) is a word, a phrase, a clause, or a sentence that completes a communicative act.

In the following extract, Debbie calls her friend Shelley at the district attorney's office. At line 03, Shelley answers the phone with "district attorney's office," which is a noun phrase that constitutes a phrasal TCU (see complete transcription key at the beginning of the book):

```
(1)  [CA ASI 2004 data—modified]
     01                      ((ring))
     02                      (5.0)
     03   Shelley:   →   district attorney's office.   phrasal TCU
     04   Debbie:    →   Shelley:,                      lexical TCU
     05   Shelley:       Debbie,=
     06   Debbie:    →   ↑what is the dea::l.           sentential TCU
     07   Shelley:       what do you ↑mean.
```

At line 04, Debbie shows recognition of Shelley's voice by saying her name. This single word "Shelley" is a lexical TCU. Debbie's question at line 06 is a sentential TCU. Note that line 05 is also a lexical TCU and line 07 a sentential TCU.

In the next example, Heidi the tutor is helping Lena to organize the various themes in her dissertation chapter into larger categories, one of which is "community." A clausal TCU is indicated at the arrowed turn:

(2)   [Waring tutoring data]
    01   Lena: The school is small.
    02   Heidi: [The size] of the school.
    03   Lena: [°yeah°]
    04   →   **but that I could put into "community" maybe.**
    05   Heidi: yeah.

At line 04, Lena's suggestion of where to place "the size of the school" is a clause that begins with the coordinating conjunction "but," and that constitutes a clausal TCU. Note that line 01 is a sentential TCU and line 02 a phrasal TCU. Lexical TCUs are found at line 03 and line 05.

Task 2

Label the types of TCUs in the transcript below: lexical, phrasal, clausal, or sentential.

(1)   [Lerner, 1991, p. 445—modified]
    01   Dan: when the group reconvenes in two weeks=
    02   Roger: =they're gonna issue strait jackets.

(2)   [Fox, 1999, p. 56-modified]
    01   Ann: D'y know what I mean? Where you=
    02   Beth: =That's like my cousin in Dayton,
    03   (0.7)
    04   Beth: y'know the place where she lives: all
    05   the hou[:ses=
    06   John: [Yeah.
    07   Beth: =there's a certain, number of,
    08   variation [s in pattern.
    09   Don: [Right.

TCUs are the building blocks of turns, but unlike building blocks, each TCU can also be a possibly complete turn. At the end of each TCU is its possible completion point (PCP). The possible completion point can make speaker transition relevant. In other words, PCP is often, though not always, a transition-relevance place (TRP). In story-telling, for example, the telling can contain multiple PCPs with one TRP at its end. Possible completion is not necessarily actual completion. An important feature of TCU is its **projectability**.

> **Projectability** is an essential feature of the turn-constructional unit that allows the recipient to calculate its possible ending.

Why is the notion of TCU projectability important in language teaching? For one thing, in order to take a turn, one has to know when others are about to stop talking. They do not hold up a green flag for you. Without the ability to project TCU completion, one runs the risk of interrupting others or not getting a word in edgewise. Knowing how to project such completion also allows one to place response tokens (e.g., *uh huh, mm hmm, yeah*) at the right moments, thereby facilitating the back-and-forth flow of a natural conversation. The question is: on what bases are we projecting the possible completion of a TCU? It turns out that we use a range of resources (Ford, 2004; Ford & Thompson, 1996; Fox, 1999):

(1) grammar;
(2) intonation;
(3) pragmatics.

A TCU may be grammatically complete, intonationally complete or pragmatically complete (Ford & Thompson, 1996). Note that nonverbal conduct also figures in projecting TCU completion although research in this area remains limited (Goodwin, 1979, 1981; Schegloff, 1984; Streeck, 1993). An utterance is grammatically complete if it could be interpreted as a complete clause in its discourse context. This utterance can be a word or a phrase such as "Juice" or "Orange juice" as a response to "What would you like to drink?" Intonation completion refers to a point at which a rising or falling intonation (as indicated by a period or a question mark) can be clearly heard as a final intonation. An utterance is pragmatically complete when it can be heard as a complete conversational action within its discourse context. All these completions do not need to be present for the TCU to be possibly complete. Consider the following:

(3)   [Schegloff, 2007, p. 270—modified]
      01   Ava: I wanted to know if you got a uh:m
      02   wutchimicawllit [what do you call it] a:: parking
      03   place °this morning.°

In real time, what one hears is successively:

(1) I
(2) I wanted
(3) I wanted to know
(4) I wanted to know if
   . . .
(5) I wanted to know if you got a . . . parking place
(6) I wanted to know if you got a . . . parking place this
(7) I wanted to know if you got a . . . parking place this morning.

As we can see, (1) projects a verb phrase (e.g., "I what?"), (2) projects either a noun phrase (e.g., "wanted what?") or a verb complement (e.g., "wanted to what?"), (3) projects a verb object (e.g., "know what?"), and (4) projects a clause (e.g., "if what?"). We use, first and foremost, our knowledge of grammar in making these projections.

By the end of (5), we have a complete sentence, and thus a possibly complete TCU. Item (5) no longer projects further elements, at least not grammatically. It is also a possibly complete TCU because Ava has by now produced a completed action, i.e., a request for information. The turn-so-far is pragmatically complete. By contrast, in (1)–(4), Ava has not yet produced a completed action. In fact, if Ava were to stop any time after (1)–(4), chances are her listener will wait for her to say more.

Despite the grammatical *and* pragmatic completions in (5), however, Ava's TCU is only *possibly* but not *actually* complete because intonationally, there is no hearable pitch drop on the word "place" (Schegloff, 1996). In (7), by contrast, the added "this morning" ends with a pitch drop as denoted in the period punctuation mark. The end of (7) is a complex transition relevance place (CTRP), where grammatical, intonational, and pragmatic completions of a TCU converge (Ford & Thompson, 1996). CTRP is also where actual turn transitions are most likely to occur.

Understanding what constitutes a TCU can be problematic for nonnative speakers. The following two TCUs are treated by the nonnative speakers as actually complete (Wong, 2004). In Extract (4), Huang is trying to give an English translation for the Chinese name *Shao*. In Extract (5), Tang asks Jim whether he received the release form for the tapes.

(4) [Wong, 2004, p. 117—modified]
    01 Huang: And work <u>hard</u> or: y'know jus- just <u>try</u> (0.2) try ev-
    02   ev- ev- everything by your- do your best way and
    03   then *shao* means uh an::: (0.6) how can I say
    04   y'know I mean uh how can I (1.2) um::
    05   (h)uh (h)uh I cannot- can't say <u>English</u>
    06 Vera: ehuh huh huh huh
    07 Huang: →   **.h that means um mm y'know and s- som- som-**
    08   **something happen <u>now</u> or ss- some- some- some-**
    09   **something will become**
    10   (0.6)
    11 Vera: Uh huh

(5) [Wong, 2004, p. 121—modified]
    01 Tang: Oh d- by the way did you get the tapes?
    02   (0.6)
    03 Jim: Oh yeah I did.
    04 Tang: →   **You di::d and uh did you get the- you know the**
    05   **stuff I sent you like (uh) (a) (.) some relea::se**
    06   (1.4)
    07 Jim   yeah.

Note that in Extract (4) Huang's turn is intonationally complete but not grammatically, and in Extract (5) Tang's turn is grammatically complete but not intonationally (see absence of the punctuation mark after "relea::se"). In other words, more is needed in each case for the TCU to be heard as complete. Not surprisingly, in each case, the native speaker uptake is delayed.

The specific resources for projecting TCU completion (i.e., grammar, intonation, and pragmatics) provide teachers with the necessary background knowledge to design awareness-raising and practicing activities that will help learners engage in turn-taking more efficiently. It is possible that turn projection is better taught to intermediate to advanced learners who already have a certain amount of grammar and vocabulary.

Task 3

Mark the possible completion points in the following transcript. For each such point, specify whether it marks grammatical, intonational, pragmatic, or nonverbal completion. Highlight CTRPs (complex transition-relevance places) if relevant.

[Waring, 2001, pp. 40–41]

01	Prof:	((lines omitted)) I want O:NE point I want people to
02		com<u>mit</u> (.) to <u>o</u>ne thi<u>ng</u> One (.) statement of
03		[some sort.=
04	Libby:	[.hhh =When when we talk
05		about committing to one statement, do we also
06		include (.) preknowledge of genre because if you
07		<u>know</u> that (.) in academic articles like Leki, she's
08		always going to make (.) a research point and a
09		pedagogical implication point. It's kind of part of (.)
10		the genre. Therefore it's not so much one point.= It's
11		it's <u>two</u> points.
12		Two interrelated points. I mean there may be <u>more</u>.
13		I'm not saying it just stops at <u>two</u> but then I say-
14		does- shall I repeat it again or does everybody get
15		me. I'm real lost Do you get me? ((turns to
16		professor))
17	Prof:	I mean- the book that she wrote was research based
18		but ((continues))

Different languages can come with different internal TCU structures. The SVO (subject–verb–object) structure in English has implications for relatively early projectability. By contrast, Japanese carries relatively late projectability due to its SOV structure (although the adverbial preceding the verb such as *completely* can provide preliminary clues to the predicate to come)

(Tanaka, 2001; Thompson & Couper-Kuhlen, 2005). While Modern Greek is characterized by flexible word order, the VSO structure can be seen as the basic word order, which suggests *very* early projectability (Vasilopoulou, 2005). The relationship between language structures and TCU projectability can be viewed on a continuum (see Figure 2.1).

It is important to remember that the varying projectability does not mean that some are less capable of accomplishing precision timing than others. Because of these variable projectabilities, speakers from different languages may orient to turn projection differently. In other words, learning to adjust expectations and practices with regard to projectability would help language learners avert cultural mishaps and fully develop their interactional competence in the second language.

> **Author's story (JW):** A graduate student of mine who teaches an advanced conversation class to adult ESL students writes about her students' turn-taking problems: "One interrupted all of the time until I spoke with her outside of class. One would just start speaking whenever she wanted to."

Compound TCU

Some TCUs are **compound TCUs**, which include a preliminary component and a final component (Lerner, 1991).

> **Compound TCU** is a two-part TCU that includes a preliminary component and a final component.

The compound TCU provides an intra-turn completion point, where a recipient can initiate anticipatory completion, resulting in a collaborative completion sequence (Lerner, 1996, p. 268). Compound TCUs take a number of formats (Lerner, 1991) (see Table 2.1).

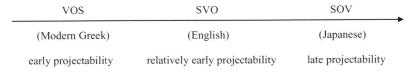

VOS	SVO	SOV
(Modern Greek)	(English)	(Japanese)
early projectability	relatively early projectability	late projectability

Figure 2.1 Projectability in Different Languages.

Table 2.1 Formats of Compound TCU

	Preliminary Component	*Final Component*
Conditional	*if X*	*then Y*
Quotation	*X said*	*Y*
List structure	*items 1, 2*	*item 3*
Disagreement preface	*preface*	*disagreement*

In the extract below, Roger provides the final component that completes the compound TCU initiated by Dan's adverbial clause:

(6) [Lerner, 1991, p. 445—modified]
```
01   Dan:    →   when the group reconvenes in two weeks=
02   Roger:  →   =they're gonna issue strait jackets.
```

Another format for compound TCUs is for the first person to introduce the reported speech and the second to deliver the actual line(s):

(7) [Lerner, 1991, p. 450—modified]
```
01   K:          Instead of my grandmother offering him a drink,
02        →      of beer she'll say
03   L:   →      want a glass of milk?
```

Compound TCUs can also be done in a list structure, where the second person provides the final item of the list:

(8) [Lerner, 1991, p. 448—modified]
```
01  L:   →   first of all they hit rain, then they hit hail,
02  R:   →   and then they hit snow.
```

Finally, compound TCUs can be structured in such a way that the first person projects a disagreement in some way and the second person articulates the disagreement itself. In the following segment, R the father begins by suggesting to his daughter C that she should talk with her parents about the potential problems of a boyfriend, C responds with "Nothing if you're sure," meaning there would be nothing wrong with this person if she knows this is the one:

(9) [Lerner, 1991, p. 449—modified]
```
01   R:         what would be good is to sit down here and tell
02              me (1.0) what is wro:ng (.) if you fi:nd
03              someone that you- (0.2)
04   C:         Nothing if you're sure.
05              (0.3)
06   R:   →     well honey
07              (0.5)
```

| 08 | | | **in this world, really truly, (.)** |
| 09 | C: | → | **you can't be sure.** |

At line 06, the father starts with a disagreement preface "well" (see Chapter 3 on preference structure). He then extends this preface with "in this world, really truly," which hints at a specific way of completing the sentence. At line 09, C provides the completion.

If you have seen the movie *When Harry Met Sally*, picture the scenes where the couple tell stories about themselves, doing so seamlessly by finishing each other's sentences. You can't help but admire the precision, rhythm, and coordination of the conversations. At the more mundane level, they were simply using compound TCUs! The ability to bring off compound TCUs is an artful skill in conversation. Without this skill, learners will remain on the edges of interactional competence.

Task 4

Locate the two components of the compound TCU (i.e., preliminary and final). Are there ways in which these examples can be used in teaching learners about turn-taking practices in ordinary conversation? Share your ideas with others in the class.

(1)		[Lerner, 1991, p. 445—modified]
01	L:	now when he gets his eyes like this and he starts
02		thinking, you know
03	K:	then you have to worry.

(2)		[Lerner, 1991, p. 446—modified]
01	A:	I just wish I were gonna eat a turkey dinner
02		someplace ahh, he, I wish that he'd say, he said, I
03		have to be back around four, because our family is
04		having something and I wish he'd say
05	B:	why don't you come over honey?
06	A:	Yeah.

(3)		[Lerner, 1991, p. 448—modified]
01	J:	Well it's a, it's a mideastern y'know it's-
02		they make it in Greece, Turke::y,
03	B:	Armenia.

(4)		[Lerner, 1991, p. 445—modified]
01	R:	If you bring it in to them,
02	C:	it don't cost you nothing.
03	R:	doesn't cost you anything=
04	C:	=right.

(5)   [Lerner 1986 handout]
01   Mom: If you should decide to live with a fellow,
02   Daughter: Mom will still talk to me.
03   Mom: I'll still talk to you but please take- but please take
04   the pill.

Unfinished TCU

Certain turns are built to be unfinished. Chavalier (2008) details the phenomenon of "unfinished turns" in French conversation. These unfinished turns are receipted without a hitch: the participants display a clear understanding of them (Chavalier, 2008). Creider (2007) describes a similar phenomenon in American English called pragmatically completed unfinished utterances (PCUUs). In the following extract, Serena has been describing her plans for the future, which involves her interest in doing international work, when Natalie asks about her fiancé John. The conversation takes place at the dinner table.

(10)   [Creider, 2007]
       01   Natalie: and what about John?
       02   (2.0)
       03   Serena: John is- loves New York. he wants to stay here. (.)
       04   and- and I think we would I would need to be
       05   [based here.   ]
       06   Natalie: →   [**yeah but you**] **could sti::ll**
       07   (0.5)
       08   Serena: mm hmm. ((smiling and nodding))
       09   (0.5)
       10   Natalie: um: but he's in linguistics too?
       11   Serena: no. not at all.

Natalie's turn has the appearance of being unfinished (see sound stretch in "sti::ll") but is treated as pragmatically complete by Serena as meaning she could still do international work.

Note that the unfinished TCU presents an interesting contrast with the nonnative examples mentioned earlier (Wong, 2004):

(a) ". . . some- some- some- something will become."
(b) ". . . did you get the- (e-) you know the stuff I sent you like (uh) (a) (.) some relea::se

While the unfinished TCU is pragmatically complete, the nonnative speaker turns are left unclear in their meanings. An unfinished TCU can also involve a trail-off, i.e., conjunctionals (*well, but, so, uh*) plus ensuing silences to signal the availability for turn transition. These conjunctionals are delivered in lowered volume and decreased tempo that can begin three or four syllables before (Local & Kelly, 1986, p. 195). The trail-off in the following example consists in a lengthened "ti:me," the conjunctional "so" delivered in lowered volume and decreased speed, and an ensuing (0.2)-second silence:

(11)   [Local & Kelly, 1986, p. 194—modified]
     01   Emma: ((lines omitted)) I couldn't uh: .hh I gotta busy sign
     02   →   all the **ti:me.** °**So:,**° **(0.2)**
     03   Lottie: From he:r?

Trail-off may seem trivial and irrelevant to language learning at first, but understanding how trail-offs work allows one to subtly yield a turn or promptly take a turn.

Task 5

Find instances of trail-off in the following segments: (1) Where does the trail-off begin? (2) What conjunctional is involved? (3) What comes after the trail-off?

(1)   [Local & Kelly, 1986, p. 194—modified]
01   Lottie: Yeh I'll see what she says about it y'know and uh:
02   (.)
03   Emma: ↑Yeah ((continues))

(2)   [Local & Kelly, 1986, p. 194—modified]
01   Emma: So: Katherine and Harry were supposed to come
02   down last night but there was a death in the family
03   so they couldn't come so Bud's asked Bill to play
04   with the company deal so I guess he can play with
05   him ↓so
06   Lottie: Oh:: goo::d.

(3)   [Local & Kelly, 1986, p. 194—modified]
01   Bud: Says he just hadn't been to ba:nk [there.]
02   Emma: [Ya:h.]
03   Bud: .hh Hadn't been up to get his [check to] deposit in
04   the ba:nk
05   Emma   [Ya: h,]
06   Bud: so
07   (0.3)
08   Emma: .hhhh Okay honey well gee tha:nks for calling and
09   I'll SEE YOU TOMOrrow.

Multi-unit Turn

Participants employ a range of techniques to build a **multi-unit turn**: (1) TCU-initial practices; (2) TCU-middle practices; (3) TCU-end practices (Schegloff, 1996).

Multi-unit turn is a conversational turn that consists of more than one TCU.

ESL/EFL learners may have difficulty holding a turn long enough to finish what they are saying. Part of the problem is the expectation that others will wait till you finish. That you only get one TCU at a time and the next speaker can start at the end of your very first TCU comes as a rude awakening for many. Holding a turn beyond its first TCU takes interactional laboring. We detail this laboring below.

TCU-INITIAL PRACTICES

Participants use various ways to mark the just-launched TCU as merely a prelude to subsequent ones:

(1) list initiating marker;
(2) story preface;
(3) pre-pre (preliminaries to preliminaries);
(4) big inbreath.

List initiating marker   One way to secure a multi-unit turn is to specify from the outset with a list initiating marker that the current TCU is only the first in a series (Schegloff, 1982, p. 75). In the following example, Libby's "first of all" at line 01 allows her to make two additional points at lines 03 and 04.

(12)   [Waring seminar data]
```
01   Libby:   →   ((lines omitted)) first of all it's generic that you
02                 kind of (.) cut back up on what you're saying just-
03                 cause >there may be limitations n'
04                 you're supposed to write about them< it's also
05                 defensive because we know very little, he's
06                 protecting himself. A:Nd, also for the
07                 same reason because >he didn't deal with
08                 motivation he didn't deal with all these things< he's
09                 gotta put that out there.
10                 [so]
11   Kelly:    °[in]conclu:sive.°
```

Story preface (Sacks, 1974, 1992b)   Another strategy for building a multi-unit turn is **story preface**.

Story preface is a device by which a prospective teller displays an intention to tell a story and secures a multi-unit turn within which the actual story may be told.

Some examples of story prefaces are (Sacks, 1992b, pp. 227–228):

- *You want to hear a joke?*
- *Something really wonderful happened today.*
- *I have something terrible to tell you.*

Story prefaces can give information about what it will take for the telling to be over. The recipient will have to wait, for example, after hearing "I have something terrible to tell you" for something terrible before responding with "Oh, how terrible!" (see Chapter 4 on story-telling).

Pre-pre   One can also build a multi-unit turn by using a **pre-pre**, i.e., preliminaries to preliminaries (Schegloff, 1980). Imagine that you are about to ask someone a question, but the question itself would not make sense without some background information. But if you give the background information first, you may lose the turn since you only get one TCU at a time. In order to solve this problem, you begin with *Can I ask you a question?* This question is the first preliminary to the second preliminary (i.e., background information) before the actual question. By using the pre-pre of *Can I ask you a question?*, one projects a multi-unit turn that ends with the final delivery of the question.

Pre-pre (preliminaries to preliminaries) is a device by which one announces an upcoming action without producing that action immediately afterwards.

Pre-pre usually takes the format of *Can I X?*, *Let me X*, or the like (Schegloff, 2007, p. 44):

- *Can I ask you a question?*
- *Can I tell you something?*
- *Can I make a suggestion?*
- *Can I ask a favor?*

In the following example, after the pre-pre at line 05, B inserts the background or preliminary information (lines 06, 09, 11) before his/her actual question, i.e., the projected action, at line 13.

```
(13)   [Schegloff, 1980, pp. 107–108—modified]
       01    B:              I've listened to all the things
       02                    that you've said, an' I agree
       03                    with you so much.
       04                    Now,
       05          →         I wanna ask you something,
       06                    I wrote a letter.
       07                    (pause)
       08    A:              Mh hm,
       09    B:              to the governor.
       10    A:              Mh hm::,
       11    B:              telling him what I thought about him!
       12    A:              (Sh:::!)
       13    B:              Will I get an answer d'you think,
       14    A:              Ye:s.
```

The pre-pre projects some action but allows the speaker to insert background information before actually producing that action. This does not mean that the speaker invariably does such insertion, however.

Big inbreath   When someone takes an inbreath, you get the sense that s/he is about to take a turn, and if s/he takes a big inbreath, you know that this is going to be a long turn. A big inbreath is another device for projecting a multi-unit turn. It is a way of signaling that what you have to say simply cannot be confined to a single TCU.

Author's story (JW): This conversation often takes place when my daughter Monica and I are driving in the car:

Jean: ((takes a big inbreath))
Monica: What?
Jean: What do you mean what?
Monica: You were about to say something?
Jean: Oh, never mind. It's not important.

In the following extract, Lena begins her response to Heidi's question with a big inbreath at line 03, as shown in the capitalized ".hhh" (the more 'h's, the bigger the inbreath), and her actual response turns out to be an elaborate account that takes up multiple TCUs:

(14) [Waring tutoring data]
    01 Heidi: Does lear:ning relate to the democratic principles in
    02   any way?
    03 Lena: → .**HHH** well it does in the sense of uhm (0.8) the
    04   intellectual pursuit you know this- this idea of
    05   ha:ving (0.3) an in<u>te</u>lligent <u>bo</u>dy
    06   [of <u>peo</u>ple that will make decisions together.
    07 Heidi: [mm
    08   °okay°
    09 Lena: and that involves <u>in</u>quiry and involves making
    10   de<u>ci</u>sion being able to weigh consequences um
    11   >I'm trying to <u>think</u> cuz-<
    12 Heidi: °Okay°
    13 Lena: <u>that</u>[question r-[ran through my mind[as <u>well</u>.
    14 Heidi: [Yeah   [<u>uh</u>   [<u>uh</u>
    15 Lena: but I thought (.) wasn't- it was <u>in</u>teresting (.) becuz
    16   (0.2) for the <u>chi</u>ldren it was a big ↑category like
    17   things that [connected to the ↑learning=
    18 Heidi: [Okay
    19 Lena: ((continues with 7 more TCUs))

Task 6

Listen for small and big inbreaths in conversations that you engage in
with others or in other people's conversations. Note what comes after
the different-sized inbreaths (e.g., story). Write down the number of
TCUs that follow, if possible. Alternatively, record a conversation and
transcribe it for this task.

TCU-MIDDLE PRACTICES

The middle of a TCU is also a place to mark the in-progress TCU as a prelude
to subsequent ones:

(1) prospective indexicals;
(2) marked first verbs;
(3) contrastive stresses or structures.

Prospective indexicals (Goodwin, 1996)

> **Prospective indexical** is an item whose referent or interpretation is to be discovered in subsequent TCUs.

In the following example, the **prospective indexical** "that" points forward to the next TCU (i.e., "='hh I came to talk to Ruthie about borrowing her:-notes. for (·) econ.").

(15)   [Schegloff, 1996, p. 62—modified]
```
01   Mark:   →   I know what you mean. Me too.<that's why I came
02                here tonight ='hh I came to talk to Ruthie about
03                borrowing her:- notes. for (.) econ.
```

Pronouns in general can work as prospective indexicals, as can phrases such as *a terrible day*.

Marked first verbs   **Marked first verbs** can also be used to foreshadow a subsequent TCU (Jefferson, 2004b; Sacks, 1992b; Schulze-Wenck, 2005).

> **Marked first verb** is the verb or set of words that functions to project multi-unit turns by implying that a second verb or set of words is in the works.

In the following segment, "were supposed to" sets up the expectation that what actually happened would appear in the next TCUs:

(16)   [Schulze-Wenck, 2005, p. 323—modified]
```
01   Emma:   →   So: Katherine and Harris WERE SUPPOSED TO
02                come down last night but there was a death in the
03                family so they couldn't come so Bud's asked Bill to
04                play with the company deal so I guess he can play
05                with him so
06   Lottie:      Oh:: goo::d.
```

Based on a corpus of 11 hours of informal American English, Schulze-Wenck (2005) found the following marked first verbs (p. 322):

- *wanted to*
- *was/were going to*
- *was/were supposed to*
- *thought/was thinking*

- *tried/was trying*
- *could have*
- *should have*

Marked first verbs display the following characteristics (Schulze-Wenck, 2005, p. 325):

(1) they express intention, plan, expectation, attempt, possibility, or obligation;
(2) they have past-time reference;
(3) they are followed by a complement that describes what was intended/ planned/expected/attempted/possible/advisable;
(4) they imply the failure of this event or action.

Vocabulary teaching in the language classroom is typically not tied to interactional concerns such as turn-taking. Incorporating information such as prospective indexicals and marked first verbs into the ESL/EFL curriculum can contribute to fostering an appreciation for the inherent connection between language and interaction.

Contrastive stress or structure   Contrastive stress or structure can also be used to project a multi-unit turn in the middle of a TCU. In the following example, the stress on "he" in "he's not going" sets up the contrast between "he" vs. "his money" in the next TCU. Similarly, "not because" foreshadows "(but) because."

(17)   [CA ASI 2004 data—modified]
```
01   Shelley:   →   So: I mean it's not because he's- he's- I mean it's
02                  not because he:s not going it's becuz (0.5) his
03                  money's not (0.5)
04                  funding me.
```

Task 7

Brainstorm some ideas for teaching the following TCU-middle practices for turn-taking to your ESL/EFL students:

(1) prospective indexicals;
(2) marked first verbs;
(3) contrastive stresses or structures.

TCU-END PRACTICES

Participants also use at least two ways to project a multi-unit turn near the end of a TCU:

(1) pitch-drop withholding;
(2) rush-through.

Pitch-drop withholding   To forestall the hearing of a TCU as complete, one can withhold the pitch drop at the end of the TCU and move directly into the next:

(18)   [Schegloff, 2007, p. 271—modified]
     01   Ava: Eh-yeah so, some of the guys who were <u>be</u>tter
     02   →   y'know went off by **themselves so** it was <u>t</u>wo girls
     03   against this one guy and he's <u>ta</u>:ll. Y'know? [.hh
     04   Bee: [Mh
     05   hm?

At line 02, if Ava were to say "the guys went off by themselves" with a pitch drop on the word "themselves" as indicated by a period, the TCU would have reached grammatical, pragmatic, *and* intonational completion. However, by not using the falling intonation, i.e., withholding the pitch drop on the word "themselves," Ava effectively bypasses the possible completion point. To appreciate the difference made by a pitch drop, try saying "some of the guys went off by themselves" as if it were the only thing you wanted to say. Then try saying the same utterance followed by "so it was," without a break between the two clauses.

Rush-through   Another TCU-end device for building a multi-unit turn is **rush-through** (Schegloff, 1996, p. 93).

> **Rush-through** is a turn-extension practice where one speeds up as s/he approaches a possible completion point, speeding through the juncture without any pitch drop or breath intake, and stopping at a point of "maximal grammatical control" (well) into the next TCU.

In the following segment, George speeds up as he approaches "on this one," goes through the possible completion point thereafter without any pitch drop or breath intake, and stops well into the next TCU.

(19)   [Waring roundtable data]
     01   George: Yea:h well- I- ↑ (I understand that but I actually
     02   →   agree with both Linda and George >**on this**

| 03 | | **one.<=<u>Ima</u>:gine what would happen, if** (.) we |
| 04 | | find out ((continues)) |

The pause after George's "if" at line 03 is a place of maximal grammatical control (e.g., after a preposition but before a noun phrase) (Schegloff, 1996, p. 93). Since the adverbial subordinator "if" strongly predicts an upcoming clause, George's right to the floor is safely preserved.

A related practice is abrupt-join, which involves a speeding up as well as a pitch and volume step-up from the last syllable of the first TCU to the first syllable of the second TCU (Local & Walker, 2004, p. 1388). Abrupt-join appears similar to "left push" or "jump start" as indicated by "<" in CA transcripts (Jefferson, 2004a, p. 29; Schegloff, 2005, pp. 470–475). It may be thought of as a rush-through on a much smaller scale:

(20)   [Local & Walker, 2004, p. 1380—modified]

01	Bee:		eh-you have anybody: that uh: (1.2) I would know
02			from the English department there
03	Ava:		mm-mh I don't think so.
04	Bee:	→	°oh,° **<DID** they get rid of Kuhleznik yet hhh
05	Ava:		no in fact I know somebody who ha:s her [now
06	Bee:		[oh my
07			godhh[hhh
08	Ava:		[yeh and she says you know he remi:nds me
09			of d-hih-ih- she reminds me .hhh of you meaning
10			me: ((continues with talk about Kuhleznik and other
11			teachers))

These devices for building multi-unit turns are particularly relevant in teaching learners the important skill of holding a turn, getting to say what needs to be said, and fending off interruptions. These are undoubtedly interactional problems for native speakers as well, but, as one can imagine, far more pronounced for second language learners. Besides, learners from different L1 backgrounds may utilize distinctly nonnative resources to build multi-unit turns and can thus benefit from the knowledge of appropriate native-like devices to accomplish the same goal. Japanese learners of English, for example, use vowel-marking as a TCU-end device to project multi-unit turns (e.g., "I don't like raining-u") (Carroll, 2005, p. 228). Takahashi (2009) also found that the "*te*-form" of verbs in Japanese is used at the end of a TCU to continue a story or describe a sequence of actions.

Task 8

Are you aware of any other strategies for building multi-unit turns in English besides those discussed above? If so, give examples. Do you know any such strategies in other languages? If so, give examples.

Turn Allocation

As we mentioned in Chapter 1, we do not take turns in conversation based on age, height, or ethnicity. How do we figure out, then, when to start talking and when to stop?

Author's story (HW): One of my graduate students recalls asking her adult ESL class the question "How do you know it's your turn to speak in a conversation?" A Turkish student responded, "I wait till there is a pause."

Waiting till there is a pause can be too late for taking the turn. Not knowing how to bring others into a conversation, take a turn at the right moment, and keep a conversation going can lead to awkward moments to say the least. These are all issues of turn allocation. In order to participate in a conversation, ESL/EFL learners can benefit from an explicit understanding of how turn allocation is managed in conversation, which we detail below.

When a TCU comes to a possible completion, speaker transition may become relevant (Sacks et al., 1974):

1. At a transition-relevance place (TRP), a set of rules apply in quick succession:

    (a) Current-selects-next.
    (b) If not (a), next speaker self-selects.
    (c) If not (b), current speaker continues.

2. Rule 1(a)–1(c) reapplies at each next transition-relevance place.

If the current speaker wants to select the next speaker, s/he is under tremendous pressure to do so before anyone self-selects. By the same token, if anyone wants to self-select, s/he is under tremendous pressure to start early in case the current speaker continues. In fact, self-selectors monitor the unfolding turn very closely and orient to its *possible*, not actual completion. Actual completion may be too late as the current speaker often engages in a variety of practices, as discussed earlier, to go beyond the initial TCU. This notion of monitoring for possible completion in order to take a turn can be particularly problematic for nonnative speakers.

In what follows, we consider the various practices for doing current-selects-next, next-speaker self-selection, and current-speaker-continues (Sacks et al., 1974).

Current-Selects-Next

A number of specific techniques are implemented to accomplish current-selects-next, and they often work in tandem:

(1) address term;
(2) initiating action with gaze;
(3) initiating action that limits potential eligible respondents.

ADDRESS TERM

The most obvious form of current-selects-next technique is address terms or explicit addressing (Lerner, 2003, p. 178). Abundant examples of this type of speaker selection can be found in the language classrooms:

(21) [Waring classroom data]
```
      01   T:          →   >Okay, < Daisuke, where do they live.
      02                   (0.8)
      03   Daisuke:        u::h the:y °live° >New York.<
      04   T:              The:y >One more time.< ((hand behind ear))
```

In ordinary conversations, however, "address terms are far from ubiquitous," and they are used primarily to do more than simply specify the addressee (Lerner 2003, p. 184). More specifically, pre-positioned address terms (e.g., *John, what about X?*) are often used to establish the availability of a recipient where such availability may be problematic, and post-positioned address terms (e.g., *What about X, John?*) are regularly used to demonstrate personal concern or some other stance (Lerner, 2003, pp. 184–187).

INITIATING ACTION WITH GAZE

The current speaker can also select the next by using an initiating action (e.g., a question) along with gaze, which is another form of explicit addressing (Lerner, 2003, p. 178). At lines 05–06 of the following segment, Michael selects Nancy as the next speaker via gaze and the question "Remember the wah- guy we sa:w?"

(22) [Lerner, 2003, p. 179—modified]
```
      01   Nancy:          You see all these (.) cars comin: (0.4) toward you
      02                   with thei[r h e a d l i g h t]s
      03   Vivian:                  [Well- thank Go ] d there weren't that
                           many.
      04   Michael:   →    ((turns to Nancy) Remember the wah- guy we
      05                   sa:w?
      05                   (0.2)
      06   Nancy:          ehh↑(h) Oh(h) he[e Y(h)a(h)a h ha ha ha ↑ha
      07   Michael:                        [huh huh
```

Author's story (HW): After our discussion on turn-taking in class, a student contacted a visually impaired friend who gives sensitivity training classes focusing on the needs of the visually impaired community. She learned that our selection via gaze in ordinary conversation "causes extreme disorientation for the visually impaired." To alleviate this problem, her friend "advises the 'seeing' participant to address the visually impaired member by name or with a light shoulder tap when selecting him/her as next speaker."

INITIATING ACTION THAT LIMITS POTENTIAL ELIGIBLE RESPONDENTS

Sometimes initiating actions appear to work alone (without any gaze) in selecting the next speaker. In the following multi-party interaction, Curt's question "Well how was the races last night" does not seem to be selecting anyone in particular, but since it is known among the participants that Mike is the only one who attended the car races, he is the only legitimate respondent. In other words, Curt's question is not *any* initiating action, but one that limits the potential eligible respondents:

```
(23)  [Lerner, 2003, p. 191—modified]
      01   Curt:   →   Well how was the races last night.
      02               (0.8) ((Mike nods head twice))
      03   Curt:       Who won   [the feature.]
      04   Mike:                 [Al won.    ]
      05               (0.3)
      06   Curt:       [(who)]=
      07   Mike:       [Al.  ]=
      08   Curt:       =Al did?
```

Lerner (2003) refers to this type of current-selects-next technique as tacit addressing (p. 179). It utilizes relevant contextual information to render very specific the addressee of the initiating action.

Next-Speaker Self-Selection

Of the three sets of turn-allocation practices, self-selection is probably the most challenging for language learners.

Task 9

How do you get a turn to talk in a multi-party conversation? List three strategies you use to get the floor:

1. _____

2. _____

3. _____

Author's story (HW): During our online discussion on whether turn-taking is worth teaching, one student wrote: "I remember once tutoring a Japanese woman who was getting her JD at Columbia Law. Her biggest concern was attending seminar classes in which she had all the content knowledge to participate but did not know how to break into the discussion. In retrospect, I think information about and practice with turn-taking strategies might have helped push her turn-taking skills forward."

In what follows, we detail a range of self-selection techniques that might have helped this Japanese lawyer-in-training "break into the discussion." The basic principle for next-speaker-self-selection is to "start as early as possible at the earliest transition-relevance place" (Sacks et al., 1974, p. 719). In order to achieve this early start, a range of practices may be implemented:

(1) overlap;
(2) turn-entry device;
(3) recycled turn beginning;
(4) nonverbal start.

OVERLAP

For early starters, a key question is, how early is not too early? Three types of overlaps are considered "legitimate" or non-intrusive within the turn-taking system: transitional, recognitional, and progressional (Jefferson, 1983). Early self-selections that do not fall into these categories are often treated by the participants as interruptions. Being able to do these overlaps requires close monitoring of the emerging turn, which may be particularly problematic for language learners.

Transitional overlap

Transitional overlap is a type of overlap that orients to the syntactic completeness of an utterance and occurs near a possible completion point.

In the following segment, Bette starts a bit before the very final sound of the word "taxed":

(24)   [Jefferson, 1983, p. 3]
     01   Andrea: The first bit of income isn't tax[ed
     02   Bette: →   [**N**o: th**at**'s right,
     03   **mm:**

Transitional overlap can occur as early as the beginning of the prior speaker's final word:

(25)   [Jefferson, 1983, p. 17—modified]
     01   Helene: <u>Jeff</u> made an asparagus pie it was s::<u>so</u>   [: <u>goo</u>:d.
     02   Tanzi: →   [**I love it.**

In this case, the adverb "so" allows the recipient to hear or anticipate an upcoming assessment adjective.

Recognitional overlap   Through **recognitional overlap**, the self-selector can start even earlier (Jefferson, 1983).

> **Recognitional overlap** is a type of overlap that occurs when a potential next speaker recognizes the thrust or upshot of the prior talk.

In the following segment, Heather begins very early during Steven's turn, that is, as soon as she recognizes where Steven is heading with "A very ha":

(26)   [Jefferson, 1983, p. 18—modified]
     01   Steven: A very ha[ppy New Ye]ar. (to the-)
     02   Heather: →   [**Th**<u>**an**</u>**k you:**] a nd a <u>happy</u> (   ).

In the next example, Sokol begins to reject the "possibility" in recognitional overlap as soon as she hears "is it possible," although her overlapping attempt is aborted soon afterwards:

(27)   [Jefferson, 1983, p. 19—modified]
     01   Bryant: With great res<u>pect</u> to your d<u>ress</u> maker <u>is</u> it
     02   p<u>o</u>ssible   [that the <u>tr</u>]imming she's used to=
     03   Sokol: →   [**No:::** it   ]
     04   = make this dress with is a little <u>vul</u>nerable
     05   to friction.

Progressional overlap   **Progressional overlap** also provides for early starts (Jefferson, 1983).

> **Progressional overlap** is a type of overlap that orients to the forward
> movement/progressivity of an utterance and occurs when that utterance
> begins to show various types of disfluency.

In the following segment, Mrs. M starts at a point where Klugman is having
trouble continuing (see sound stretch and silence filler "uh"), and he is not
anywhere near a possible completion point.

(28) [Jefferson, 1983, p. 22—modified]
      01 Mrs. M.:   Nah I think he was just appa:lled at the turn that
      02   things have taken y'know.
      03 Klugman: Oh yes::. Someti:mes uh[:
      04 Mrs. M.   **[Cuz this . . .**

In the next example, Helen's progressional overlap starts immediately after
Doreen's stutter " "Theh-: the":

(29) [Jefferson 1983-p. 25—modified]
      01 Doreen: No well they fidget. Theh-: the
      02   [y
      03 Helen: →   **[Yes they do.**

Task 10

Decide which types of overlap (transitional, recognitional or progressional) characterize the turns at the arrows.

(1) [Waring tutoring data]
      01 Jeff: ((reading)) learners including ELL- ↑now,
      02   u:::m (0.2) you talked about no child left
      03   behi[:nd,]
      04 Caitlin: →   [>m]hm?<
      05   (0.5)
      06 Jeff: You mention it- but you don't- really explain
      07   what it is.
      08   (0.2)
      09 Caitlin: Okay.
      10   (0.5)
      11 Jeff   S' I think that (.) you nee: d to: (0.5) expand
      12   upon what is no child left behind.
      13   [.hhh >so it's<] legislation that wa:s
      14 Caitlin: →   [o k a: y?   ]

(2)   [Waring tutoring data]
```
01   Priya:         Where are we.
02   Liam:          Ah::m (0.5) >My only< [comment
03   Priya:    →                         [Is it bad?
04                  (1.0)
05   Liam:          W↑ell- what I think you need to focus on (.) is
06                  tighten it up a little bit, there's like a lo:t'v
                    (0.5) >I don't know< how important everything is.
07                  (.)
08                  when you discuss it. ((7 lines omitted))
09   Liam:          [Each one of them has to have- has to be =
10   Priya:    →    [That's-
11   Liam:          = like a building block of what you're sa:ying.
12   Priya:         But that's what- is not th↑e:re.
```

(3)   [Waring, 2007, pp. 384–385]
```
01   Heidi:         >so you say ↑working together an' then give a
02                  couple of quotes of [working together.< an::=
03   Lena:     →                        [°mhm?°
04   Heidi:         =>↑helping each other=a' give a couple of
05                  quotes [of that.<
06   Lena:     →           [Got it.
07   Heidi:         an' then town meeting. >↑whatever.<
08   Lena:          I hear you.
09                  [(              ) community.]
10   Heidi:    →    [so that's your (.) internal organiza]tion.
11                  °(y)eah.°
12   Lena:          ((writing)) °i:nto: (1.0) subthemes
13                  [of (0.8) helping, being together,=
14   Heidi:         [mm
15   Lena:          =that makes sens:::e.°=
16   Heidi:         =That also gives you a- a look of (.) [text,
17   Lena:     →                                          [mhm?
18   Heidi:         text data text data >instead of text ↑boom
19                  boom boom boom boom< a whole bunch of
20                  data .hhh
21                  (1.0)
22                  you're basically
23                  [helping the reade]r to proce[ss.
24   Lena:          [yeah.   yeah.    ]          [>Ye.< I mean
25                  ↑this was my first (.) like shot at it
                    ((continues))
```

TURN-ENTRY DEVICE

Now that we have answered the question of when to make an early start, let us consider the "what" of early starts. One set of items that can be used in doing early starts, also referred to as pre-starts, are **turn-entry devices** (Sacks et al., 1974, p. 719).

> **Turn-entry device** is a turn-initial item such as *well, but, and, so, you know*, or *yeah* which does not project the exact plan of the turn's construction.

Turn-entry devices are unique in that they begin a turn without giving away the precise content of that turn although they can signal a general orientation (e.g., *but* suggesting something contrastive). In other words, they allow early starters to begin without being completely ready. Because of lack of content of turn-entry devices, they also serve to minimize any damage incurred by an overlap. In the following segment, Ellen begins her overlapping turn with the turn-entry device "well" but manages to place her actual turn beginning (i.e., "that's") in the clear.

(30) [Waring seminar data]
```
      01   Tamar:       so that could be related to the oral tradition how you
      02                tell a story not just to how you process the
      03                infor[mation.]
      04   Ellen:   →        [Well    ] that' why it's narrative structure
      05                we're talking about discourse knowledge?
      06   Tamar:       Yeah.
```

Turn-entry devices accomplish "the absorption of overlap with prior turns, without impairing an actual turn's beginning" (Schegloff, 1987a, p. 74).

RECYCLED TURN BEGINNING

Another overlap-absorption technique is **recycled turn beginning** (Schegloff, 1987a, p. 80).

> **Recycled turn beginning** is a practice that involves repeating the part of a turn beginning that gets absorbed in overlap.

Recycled turn beginning can be used to absorb overlap resulting from either the current speaker's continuation or the next speaker's early start. If what gets buried in overlap is substantive, it would warrant repeating, and that is when recycled turn beginnings become useful:

(31)   [Schegloff, 1987a, p. 75]
```
01   R:        Well the uhm in fact they must have grown a
02             culture, you know, they must've- I mean how long-
03             he's been in the hospital for a few days, right? Take
04             a[bout a week to grow a culture]
05   K:   →    [I don't think they grow a    ] I don't
06             think they grow a culture to do a biopsy.
```

The need to teach language learners when and how to start a turn is in part evidenced in Gardner's (2007a) finding on the "broken starts" or "bricolage" of nonnative speakers' turn beginnings:

(32)   [Gardner, 2007a, p. 64—modified]
```
01   Ann:  →   .hhh U:m ↑last wee:k-h (0.5) ↓uhm: (0.8) kh
02             uh ↑there ↓we:re (0.3) ↑three funeral:s; (.)
03             in the church.
```

NONVERBAL START

One can also achieve early starts via a range of pre-beginning nonverbal cues such as gaze direction, head turning, facial expression, lip parting, cough or throat clearing (Schegloff, 1996, pp. 92–93). The use of gestures in self-selection is not unique to the English language. Streeck and Hartge (1992) show that gestures are deployed in a Philippine language not only to display the intent to speak but also to provide "a preview of the type of talk" that is upcoming (p. 139). Based on a corpus of French multidisciplinary work meetings, Mondada (2007) also found that participants used the pointing gesture (at the maps or other documents on the table) as a resource for self-selection. An example from classroom discourse is shown below, where the teacher's nonverbal self-selection well precedes her actual talk:

(33)   [Waring, 2008, p. 582]
```
01   T:            ((looks up at Class)) Nu::mber three::::
02                 Kevin.
03                 (1.0)
04   Kevin:        "Wow. I didn't know (.) you were married."
05                 (0.8)
06                 "Ho:::w lo:ng
07                 have you:::[::::::(.) b : e e n m a r r i e d ." ]=
08   T:    →       [(((slight nod turns into large
09                          encouraging nods)) ]
10                 =$Very good=how long have you been married.$
11                 =Very good. Nu:mber four. Mai,
```

Before we move on to current-speaker-continues techniques, let us point out that self-selectors can find themselves benefiting from two conditions:

(1) second-starter supersession;
(2) last as next bias.

Although "first starter goes" is the general provision, there are cases where the **second starter supersedes** the first and gets the turn. This happens when the second starter targets a problem in understanding the prior utterance (Sacks et al., 1974, p. 720) (also see Chapter 7 on repair).

Second-starter supersession refers to the case where the second starter succeeds in getting the turn by addressing a problem in understanding the prior utterance.

In the segment below, D starts well after K, but because s/he starts with a question, his/her turn gets to be said in the full and gets responded to.

(34)   [Sacks et al., 1974, p. 720]
      01   R: Hey::, the place looks different.
      02   F: Yea::h.
      03   K: Ya have to see all ou[r new-
      04   D: →   **[It does?**
      05   R: Oh yeah.

Thus, second-starter supersession may be strategically invoked by self-selectors to overcome their lateness. A second turn-taking feature that may work to the advantage of the self-selector is the **last as next bias** (Sacks et al., 1974, p. 712).

Last as next bias refers to the turn-order bias that selects the one who spoke before the current speaker as the next speaker in multi-party interactions.

The bias is routinely observed in classroom discourse, where the student who just spoke often has the advantage to speak again next. In the following example, Miyuki capitalizes her status as the last speaker to raise her question at line 08:

(35)   [Waring, 2009, p. 808]
      01   Miyuki: ((completing an exercise)) How long have you been
      02   diving in <u>Ma</u>drid.
      03   Teacher: Ma<u>drid</u>.
      04   (.)
      05   ↓Very g̲ood.

```
06   Miyuki:       ° (syll syll)°-
07   Teacher:      [>°Does anybody°-<          ]
08   Miyuki:    →  [I have one ((raises hand)) ][ques]tion,
09   Teacher:                                  [Yes. ]
```

In other words, in multi-party interaction, whoever just spoke is likely to get the turn to speak again. What this means for self-selection is that those intending to self-select should capitalize on their status as the "last" speaker in achieving their status as the "next."

The range of turn-taking techniques can be eye-opening for even highly advanced nonnative speakers:

Author's story (HW): In response to reading a preliminary draft of this chapter, one graduate student from China writes: "I used to think turn-taking is totally a personality thing." Another from Taiwan writes, "When I first started to learn English, I thought it was the English proficiency part that was giving me a hard time [in turn-taking]."

Current Speaker Continues

While the self-selection techniques give learners the knowledge of when to jump in and how to jump in, the current-speaker-continues techniques are aimed at keeping the conversation going, thereby minimizing gaps and silence (which may be culturally specific). This can be done by:

(1) starting a new TCU;
(2) adding an increment.

STARTING NEW TCU

The first method of current-speaker-continues is starting a new TCU. In the following tutoring example, Liam's first TCU at line 01 is followed by a second new TCU at line 02: "You just have to discover it." Note that this second TCU is launched after Priya bypasses the self-selecting option after Liam's "relationship."

(36) [Waring, 2005a, p. 147]
```
01     Liam:      In m↑y mi:nd there's a re↑lationship.
02        →       You just have to- (0.5) °discover it.°
03     Priya:     What ↑is the relationship.
```

Although Liam ends up producing two TCUs in a row, how he arrives at this multi-unit turn is very different from the speaker-initiated methods of building multi-unit turns discussed earlier (e.g., rush-through) (Schegloff, 1982,

p. 76). In Liam's case, the multi-unit turn "falls into his lap," so to speak, and is in this sense recipient-initiated (Schegloff, 1982, p. 77), i.e., as a result of Priya's failure to self-select.

ADDING AN INCREMENT

The current speaker can also continue by adding an **increment** (Schegloff, 1996, p. 59; Walker, 2007, p. 2218).

> **Increment** refers to a grammatically fitted continuation of an already completed TCU.

Guy's adverbial continuation below in the form of a prepositional phrase "by any chance" is an increment. It becomes the adverbial within the now larger sentence "Have you got X by any chance?"

```
(37)   [Thompson & Couper-Kuhlen, 2005, p. 495-modified]
       01     Guy:          Why don't I: uh (0.6) I'll call uh (.)
       02                   Have you got (.) uh: Seacliff's phone number? h
       03                   (1.1)
       04     Guy:    →     by any chance?
       05                   (0.3)
       06     Jon:          Ye:ah?
```

Increments can take on a variety of syntactic forms such as "[adverbial] NPs, adverbs, adverbial phrases, prepositional phrases, relative clauses, and adverbial clauses" (Ford, Fox & Thompson, 2002, p. 18).

Task 11

Consider the following extract (T=teacher). How does each speaker come to have the turn? (1) Did the prior speaker select him/her? If so, how? (2) Did s/he self-select? If so, what, if anything, in the prior talk might have prompted the self-selection? (3) Did the preceding current speaker continue?

```
[Waring classroom data]
01    T:     U:::hm (1.0) °right so: wha-° so >that leaves us
02           with< one two three a:nd seven.
03           (0.5)
04    T:     I thought number one wasn't too bad.
05           (0.8)—((looks to Mindy))
06           [°right?°          ]
```

07	Mindy	[((looks up to T))]°for me it was the wors(h)t.°
08	T:	Oh yeah? $Okay$ that's funny.=because I- I- >there
09		were- there were some other ones that I thought
10		were really bad.< In fact,
11		((looks to Nancy)) number four was one of the
12		ones °↑I didn't like. °((away from Nancy and
13		down to textbook)) but Nancy said she thought that
14		was ok[ay.
15	Mindy:	[I did- the first one (·) the last.
16	T:	Number one was the worst, $yeah? Okay.
17		a:::hm$ (·) well we- we can come b↑ack to number
18		one I su- ppo:se? >Mindy so what do you
19		recommend then. =what's the next one we should
20		look at.<

As can be seen, turn allocation alone engages a complex set of interactional resources. Knowing what to do as a turn approaches its completion is integral to one's interactional competence. Language learners can, for example, benefit from the rich array of self-selection techniques to overcome the difficulty of getting a word in edgewise.

Teaching Turn-taking Practices

As the core component in our model of interactional practices, turn-taking practices are indispensable tools for participating in the very task of language learning. To render the turn-taking system teachable, we first need to prioritize what to learn from its vast array of complexities. Although a comprehensive understanding of how the system works should constitute the foundational knowledge of the language teacher, not every element of the system presents equal challenges to every language learner. Carroll (2004), for example, showed that Japanese novice speakers of English used recycled turn beginnings and increments in ways similar to those of native speakers of English. It might be more expedient, then, to focus on those practices that are of particular importance to language learners, such as getting a turn and holding a turn, which involve the ability to (a) project turn completions, (b) self-select, and (c) build multi-unit turns.

Projecting Turn Completion

Awareness-raising Activity: *When does a Turn End?*

(1) Brainstorm answers to the following question (in learners' native languages if necessary): How do you know someone is about to stop speaking?

(2) Pick an actual turn from a CA transcript such as "I wanted to know if

you got a uh:mwutchimicawllit [what do you call it] a:: parking place °this morning.°" See Schegloff (2007) for a complete transcript of the "Ava and Bee" conversation, as well as its online sound file. The transcript may be modified to facilitate reading for learners. Gradually reveal the turn word by word from left to right. The same can be done with an actual recording (e.g., excerpt from a TV show, your answering machine messages, etc.), where you stop after each word. With each revelation, ask: (a) Is s/he about to stop? (b) How do you know? Introduce the concept of *possible* completion point, and as the exercise unfolds, discuss grammatical, intonational, pragmatic, and nonverbal completions.

(3) Identify the possible completion points in the dialog below (Schegloff, 2007—modified). Explain that in the transcript a period indicates falling intonation, a question mark indicates rising intonation, and a comma indicates continuing intonation.

01	Ava:	You know half the group that we had last term was
02		there and we were just playing around.
03	Bee:	Uh fooling around.
04	Ava:	Eh yeah so, some of the guys who were better you
05		know went off by themselves so it was two girls
06		against this one guy and he's tall you know?
07	Bee:	Mm hm?
08	Ava:	And, I had I was I couldn't stop laughing it was the
09		funniest thing but you know you get all sweaty up
10		and everything we didn't think we were gonna play,
11		hh and oh I'm knocked out.

(4) Ask learners whether the same resources for projecting turn completions apply to their native languages. Discuss potential cross-cultural variations.

Variation

The teacher starts a turn on the board with one word (e.g., "The"), and the students provide the next possible word. Guessing each successive word continues until the class decides they have finished the turn. Throughout the process, ask on what bases they are making their predictions. Introduce grammatical, intonational, and pragmatic completions if necessary.

Practicing Activity: *Monitoring Turn Completion* (adapted from Carroll, forthcoming)

(1) Put each answer below on a separate index card. If you have 10 students, make two sets of cards so that two students will have the same answer card.

Q: How was your weekend?	A: Great. Thanks.
Q: What did you do?	A: Oh, I went to a party.
Q: Who did you go with?	A: I'm not telling.
Q: Where was the party?	A: Nowhere.
Q: Why are you being so secretive?	A: It's just the way I am.
Q: How long have you been this way?	A: Forever.
Q: Has it really always been this way?	A: I think so.
Q: Why can't you lift this box again?	A: Well, I'm pregnant.
Q: When did that happen?	A: Yesterday.
Q: Do you have any idea what it means?	A: Not really.

(2) Have students stand up and be ready to respond to the teacher's questions with the utterances on their cards. The teacher reads the questions one by one. The students closely monitor the unfolding question in order to deliver their answers as early as possible. Whoever delivers the earliest appropriate answer for any particular question sits down. (Note that some of the answers can be fitted to more than one question). The game continues until everyone sits down.

Variation

The difficulty level may be decreased or increased by adjusting the content and length of the conversation. To lower the difficulty level, one can make the conversation shorter, slow down the delivery, use simpler vocabulary, or limit the questions to one type (e.g. yes/no, *what, when,* or *where*). To raise the difficulty level, one can make the conversation longer, use more complex questions, speed up the delivery, or give each student more than one card to choose from as their potential responses.

Self-Selection

Awareness-raising Activity: *Early Start*

(1) Brainstorm answers to the following questions: (a) Is it okay to start talking before the other is finished? (b) If yes, how early can one start? How early is not too early?

(2) Have students consider the following three exchanges adapted from Jefferson (1983). Can the speakers at the arrowed turns start any earlier? If yes, where?

(a)
01 Andrea: The first bit of income isn't taxed.
02 Bette: → No that's right, mm

(b)
01 Helene: Jeff made an asparagus pie it was so good.
02 Tanzi: → I love it.

(c)
01 Steven: A very happy New Year to you.
02 Heather: → Thank you and a happy New Year to you too.

(3) Show the actual transcripts below. Explain that the brackets mark where simultaneous talk (i.e., overlap) begins and ends. Establish the understanding that a self-selector can start *before* the end of other's turn as soon as s/he recognizes what the other is about to say. This is not considered inappropriate in English.

(aa)
01 Andrea: The first bit of income isn't tax[ed.
02 Bette: →   [**No that's**
03   **right, mm**

(bb)
01 Helene: Jeff made an asparagus pie it was so [**good.**
02 Tanzi: →   [**I love**
03   **it.**

(cc)
01 Steven: A very ha[ppy New Year to you.]
02 Heather: →   [**Thank you and a ha**]**ppy New**
03   **Year to you too.**

(4) Discuss cross-cultural variations in self-selection techniques if relevant.
(5) Assign as homework the task to collect two examples of overlap talk in English conversations from daily life or radio/television programs. Indicate exactly where the overlap begins.

Practicing Activity: *Precision Timing* (Carroll, 2005)

(1) Self-selection needs to be precisely timed to disallow any uncomfortable silence between the turns. Have learners form a circle and count off from one to ten. Practice until the counting is smooth and sounds as if only one person were counting. Build up the speed. This will sensitize learners to the need to minimize gaps between turns in English.
(2) Have groups of three stand around a desk and take turns picking up and putting down a ball, which symbolizes a conversation turn. Tell them that the time the ball is on the desk, like silence in conversation,

is to be minimized. They are likely to begin by taking "ordered" turns in a circular fashion. Ask them if this is how actual conversation works. They will notice or realize that it is not.

(3) Have learners take turns again, but now compete for the turns without going around in an orderly fashion. As they become more "fluent," build up the speed.

(4) Once the nonverbal simulations are completed, learners may start talking for real. With beginning-level learners, we may experiment with simple "conversations" such as "I like pizza," "I like sushi," "I like hamburgers," etc.

Variations

(i) For intermediate to advanced learners, role-play the exchanges in (3) under "Awareness Raising Activity: Early Start" above. The goal is for the second speaker to practice starting at the earliest possible moment. Use additional transcripts from the chapter as necessary.

(ii) For intermediate to advanced learners, practice in pairs the following exchanges adapted from Lerner (1991). The goal is to finish each other's sentences without any gap in between. The students can also come up with their own exchanges.

(a)
01   A: If you bring it in to them,
02   B: it doesn't cost you anything.

(b)
01   A: So if one person said he couldn't invest,
02   B: I'd have to wait.

(c)
01   A: When the group reconvenes in two weeks,
02   B: they're gonna get tough.

(d)
01   A: If you don't put things on your calendar,
02   B: you're out of luck.

(e)
01   A: When he gets his eyes like this and he starts
02   thinking,
03   B: then you get to worry.

Building Multi-Unit Turns

Awareness-raising Activity: *Preliminaries to Preliminaries*

(1) Brainstorm answers to the following questions (in learners' native languages if necessary): (a) How long do you get to talk once you get a turn? (b) What do you have to do to get a long turn to talk?

(2) Ask learners to look at the radio talk show excerpt below adapted from Schegloff (1980). B is the caller, and A the radio host.

```
01   B:   I've listened to all the things that you've
02        said, and I agree with you so much.
03        Now,
04        I want to ask you something,
05        I wrote a letter.
06        (pause)
07   A:   Mh hm,
08   B:   to the governor.
09   A:   Mh hm,
10   B:   telling him what I thought about him!
11        Will I get an answer do you think,
12   A:   Yes.
```

Pose the following questions:

(a) What is B calling about?
(b) What question does B ask the talk show host?
(c) When (at which line) does B let A know s/he has a question to ask? When does s/he actually ask the question? How come s/he does not ask the question earlier?

(3) Explain that English speakers use utterances such as *I want to ask you something* as a way to get the floor for an extended period of time.

This practice allows the speaker to provide background information before, for example, asking the question or making the suggestion. Elicit from learners other examples of this type of utterances (see "Pre-pre" section in the chapter).

(4) Ask learners whether they use similar or different strategies or utterances in their native languages.

(5) Assign as homework the task to bring in two examples of these preliminary utterances from daily conversation or the media.

Practicing Activity: *Rush-through*

(1) The following is a sample exchange from a sales call. The salesperson A would try to say as much as possible before B hangs up.

A: Hi, My name is <u>Darcy. I'm calling from ZMW Insurance. I'd</u> like to ask you a few questions.
B: I'm sorry I'm on another line.((hangs up))

Make two sets of index cards. Set A should have A's turn written on them, and Set B should have B's turn. Include the following instructions on the reverse sides of the cards:

Set A:
>   Try to say your lines in one turn by speeding up at the underlined portion.

Set B:
>   Try to deliver your lines as early as possible without interrupting the other person.

(2) Divide the class into Group A and Group B. Group A receives Set A and Group B Set B. Members of Group A should talk to all members of Group B. Each Group A member should receive one point for completing the turn each time, and each Group B member should receive one point for not letting the other complete the turn each time. After all members of Group A have spoken to all members of Group B, add up the individual scores for each group to determine the group winner.

(3) Switch groups and repeat the same activities as needed; between each round reflect on the strategies as a whole class.

Chapter Summary

Turn-taking practices lie at the core of our model of interactional practices. Despite its importance, the topic of turn-taking in pedagogical materials or classroom instruction is difficult to find. This may be due to a general lack of understanding of how turn-taking works. The turn-taking system is comprised of a turn construction component and a turn allocation component. The basic unit of a turn is a turn-constructional unit (TCU), and as each TCU unfolds, it comes to a possible completion point (PCP), which may become a place for speaker transition. TCUs can also be compound or unfinished. The resources for projecting their possible completions are grammar, intonation, pragmatics, or nonverbal conduct. A wide range of devices are used to build multi-unit turns. Turn allocation is implemented in three successive procedures: current-selects-next, next-speaker-self-selection, and current-speaker-continues. Each procedure engages a variety of practices. For the language teacher, understanding these complexities constitutes a first step towards helping learners master the basic skill of managing turn-taking. Pedagogical decisions on what to teach or how to teach should be tailored to specific learner populations. Specific activities may be designed to teach learners the skills to project turn completions, do self-selections, and extend their turns. Our suggestions are meant to provide an initial template from which additional or alternative pedagogical visions may be generated.

Key Concepts

- **Compound TCU:** A two-part TCU that includes a preliminary component and a final component.
- **Increment:** A grammatically fitted continuation of an already completed TCU.

- **Last as next bias:** The turn-order bias that selects the one who spoke before the current speaker as the next speaker in multi-party interactions.
- **Marked first verb:** The verb or set of words that functions to project multi-unit turns by implying that a second verb or set of words is in the works.
- **Multi-unit turn:** A conversational turn that consists of more than one TCU.
- **Pre-pre (preliminaries to preliminaries):** A device by which one announces an upcoming action without producing that action immediately afterwards.
- **Progressional overlap:** A type of overlap that orients to the forward movement/progressivity of an utterance and occurs when that utterance begins to show various types of disfluency.
- **Projectability:** An essential feature of the turn-constructional unit that allows the recipient to calculate its possible ending.
- **Prospective indexical:** An item whose referent or interpretation is to be discovered in subsequent TCUs.
- **Recognitional overlap:** A type of overlap that occurs when a potential next speaker recognizes the thrust or upshot of the prior talk.
- **Recycled turn beginning:** A practice that involves repeating the part of a turn beginning that gets absorbed in overlap.
- **Rush-through:** A turn-extension practice where one speeds up as s/he approaches a possible completion point, speeds through the juncture without any pitch drop or breath intake, and stops instead at a point of "maximal grammatical control" (well) into the next TCU.
- **Second-starter supersession:** The case where the second starter succeeds in getting the turn by addressing a problem in understanding the prior utterance.
- **Story preface:** A device by which a prospective teller displays an intention to tell a story and secures a multi-unit turn within which the actual story may be told.
- **Transitional overlap:** A type of overlap that orients to the syntactic completeness of an utterance and occurs near a possible completion point.
- **Turn-constructional unit (TCU):** A word, a phrase, a clause, or a sentence that completes a communicative act.
- **Turn-entry device:** A turn-initial item such as *well, but, and, so, you know*, or *yeah* which does not project the exact plan of the turn's construction.
- **Turn-taking practices:** Way of constructing a turn and allocating a turn.

Post-reading Questions

1. What is the basic unit of a turn? What resources are used for projecting the possible completion of a turn?
2. What are the devices for building multi-unit turns?
3. What is the set of procedures for turn allocation? What practices are available for implementing each procedure?

4. How has the content presented in this chapter changed your understanding of turn-taking in conversation?
5. Select one of the suggested readings listed below and present the article in class, summarizing the article's key points and offering your questions and concerns. Consider how the points raised in the article might be related to issues in language teaching.
6. What other ways of teaching turn-taking can you think of?
7. Having read the chapter, what questions or concerns do you still have about turn-taking?

Suggested Readings

Carroll, D. (2004). Restarts in novice turn beginnings: Disfluencies or interactional achievements? In R. Gardner & J. Wagner (Eds.), *Second language conversations* (pp. 201–220). London: Continuum.

Ford, C. E., & Thompson, S. A. (1996). Interactional units in conversation: Syntactic, intonational, and pragmatic resources for the management of turns. In E. Ochs, E. A. Schegloff, & S. A. Thompson (Eds.), *Interaction and grammar* (pp. 135–184). Cambridge: Cambridge University Press.

Gardner, R. (2007a). Broken starts: Bricolage in turn starts in second language talk. In Z. Hua, P. Seedhouse, L. Wei, & V. Cook (Eds.), *Language learning and teaching as social inter-action* (pp. 58–71). London: Palgrave.

Lerner, G. H. (2003). Selecting next speaker: The context-sensitive operation of a context-free organization. *Language in Society, 32*(2), 177–201.

Sacks, H., Schegloff, E. A., & Jefferson, G. (1974). A simplest systematics for the organization of turn-taking in conversation. *Language, 50*(4), 696–735.

Schegloff, E. A. (1996). Turn organization: One intersection of grammar and interaction. In E. Ochs, E. A. Schegloff, & S. A. Thompson (Eds.), *Interaction and grammar* (pp. 52–133). Cambridge: Cambridge University Press.

Tanaka, H. (2001). Adverbials for turn projection in Japanese: Toward a demystification of the "telepathic" mode of communication. *Language in Society, 30*(4), 559–587.

Wong, J. (2004). Some preliminary thoughts on delay as an interactional resource. In R. Gardner & J. Wagner (Eds.), *Second language conversations* (pp. 114–131). London: Continuum.

Chapter 3

Sequencing Practices and Language Teaching I

Basic Sequences

Pre-reading Questions

1. What are some routine tasks (e.g., request, apology, compliment, etc.) that second language learners need to perform as members of the target speech community?
2. What are some problems that ESL/EFL learners face in getting the routine tasks done in English?
3. How authentic are the textbook materials on teaching learners how to request or engage in any other activity in English?
4. If you were to design a course in speaking, what real-life tasks would you envision that your learners would need to accomplish with the newly acquired speaking skills?

Chapter Overview

This and the next chapter provide an overview of sequencing practices. In this chapter, we offer a conversation analytic account of how participants manage to foreshadow, initiate, respond to, and expand upon their own and others' talk while conducting a wide range of social actions such as announcing, complaining, complimenting, inviting, offering, and rejecting. How to do these social actions has been a consistent focus of ESL/EFL materials and classroom instruction for quite some time now. With a focus on the microanalyses of actual talk, CA findings can help to invigorate teachers' interest in achieving a nuanced sense of language and social interaction. In turn, teachers can offer learners a more specific, more situated, and more complex picture of how sequencing works. Transcripts of naturally occurring talk showcasing real-life sequencing practices are used for illustration. The pedagogical relevance of the various sequencing practices is considered throughout the chapter. We provide a range of awareness-raising and practicing activities for teaching sequencing at the end of the chapter.

Sequencing Practices

As discussed in Chapter 1, **sequencing practices** constitute another key component in our model of interactional practices.

> **Sequencing practices** are ways of initiating and responding to talk while performing actions such as requesting, inviting, story-telling or topic initiation.

In this chapter, we focus on the basic sequences within sequencing practices.

While turn-taking practices provide the essential platform for interaction, knowing how to get a turn and construct a turn is only the first step towards full participation in the target speech community. One still has to know what to do with the turn at hand. One has to know what actions to perform and how. Sequencing practices are the resources with which social actions such as announcing, inviting, complimenting, complaining, agreeing, or disagreeing are implemented and responded to, and mastering these resources is a central goal of ESL/EFL learners.

> **Author's story (JW):** One of my students from Turkey writes about her traumas of being shuffled from a canceled flight to a bus upon her first arrival in the United States: "I was still crying on the bus. The person next to me handed me a tissue. When I thanked him, he said, 'You're welcome.' I wondered why he was welcoming me until I heard others on the bus use the same expression in response to 'Thanks.' In Turkey, I was taught to say 'Not at all.' "

The practices of sequencing lie at the heart of Communicative Language Teaching (CLT) (Savignon, 2001). An important contribution to CLT has come from researchers in cross-cultural and interlanguage pragmatics, who showed how speech acts such as apologies, complaints, refusals, requests, compliments, and compliment responses are performed by native and non-native speakers of English (e.g., Beebe, Takahashi, & Uliss-Weltz, 1990; Blum-Kulka, House, & Kasper, 1989; Boxer, 1996; Gass & Neu, 1999; Herbert, 1989, 1990; Kasper & Blum-Kulka, 1993; Trosborg, 1995). More recently, Kasper (2006b) has argued for a "discursive pragmatics" that studies speech acts from a conversation analytic perspective. Using CA-based materials to teach pragmatics can provide students with empirically researched rather than intuitively generated information, raise their awareness of pragmatic transfer, enhance their ability to understand and produce relevant next turns, and ultimately, help them prevent cross-cultural miscommunications (Huth, 2006, pp. 2045–2046; Huth & Taleghani-Nikazm, 2006). In what follows, we show what discursive pragmatics might look like by describing how sequencing is done in interaction. We organize our account by (1) generic sequencing practices (i.e., adjacency pairs and preference organization); (2) type-specific sequencing practices (e.g., requests); (3) response tokens.

Generic Sequencing Practices

Generic sequencing practices are the practices that underpin all other type-specific sequences such as requests or offers. In this section, we introduce two concepts central to these generic practices: (1) adjacency pair; (2) preference.

Adjacency Pair

Just like a basic building block of a turn is a TCU (turn-constructional unit), a basic building block of a sequence is an **adjacency pair**. In the following extract, lines 01–02 are one adjacency pair, and lines 03–04 another (see complete transcription key at the beginning of this book):

(1)   [CA ASI 2004 data]
01   ((ring))
02   Nancy: H'llo:?
03   Hyla: Hi:,
04   Nancy: ↑HI::.

Adjacency pair (AP) refers to a sequence of two turns produced by different speakers and ordered as first pair-part (FPP) and second pair-part (SPP), where a particular type of FPP requires a particular type of SPP.

Upon the production of a first pair-part, a second pair-part is made conditionally relevant (Schegloff, 1968). That is, a particular type of first pair-part calls for a particular type of second pair-part. For example, a question makes an answer conditionally relevant, a greeting makes a return greeting conditionally relevant, and an offer makes an acceptance or refusal conditionally relevant. Classic examples of adjacency pairs are the four core sequences in telephone openings: summons–answer, identification–recognition, greeting sequence, *how-are-you* sequence (see Chapter 5).

It is important to note that the pairs do not always occur adjacently. The adjacency pair organization is a normative framework, not an empirical generalization: it shapes the expectations, understandings, and actions of participants (cf. Conversational Maxims in Grice, 1975). In other words, it is not that a particular first pair-part is always followed by its second pair-part, but that the absence of that second pair-part (e.g., not saying *Hi* back to someone's greeting) becomes noticeable for the participants. In the following exchange between Charlie Gibson of the *ABC News* and the vice presidential candidate Sarah Palin, Gibson's question (FPP) at line 01 does not receive an immediate answer at line 02, but an answer remains relevant over the next 12 lines. That Sarah Palin's second pair-part was not immediately forthcoming dominated the national news for at least a week or so. It became a basis for inferring her intelligence, competence, and readiness for the vice presidency:

(2)   [Bush Doctrine, ABC, September 2008]

```
01    Charlie:    →    >Do you agree with the< Bush Doctrine?
02                     (1.5)
03    Sarah:           In what respect Charlie,
04                     (0.8)
05    Charlie:         Bush- wh- wh- what d'y- what d'y interpret it
06                     to be.
07                     (0.2)
08    Sarah:           his wo:rld vie:w?
09                     (0.2)
10                     [( °y' mean,° )    ]
11    Charlie:         [>No.=the< Bush] doctrine. enunciated
                       September
12                     (.) two thousand two. ° for the Iraq war.°
13                     (0.8)
14    Sarah:    →    I believe that ((continues))
```

Task 1

Consider the following telephone opening jotted down immediately after the call. Identify the adjacency pairs. Are there any missing first or second pair-parts?

```
01                     ((phone rings))
02    Hansun:          Hello?
03    Charlie:         Hello?
04                     ((silence))
05    Hansun:          Who is this?
06    Charlie:         Charlie.
07                     ((silence))
08    Hansun:          Oh, Michael's not home.
```

Nonnative speakers may have difficulty supplying the appropriate second pair-part of an adjacency pair, as shown in the following data taken from a language proficiency interview, where the ESL student answers a *wh*-question with "Yeah" twice:

(3)   [He, 1998, p. 106]
    01   Interviewer: So what was your concentration=
    02   Interviewee: →   **=Yeah.**
    03   Interviewer: in China?
    04   Interviewee: →   **Yeah.**
    05   Interviewer: What con- what did you concentrate on=
    06   Interviewee: =Physical chemistry.

An adjacency pair can be expanded, and such expansions can come before, between, and after the base adjacency pair as **pre-expansions**, insert-expansions, and post-expansions (see Schegloff, 2007 for a detailed account of these expansions).

Pre-expansion is an adjacency pair positioned before the base adjacency pair designed to ensure its smooth running.

In the following segment, taken from a multi-party dinner conversation, Don's request for Jerry to pass the salt at line 04 is prefaced by the pre-expansion begun at line 01:

(4)   [Schegloff, 2007, p. 50]
    01   Don: → **Hey Jerry?**
    02   Jerry: → **[((looks to Don))**
    03   Beth: [An' it- [he- he- it-]
    04   Don: [Will you pass] that uh,
    05   Jerry: Uh this?
    06   Don: This one here,

Author's story (HW): This used to be a typical scenario between my husband and me: I would ask a question, receive either a "huh?" or complete silence. I would then complain that he just didn't pay attention, and because this happened again and again, I would protest that he never listened. What was missing, of course, was the pre-expansion.

Some pre-expansions are specific to the kinds of sequences (e.g., invitation) they preface. These will be discussed along with the type-specific sequences later in the chapter.

Additional adjacency pairs can also come between the base adjacency pair.

> **Insert-expansion** is an adjacency pair that comes between the first and second pair-parts of the base adjacency pair to either clarify the first pair-part or seek preliminary information before doing the second pair-part.

In the following example, the first pair-part of the **insert-expansion** at line 02 points specifically backwards to the first pair-part of the base adjacency pair, seeking clarification of Debbie's "What is the deal.":

(5)   [CA ASI 2004 data—modified]
    01   Debbie: What is the dea::l.
    02   Shelley: →   **What do you mea::n.**
    03   Debbie: →   **You're not gonna go::?**
    04   (0.2)
    05   Shelley: well -hh now: my boss wants me to go: an:
    06   uhm finish this >stupid< trial thing, uhm

In the following example, before responding to the customer's request for a drink, the server checks the customer's drinking eligibility with the first pair-part of an insert-expansion:

(6)   [Schegloff, 2007, p. 109—modified]
    01   Cus: May I have a Budweiser?
    02   Ser: →   **Are you twenty-one?**
    03   Cus: →   **No.**
    04   Ser: No.

An adjacency pair may also be expanded beyond its second pair-part with a **post-expansion**.

> **Post-expansion** is a turn or an adjacency pair (AP) that comes after and is still tied to the base AP. Post-expansion can be minimal or non-minimal.

The minimal post-expansion is also referred to as **sequence-closing third (SCT)**.

> **Sequence-closing third (SCT)** is an additional turn (e.g., *oh, okay,* or *great*) beyond the second pair-part designed to terminate the sequence.

(7) [Schegloff, 2007, p. 283—modified]
```
01   Ava:              Where's he going.
02   Bee:              To Wa:shington.
03   Ava:    →    Oh.
```

Other examples of SCT are typically *Okay, Good*, or a combination such as *Oh okay great*.

The non-minimal post-expansion does exactly the opposite of the minimal post-expansion. Instead of closing down the sequence, it keeps the sequence open. It is typically done because the second pair-part of the base sequence is treated by the recipient as unsatisfactory in some way. In the tutoring interaction below, Heidi's advice at lines 01–02 is not immediately accepted by Lena (lines 03, 05, and 07–08):

(8)   [Waring tutoring data]
```
01   Heidi:         ((lines omitted)) Yeah you need to re(.)phrase the
02                  questions.
03                  (0.8)
04                  if that's what you (.) wanna do.
05   Lena:          I'll think about it. [((laugh)) cuz that-
06   Heidi:                              [If- yeah yeah
07   Lena:          You don't know what it- took (.) for us to get to
08                  these=
((lines omitted))
09   Heidi   →    Yeah for now, if you can just do this. If you think
10                that's (   ).=
11   Lena:   →    = >↓I ↑can do th↑at.<
12   Heidi:        Yeah. Whatever order you want.
```

At lines 09–10, Heidi begins a post-expansion by making her initial advice more acceptable, which immediately receives a favorable response from Lena in the next turn (line 11).

Task 2

Identify all the relevant sequence types (e.g., base sequence and pre-, insert-, or post-expansion) in the following Skype chat exchange. Hansun and Michael are packing for their trip to Savannah, Georgia. Consider the timing in the brackets in your analysis.

```
[11:40:59 AM] Hansun says:
            01              Can you carry my boots in your backpack?
[11:41:33 AM] Michael says:
            02              What boots? and do we need boots?
[11:41:50 AM] Hansun says:
            03              To go with my outfit for dinner.
```

[11:43:40 AM] Hansun says:
        04   I'll carry all your reading materials.
[11:44:16 AM] Michael says:
        05   Okay.
[11:44:27 AM] Hansun says:
        06   Okay.

Preference Organization

Also generic to sequencing practices is an important organization called **preference** (Pomerantz, 1984; Sacks, 1987). In what follows, we first define preference, then discuss the criteria for deciding what is "preferred," and finally, address two sets of complications related to preference.

> **Preference** is a structural organization in which the alternatives that fit in a certain slot in a sequence are treated as nonequivalent (i.e., preferred vs. dispreferred).

Preferred actions are the "natural," "normal," or "expected" actions. Their absence is noticeable. The absence of a preferred action is a basis for inferring the presence of a dispreferred one. For example, after an invitation, acceptance is preferred and refusal dispreferred. The absence of acceptance is the basis for inferring refusal. To accurately understand the concept of preference, a few more specifications are in order:

(1) preference applies to both first and second pair-parts;
(2) preference is not a psychological concept;
(3) preferred actions minimize "face" threats;
(4) preference is context-dependent;
(5) not all adjacency pairs are subject to the preference organization.

First, preference applies to both first and second pair-parts. When we speak of preference, we often use this example: as second pair-parts in response to an invitation, acceptance is preferred over rejection. First pair-parts, however, can also be preferred or dispreferred. For instance, as first pair-parts, offers are preferred over requests. Requests are often withheld to maximize the possibility that someone will do the offering. Second, preference is not a psychological concept indicating one's personal desires. A refusal is dispreferred not because one hates rejecting an invitation (i.e., s/he might not want to go to the party in the first place). Third, preferred actions are designed to minimize face threats, maintain social solidarity, and avoid conflicts (Heritage, 1984a, p. 265). Fourth, what is preferred varies from context to context. After self-deprecation (e.g., "My English is not very good"), what is preferred is disagreement, not agreement. In oral proficiency interviews, however, self-deprecation is not followed by disagreement (or agreement) (Lazaraton, 1997). Finally, not all adjacency pairs are subject to the preference organization. Preference becomes relevant when the first pair-part "makes conditionally relevant distinct alternative types of responding actions" (e.g., agree/disagree, accept/reject) (Schegloff & Lerner, 2009, p. 113). Many *wh*-questions, for example, do not seem to involve alternatives that can be "compellingly characterized" as preferred or dispreferred (Schegloff & Lerner, 2009, p. 113).

DECIDING WHAT IS PREFERRED

How do we decide, then, what is preferred (i.e., natural or expected) in a given context? Three criteria may be used:

(1) regularity of occurrence;
(2) potential for sequence-closing;
(3) unmarked turn shape.

First, what is preferred often refers to what is frequently done. For example, overwhelmingly, greetings are returned. Return greetings are thus preferred. Second, what is preferred is also what expedites the closing of a sequence. In the case of advising, advice is offered to be accepted, and acceptance of advice is the quickest way to close the sequence, and thus preferred. Third, preferred actions are regularly packaged in unmarked turn shapes: without any delay, mitigation (i.e., softening devices) or accounts (i.e., explanations). In the extract below, Priya's advice acceptance is done immediately and succinctly:

(09) [Waring tutoring data]
    01   Liam: Okay be↑fore I lose this, go through all of
    02   those. Periods. Double space.
    03   Priya: →   **Oh yeah I will.**
    04   Liam: Okay.

Dispreferred actions, on the other hand, are produced in marked formats with delay, mitigation, or accounts. In the next extract, Lena's advice rejection is produced with the delay (i.e., silence) at line 03, the further within-turn delay ("I'll think about it") and the mitigating laughter at line 05 as well as the account at lines 07, 09–11:

(10) [Waring tutoring data]
    01   Heidi: ((lines omitted)) Yeah you need to re(.)phrase the
    02   questions.
    03   (0.8)
    04   if that's what you (.) wanna do.

```
05  Lena:   →   I'll think about it.  [((laughs)) cuz that-
06  Heidi:                           [If- yeah yeah
07  Lena:       You don't know what it- [took (.) for us [to get=
08  Heidi:                              [Yeah           [I kno:w.
09  Lena:       = to these three questions. u- u- you know. Over
10              a year of going back and
11              [forth of different things.
12  Heidi:      [O- O- O-
13              Okay.
```

Second language speakers may have a limited range of resources to conduct a dispreferred action (Gardner, 2004).

Author's story (HW): The difficulties that Japanese speakers face in giving dispreferred responses became a salient topic of online discussion in my CA class. Some anecdotes that came up include: a Japanese woman said "I don't think so" and left when invited to lunch by her American co-worker, another replied with a curt "No!" when asked if she needed any help by a salesperson, and a Japanese businessman with low-level English expressed trouble saying "no" to someone asking for a cigarette in the street. In accounting for her experience working with a Japanese tutee, one student wrote: "she did not know how to say 'no' without being rude. We spent almost an hour talking about hedges, delays, accounts, pro-forma agreements, blocking responses, etc, and we re-recorded the role-play many times so that she could practice turning me down. She was very excited to learn how to refuse people!"

TWO COMPLICATIONS

Preference is not determined *a priori*. Participants play an important part in jointly shaping and reshaping whatever is normally taken to be preferred or dispreferred. More specifically, two complications enter the picture:

(1) preference may be manipulated via turn designs;
(2) any preferred action may be produced in a dispreferred format, and vice versa.

For example, *yes/no* questions generally prefer a *yes* answer. Hansun was recently visiting Jean, and as they were driving around, Hansun asks, "So do you have neighborhood barbecue and stuff like that?" "U:m, not that much," Jean answered. Note that Jean's *no* response to Hansun's *yes/no* question is done in a mitigated format. In other words, it treats Hansun's question as preferring a *yes* answer. In the extract below, however, this preference for *yes* is reversed to *no* with the use of the adverb "yet":

(11)   [Schegloff, 2007, p. 273]
01   Bee: →   **Oh did they get rid of Kuhleznik yet hhh**
02   Ava: No in fact I know somebody who ha:s her now.

Consider another example: the speaker redesigns his/her question at line 03 to reverse the preference so that the negative answer is preferred:

(12)   [Sacks, 1987, p. 64]
01   A: →   **Good cook there?**
02   ((pause))
03   A: →   **Nothing special?**

Aside from the fact that preference may be manipulated via turn designs, a normally preferred action may be done in a dispreferred format. The following is an example where the preferred action of granting permission is done as if it were dispreferred:

(13)   [Schegloff lecture CA ASI 2004]
01   A: Can I go over to Doug's house?
02   B: →   **Well, it's pretty close to dinner . . . well, okay.**

B's response sets A up for rejection but offers what is sought in the end, thereby creating the image of being extra nice. On the other hand, a dispreferred action may be done in a preferred format, which would incur the image of someone being extra difficult or the like. In the next example, Bee's *yes/no* inquiry, which prefers a *yes* response, receives the dispreferred *no*. Notably, the *no* is done immediately without any mitigation or accounts. It is, in other words, done as if it were a preferred response:

(14)   [Schegloff, 2007, p. 273]
01   Bee: You have anybody that I would know
02   from the English department?
03   Ava: →   **>mm< I don't think so**

Preference is a complex concept. Unfortunately, it is often understood in a dogmatic way. The urge to call any turn in conversation preferred or dispreferred without considering what kind of sequence that turn is in, whether preference is relevant to that sequence, what is treated as preferred or dispreferred by the participants in that sequence, and how that treatment is used to perform particular social actions, is common among beginning students of CA. Understanding the above complications would allow language teachers to steer clear of the simplistic route of mapping forms to functions and give their students the truly dynamic gift of using language as a resource. For example, it is important to understand that rejections are not always done with delay, mitigation, or accounts. If someone says a simple *no* to your invitation, it can

be meant as a joke or to be purposely nasty. ESL/EFL learners do not necessarily know these subtleties.

Task 3

Consider the following exchange, where line 01 is the first pair-part
(FPP) of an adjacency pair: (a) What action does this FPP perform?
(b) What kind of second pair-part (SPP) does it prefer? How do you
know? (c) Where is its SPP in the transcript? (d) Is it the preferred or
dispreferred option? How can you tell?

```
[CA ASI 2004 data—modified]
01  Bee:   You sound HA:PPY,
02  Ava:   uh- I sound ha:p [py?
03  Bee:                    [Ye::ah.
04         (0.3)
05  Ava:   No:.
```

Type-specific Sequencing Practices

Type-specific sequences are those addressed to particular actions such as
requests or compliments. These are exactly the foci of many ESL/EFL textbooks and classroom instruction. In this section, we introduce these sequences
alphabetically: agreement and disagreement, announcement, complaint, compliment response, invitation and offer, and request.

Agreement and Disagreement

As assessments, agreement and disagreement are not treated as equivalent
by participants: agreement is preferred, and disagreement dispreferred. As a
preferred action, agreement is typically done without delay, mitigation, or
accounts (Pomerantz, 1984). The three ways of doing agreement are:

(1) upgrade;
(2) same;
(3) downgrade:

(15) [Pomerantz, 1984, p. 65—modified]
      (upgrade)
      01   A: It's a beautiful day out isn't it?
      02   B: →   **Yeh it's just gorgeous . . .**

(16) [Pomerantz, 1984, p. 67]
      (same)

```
        01   A:              . . . She was a nice lady—I liked her.
        02   B:       →      I liked her too.
```

(17)   [Pomerantz, 1984, p. 68]
       (downgrade)
```
        01   A:              That's beautiful.
        02   B:       →      Isn't it pretty.
```

Disagreement, on the other hand, generally features delay and mitigation. As shown in the examples below, delay can be done through

(1) silence;
(2) questions;
(3) reluctance markers (e.g., "uh" or "well");
(4) agreement prefaces (e.g., "yeah but").

The first two features are seen in Extract (18) below and the third and fourth features in Extract (19):

(18)   [Pomerantz, 1984, p. 71—modified]
```
        01   A:       . . . You sound very far away.
        02        →   (0.7)
        03   B:   →   I do?
        04   A:       Yeah.
        05   B:       No I'm no:t,
```

(19)   [Pomerantz, 1984, p. 72—modified]
```
        01   A:       We've got some pretty [(good schools.)
        02   B:   →                         [Well, yeah but where in
        03            the heck am I gonna live.
```

Mitigation of disagreement is done with "qualifications, exceptions, additions, and the like" (Pomerantz, 1984, p. 74):

(20)   [Pomerantz, 1984, p. 75—modified]
```
        01   A:       But you admit he is having fun and you think
        02            it's funny.
        03   B:   →   I think it's funny, yeah. But it's a ridiculous
        04            funny.
```

(21)   [Pomerantz, 1984, p. 75—modified]
```
        01   C:       . . . You've really both basically honestly gone
        02            your own ways.
        03   D:   →   Essentially, except we've had a good
        04            relationship at home.
```

Author's story (HW): In arguing for the importance of teaching preferred and dispreferred responses even at a lower level, one of my graduate students wrote: "Students find it mystifying that they should at first agree with a stranger's unprompted initiation (such as a complaint about how bad a class is, for example) even when they completely disagree . . . many students coming to America assume that we value directness."

Task 4

Consider the following textbook materials on teaching disagreement taken from *Speaking Naturally*. Given what you have just read about agreement/disagreement, in what ways do they reflect how disagreement is done in real life, and in what ways do they not? How would you modify these materials if necessary?

Direct
01   Mary: The show finishes at ten o'clock.
02   Chuck: No, it doesn't. They told me eleven.

Indirect
01   Mary: The show finishes at ten o'clock.
02   Chuck: Oh, really? That's strange. They told me it would be
03   around eleven.

In ESL/EFL texts, the teaching of disagreement typically does not include issues of timing, i.e., saying an utterance early versus late. Doing a disagreement without any hesitation can be seen as rude, aggressive, or uncooperative. For example, the direct utterance in the task above "No, it doesn't. They told me eleven." may be viewed by its recipient Mary as (somewhat) impolite precisely because it was delivered without any prefacing silence or uncertainty markers. The issue of timing is particularly difficult for ESL/EFL learners because they are still struggling to comprehend a message as well as respond to it.

Announcement

The announcement sequence consists minimally of the following adjacency pair:

(D = deliverer; R = receiver)
D: Announcement of News
R: Response to Announcement

This base adjacency pair can take on pre-, insert-, and post-expansions, result-ing in the following expanded sequence (Maynard, 2003; Terasaki, 2004):

```
     D:   Pre-announcement FPP ⎤
     R:   Pre-announcement SPP ⎦
 ⎧D:     Announcement of News
 ⎩R:       Insert sequence FPP ⎤
     D:       Insert sequence SPP ⎦
     R:   Response to Announcement
     D:   Elaboration of News (Post-announcement FPP) ⎤
     R:   Assessment of News (Post-announcement SPP) ⎦
```

In the following example, the braces on the left mark the two base announce-ment sequences, and the three on the right mark respectively pre-, insert-, and post-expansions:

(22)   [Terasaki, 2004, p. 176—modified]
    01   D: I forgot to tell you the two best things that ⎤ Pre-announcement
    02   happened to me today.   ⎦ sequence
    03   R: Oh super-What were they.
    04   D: ⎧I got a B plus on my math test.
    05   R: ⎩On your final? ⎤ Insert sequence
    06   D: Uh huh? ⎦
    07   R: Oh that's wonderful!
    08   D: ⎧hh And I got athletic award.
    09   R: ⎩REALLY?!?
    10   D: Uh huh. From Sports Club. ⎤ Post-announcement
    11   R: Oh that's terrific Ronald. ⎦ sequence

PRE-ANNOUNCEMENT

In the first pair-part of the pre-announcement (henceforth "Pre-announcement First"), the speaker strives to project some news to come without actually delivering the news (Terasaki, 2004, p. 182). Pre-announcement First serves to gauge the potential news-worthiness of the announcement and give the recipient an opportunity to preempt the telling in case it is not news for him/her. The features of Pre-announcement First are:

(1)   naming the projected sequence (e.g., "news");
(2)   characterizing the news (e.g., "great" news);
(3)   referring to its recency (e.g., "today");
(4)   offering to tell (e.g., "You wanna know X?").

These features are shown in the following two examples:

(23)   [Terasaki, 2004, p. 184—modified]
    01   D: →   **Did you hear the terrible news?**
    02   R: no, what.

(24)   [Terasaki, 2004, p. 184—modified]
    01   D: →   **Toni and Bill I have something to tell you.** You
    02   probably heard about it already but just in case you
    03   haven't.

The preferred second pair-part of the pre-announcement sequence (henceforth "Pre-announcement Second") is a solicitation of the news (henceforth "**Solicit**"), and such Solicits are routinely formulated as *wh-*questions:

(25)   [Terasaki, 2004, p. 193]
    01   D: Hey we got good news.
    02   R: →   **What's the good news.**

(26)   [Terasaki, 2004, p. 193]
    01   D: Y'wanna know who I got stoned with a
    02   few(h)weeks ago? hh!
    03   R: →   **Who.**

Solicit is the preferred second pair-part of the pre-announcement sequence, where one requests the news with a *wh-*question.

Task 5

Using what you have just read in the prior section, explain why the following exchange from *Everybody Loves Raymond* is funny.

    01   Marie: Guess what?
    02   Other family members: What?
    03   Marie: Guess.
    04   ((audience laughter))

ANNOUNCEMENT RESPONSE

In responding to an announcement, one can encourage elaboration, discourage elaboration, or remain ambivalent (Maynard, 2003, pp. 98–107). The three types of announcement responses are:

(1) newsmark (e.g., *Really?*);
(2) news receipt (e.g., *Oh*);
(3) standardized *oh*-prefaced assessment (e.g., *Oh good.*).

Newsmark is a type of announcement response that encourages elaboration in the following forms:

(1) *oh* + partial repeat (e.g., *oh do they?*)
(2) *really?*
(3) *yes/no* questions (e.g., *did she?*)

In the following extract, R encourages elaboration with "REALLY?!?":

(27) [Maynard, 2003, p. 102]
    01   D: ° hh And I got athletic award.
    02   R: →   **REALLY?!?**
    03   D: Uh huh. From Sports Club.
    04   R: Oh that's terrific Ronald.

News receipts, by contrast, may receive a confirmation with no elaboration in the next turn (Maynard, 2003, p. 101).

News receipt is a type of announcement response that discourages elaboration in the following forms:

(1) *oh*
(2) *oh really*
(3) uninverted *yes/no* question (*she did?*)
(4) *oh* + assessment (*oh great*)

---

(28) [Maynard, 2003, p. 101—modified]
    01   Emma: Hey that was the same spot we took off for
    02   Honolulu. (0.4) where they put him on, at that
    03   chartered place,
    04   Nancy: → **Oh really?**
    05   Emma: Y:ea::h.
    06   Nancy: Oh:? For heaven sakes.

(29) [Maynard, 2003, p. 101—modified]
    01   Ida: .hhh Well there's a: few things arrived for you.
    02   Jenny: → **Oh goo:d [.hhh**

```
03   Ida:                    [Yes.
04   Jenny:          Oh cuz the boys were asking how long they'd been
05                          . . .
```

Finally, although *oh*-preface assessments usually function as news receipts that discourage elaboration, when *oh good* is used to respond to good news and *oh dear* to bad news, they are each designed to be ambivalent about encouraging or discouraging elaboration (Maynard, 2003, p. 103). According to Maynard (2003), both *oh good* and *oh dear* have an "abstract and laconic quality that endows them with a utility for responding to very diverse kinds of news" (p. 103). We show one case using *oh good*:

```
(30)   [Maynard, 2003, p. 104—modified]
       01   Mum:              Auntie Vi is he::re=
       02   Leslie:    →      =h- ↑Oh goo[d,
       03   Mum:                         [She's been here all [the wee:k ['n
       04   Leslie:                                           [° hhhh    [Oh:
       05                      how nice.
       06                      (.)
       07   Mum:              M[m:.
       08   Leslie:           [.hhhh Are you having her dinner? hh
```

Task 6

Look for announcement sequences (e.g., giving or telling information/news and responding to information/news) in ESL/EFL textbooks. Compare them with the information given in the above section. Do you find pre-announcements, insert sequences, and post-announcements? Do you find newsmarks and news receipts? If there is a discrepancy between the textbook materials and what is presented here, how would you modify your instruction?

Teaching ESL/EFL students the subtle differences between newsmarks and news receipts can help them become better participants in conversation so that they do not look as if they were interested when they are not, or vice versa.

Author's story (HW): My cousin from China who has a limited command of English visited us last summer. She would respond to everything my husband and I said with "Oh really?" regardless of whether it was anything newsworthy or surprising. I remember thinking it was a bit odd.

Complaint

Complaints may be launched directly against a co-participant or indirectly about a third party (e.g., Drew, 1998; Stokoe, 2009). In the conversation analytic literature, "complaint" is also used to characterize talk about oneself such as *I'm so tired* or *I have so much work* (Mandelbaum, 1991/1992). Our focus is on direct complaints. Schegloff (1988) offers an elaborate account of how Sherri's turn at line 05 below is produced and recognized as a complaint:

```
(31)   [Schegloff, 1988a, pp. 119–120—modified]
       01                ((door squeaks))
       02   Sherri:      Hi Carol.=
       03   Carol:       =[Hi::.    ]
       04   Ruthie:       [CA:RO] L, HI::
       05   Sherri:  →   You didn't get an icecream sandwich,
       06   Carol:       I kno:w, hh I decided that my body didn't need it.
       07   Sherri:      Yes but ours di:d=
       08                =hh heh heh heh [heh heh heh .hhih
```

At line 05, Sherri notices a negative event, and more specifically, a failure on the part of Carol to bring back an icecream sandwich. This specific type of noticing appears to be a practice for doing complaining (Schegloff, 1988a, pp. 120–121). In addition, line 05 is also treated as a complaint by Carol. While a simple noticing would get a response such as *oh* or agreement, a complaint makes conditionally relevant a range of responses such as accounts, apologies, or remedies. Carol provides an account at line 06, showing that she treats line 05 as a complaint. The sequence goes on to include multiple accounts and remedies from Carol and multiple rejections by Ruthie and Sherri, yielding further evidence for the participants' understanding of line 05 as a complaint. We only show part of the ensuing interaction below:

```
(32)   [Schegloff, 1988a, p. 128—modified]
       01   Carol:   →   hh alright give me some money and you can
       02                treat me to one and I'll buy you all some
       03                [too.        ]
       04   Sherri:      [I'm kidding,] I don't need it.
       ((lines omitted))
       05   Carol:   →   I know an icecream sandwich is better, but I don't
       06                feel like going down to Parking Level and seeing
       07                all those weird people and
       08                have them st[a:re at me.
       09   Ruthie:                  [in your slippers,
       10                (0.3)
       11   Carol:       Yeah.
       12                (0.8)
       13            →   I don't want them to see me when I look this
```

```
14                    good.
15                    (0.4)
16   Ruthie:          Hhuh hhhh=
17   Carol:           =no one deserves it.
```

At lines 01–03, Carol offers a remedy which gets rejected by Sherrie at line 04. At lines 05–08, Carol gives another account for her unwillingness to go downstairs for the icecream sandwich, which is continued at lines 13 and 17.

The most comprehensive treatment of complaint sequences can be found in Dersley and Wootton (2000), where complaints of an acrimonious nature more akin to accusations are investigated with a focus on the first four positions: complaint, response to complaint, rebuttal to complaint response, and response to rebuttal. They show three types of responses to complaints and found that the most frequent response (85 percent) is (2) below:

(1) *didn't do it*;
(2) *not at fault* (i.e., excusable);
(3) alternative characterization of the offense.

The *didn't do it* option exhibits preferred turn features (i.e., without delay, mitigation, or accounts); whereas the *not at fault* option manifests dispreferred features (i.e., with delay, mitigation, or accounts). In the following segment, Clara responds to Milly's complaint immediately with a straightforward *didn't do it* denial:

(33)   [Dersley & Wootton, 2000, p. 381—modified]
```
       01   Milly:          people don't like you putting down other people
       02                   [to make yourself look good.
       03   Clara:   →      [I did not ((slow deliberate prosody through to 09))
       04                   (.)
       05                   put=
       06   Milly:          =yes you [did
       07   Clara:                   [ANYONE
       08                   (.)
       09   Clara:          DOWN.
```

By contrast, Dave's complaint that his wife is not making enough money is received with a delayed *not at fault* excuse that shifts the blame to the recession:

(34)   [Dersley & Wootton, 2000, p. 384—modified]
```
       01   Dave:           forty-five a day.
       02   Gemma:          uh ° uh °
       03                   (0.7)
       04   Dave:           That's what you yourself should be making (0.3)
       05                   profit
```

```
06              (0.2)
07  Gemma:      ° uh °
08              (2.6)
09  Wife:   →   there's a recession on at the moment
10              [you don't do it all the ti::me?
11  Dave:       [I kno:w yeah.
```

The third type of initial response to complaints is an alternative characterization of the offense:

```
(35)  [Dersley & Wootton, 2000, p. 385—modified]
      01  Colin:      you were- just (0.2) y'know sort- of (.) blanking her
      02              out I don't understand [(you)
      03  Mum:    →                         [I'M NOT BLANKING
      04              HER OUT I'M BUSY.
```

While the *didn't do it* option can jump-start a series of oppositional assertions, the *not at fault* option can receive more diverse responses from the complainer in the third position (i.e., rebuttal to complaint response), as seen in Table 3.1 below.

The third position can determine whether subsequent interaction becomes

Table 3.1 Complaint Sequence

Position	Participant		Activity	
1st position	Complainer		Complain	
2nd position	Complainee	*didn't do it* (5%)	*not at fault* (85%)	alternative characterization of "offense" (10%)
3rd position	Complainer	Successive oppositional assertions	(1) finds in defense warrant for furthering the complaint (2) ridicules defense (3) ignores defense (4) explicitly and directly dismisses defense (5) disputes defense without explicitly rejecting it	
4th position	Complainee		Some responses are more conciliatory (e.g., after (5) above) and some are less so (e.g., after (2) and (3) above).	

more or less conciliatory. If the complainer disputes the offense without explicitly rejecting it in the third position, the ensuing talk can become more conciliatory. Prior to the following, Kevin has complained about not having access to "the tape" in which an allegedly untoward action on the part of Kevin took place, and Rob launched a defense by saying that the transcript is sufficient. The segment begins with the third position in the complaint sequence, where Kevin preserves his complaining stance without denying the usefulness of the transcript:

(36)   [Dersley & Wootton, 2000, pp. 395–396—modified]
```
01   Kevin:   →   =well- for example I might hear::d- uh s:o-
02                eh- you've got me saying resign resign I might
03                say (.) well that's somebody:: (.) that
04                that is the voice of somebody I kno:w.
05   Rob:        but [ (    )
06   Kevin:          [and this person is he:r:e toda::y.
07                (0.3)
08                you know to- to state that .hh but I'm not able to
09                say that [if I can't hear the tape in advance=
11   Rob:                 [Well-
12                =well that's that's a point that you'll have to bring
13                to the meeting then.
```

As can be seen, in the next turn (lines 11–13), Rob takes a more conciliatory stance by implicitly acknowledging that Kevin's point might have some merit and is worth taking to the meeting.

By contrast, the options of "ridicule" or "ignore" in the third position can contribute to an acrimonious tone of the interaction:

(37)   [Dersley & Wootton, 2000, p. 397—modified]
```
01   Wife:    so- you don't know what family life is.
02            (0.3)
03   Dave:    and you do?
04   Wife:  →  I blame your ↑ p[a:rent-
05   Dave:                     [((curse word))
```

Wife's turn in the third position essentially ignores Dave's counter at line 03, in response to which comes Dave's outburst in the fourth position at line 05. For a more detailed description of complaint sequences that take the acrimonious trajectory, see Dersley and Wootton (2000).

ESL/EFL texts aimed at teaching complaints tend to focus on the specific strategies of formulating a complaint such as "state the problem" (e.g., "There is a fly in my soup"). Competent participation in a complaint event, however, requires the ability not only to launch the initial complaint but also to manage the subsequent interactions such as responding to a complaint, reacting to the complaint response, and so on. Understanding, for example, that complaint responses can come in three formats (i.e., *didn't do it*, *not at fault*, and alternative characterization of offense) makes it possible to specify this ability and thereby render it teachable.

Compliment Response

Task 7

How do you think speakers of English respond to compliments? If you were to design a lesson teaching learners how to respond to compliments, what would that lesson look like? What are the specific wordings or strategies used by native speakers of English in their compliment responses?

Contrary to the misconception that native speakers of English always respond to compliments with *Thank you*, two competing preferences govern the production of compliment responses in American English (Pomerantz, 1978):

(1) preference for agreement;
(2) preference for avoiding self-praise.

Agreeing with the compliment would mean lacking modesty. Because of this tension, actual compliment responses seem a bit wishy-washy. The two main solution types to manage these competing preferences are (Pomerantz, 1978):

(1) praise downgrade;
(2) referent shift.

PRAISE DOWNGRADE

The responses that use the "praise downgrade" strategy typically contain both agreement and disagreement elements. By straddling these contrasting positions, the participant is able to accept or reject the compliment without fully committing to either:

(38) [Pomerantz, 1978, p. 102]
```
    01   A:         Oh it was just beautiful.
    02   B:    →    Well thank you uh I thought it was quite nice.
```

(39) [Pomerantz, 1978, p. 99]
```
    01   A:         Good shot.
    02   B:    →    Not very solid though.
```

Author's story (HW): After reading a preliminary draft of this chapter, an MA student from China remarks in disbelief, "Do Americans really do 'praise downgrade'? I was taught the opposite, and I always upgrade any compliment I received!"

REFERENT SHIFT

Participants also attend to both preferences by shifting the target of the praise in two ways (Pomerantz, 1978, pp. 101–106):

(1) reassigning target of praise;
(2) returning praise.

(40) [Pomerantz, 1978, p. 102]
    (reassign)
    01   A: You're a good rower, honey.
    02   B: →   **These are very easy to row. Very light.**

(41) [Pomerantz, 1978, p. 102—modified]
    (return)
    01   A: You're looking good.
    02   B: →   **Great. So are <u>you</u>.**

Methods of compliment responses can vary cross-culturally. Germans, for example, tend to use a greater variety of strategies for agreement or acceptance (e.g., provide an assessment, offer confirmation, or give a stronger second assessment and elicit more) (Golato, 2002):

(42) [Golato, 2002, p. 557]
    (provide assessment)
    01   A: but it was nice this evening here at your place.
                Aber heute abend hier war's schoen bei euch
    02   B: →   **that's nice.**
                schoen.

(43) [Golato, 2002, p. 557]
    (offer confirmation)
    01   A: You have such a nice onion pattern here.
                 ihr habt ja so en schoenes zwiebelmuster hier,
    02   B: →   **Yes.**
                 joa:

(44) [Golato, 2002, p. 558]

(give stronger second assessment)

```
01  A:        by the way the meat was excel[lent.
              übrigens (.)da s fleisch exzel  [lent
02  B:                                        [super, right?
                                              [super ne?
03  A:  →   excellent.
            exzellent
04  B:      Yeah.
            joa.
```

Because of these cross-cultural differences, Germans may sound to Americans as if they lacked modesty. According to Golato (2002), the reason why Germans appear more willing to accept compliments is that compared to Americans, who often compliment to maintain good social relationships, Germans only give compliments when they actually mean it. In other words, German compliments are more "truthful," which makes their acceptance easier or more warranted, so to speak. In fact, Germans are often puzzled by the "excessive" compliments Americans give. (For a sociolinguistic analysis of compliments, see Wolfson, 1981).

Invitation and Offer

Task 8

Imagine you are preparing a lesson on teaching ESL/EFL students how to give and respond to invitations in conversation. In groups of three or four, create two conversations that best model an invitation sequence for your students—one that involves acceptance and one rejection. Write down your conversations below:

Conversation 1:

A: _____
B: _____
A: _____
B: _____
A: _____
B: _____

. . .

Conversation 2:

A: _____
B: _____
A: _____
B: _____

```
A: _____
B: _____

. . .
```

Invitations and offers make conditionally relevant acceptance or rejection. Participants work hard to maximize acceptance and minimize rejection. In what follows, we describe how invitations and offers are foreshadowed and produced, and how rejections are responded to (for how rejections are done, consult our earlier section on dispreferred actions).

PRE-SEQUENCES TO INVITATION AND OFFER

Pre-invitation   In the following segment, the actual invitation at line 06 is preceded by a pre-invitation sequence at lines 04–05.

```
(45)   [Schegloff, 2007, p. 30—modified]
       01    Clara:          Hello
       02    Nelson:         Hi.
       03    Clara:          Hi.
       04    Nelson:   →     What are you doing.
       05    Clara:    →     Not much.
       06    Nelson:         You wanna drink?
       07    Clara:          Yeah.
       08    Nelson:         Okay.
```

Clara gives at line 05 a go-ahead, which facilitates the production of the actual invitation and foreshadows its acceptance. There are three types of responses to a pre-invitation or pre-offer (Schegloff, 2007):

(1) go-ahead;
(2) blocking;
(3) hedging.

Clara could have produced a blocking response such as "I'm studying for CA," which blocks the forthcoming invitation. Or she could also have produced a hedging response such as "why," which leaves room for her to do accept or reject based on the nature of the invitation. Thus, pre-invitation minimizes the possibility of an actual rejection.

In the pre-invitation, the inviter can gauge the possibility of acceptance or rejection from the invitee by giving or asking for a report (Drew, 1984):

```
(46)   [Drew, 1984, p. 133—modified]
       01    J:     →     So who are the boyfriends for the week.
       02                  (0.2)
```

```
03   M:        hhhh- Oh: go::d you this one and that one y'know,
04             I just, y'know keep busy and go out when I wanna
05             go out John it's nothing .hhh I don' have anybody
06             serious on the string,
07   J:        So in other words you'd go out if I::: asked you out
08             one of these times.
09   M:        Yeah! Why not.
```

J solicits reporting at line 01, which M provides at lines 03–06. At lines 07–08, J formulates the upshot of M's reporting as her availability to go out with him, which M then confirms at line 09. An invitation and acceptance are thereby achieved at lines 07–09, preceded by the pre-invitation sequence. In cases where the reporting implies unavailability, the potential inviter may opt to treat the reporting as just that, thereby masking his/her intent to invite in the first place. The goal of minimizing rejection is also achieved by the inviter's own reporting:

```
(47)  [Drew, 1984, pp. 141–142—modified]
      01   M:        Ye:h I I wa:s, (.) and n:ow I'm take- I have taken a
      02             leave and I'm: uh (0.2) I'm doing drug counseling
      03             down in Venice:.
      04             (0.2)
      05   M:   →    which I really (0.6) am crazy abou:t and as a
      06             matter of fact (0.3) we have written a pla:y, and
      07             we are putting that on on the tenth of December.
      08   R:        Can I go see it?
      08   M:        Love to S:- Oh: that'd be great.
```

By simply reporting an upcoming event, M is able to secure R's self-invitation at line 07 without being intrusive and imposing the invitation on R.

Pre-offer   In the following segment, Gary's offer at line 06 is preceded by a pre-offer at line 04, which receives Cathy's go-ahead at line 05:

```
(48)  [Schegloff, 2007, p. 35—modified]
      01   Cat:       I'm gonna buy a thermometer though [because I=
      02   Les:                                          [But-
      03   Cat:       =think she's [got a temperature.
      04   Gar:   →                [We have a thermometer.
      05   Cat:   →   You do?
      06   Gar:       Want to use it?
      07   Cat:       Yeah.
```

Again, Cathy could have produced a blocking response such as "Oh we should have one in the house anyway." or a hedging response such as "What kind?"

By giving a pre-offer, Gary is able to gauge the likelihood in which Cathy may accept the offer and thereby pre-empts a rejection.

Note that pre-sequences are one resource for doing being indirect in interaction. In the interlanguage pragmatics literature, indirectness is sometimes discussed in terms of learners' repertoire of internal or external modifiers within the turn (e.g., *I wonder if*... or *Can I ask you a favor?*) (Blum-Kulka et al., 1989). The notion that indirectness may be achieved sequentially has not yet received much attention within applied linguistics. In fact, a fair amount of pragmatic problems for ESL learners may be attributed to their lack of competence in using pre-sequences, but pre-sequences are rarely included in ESL/EFL textbook dialogs (Bernsten, 2002).

DOING INVITATION AND OFFER

The actual formulation of invitation such as *Would you like to do X?* or *Wanna do X?* has not received much attention in CA research. There is, however, some work on the formulation of offers. Curl (2006) describes the specific syntactic formats of the offers in telephone openings and closings. These offers function as solutions to problems.

Offers that occur in the opening segments are typically made with the conditional *if* (e.g., "If there's anything we can do, let us know."). In the following segment, Ilene's offer emerges at line 12:

```
(49)   [Curl, 2006, p. 1264—modified]
       01   Jane:         hello?
       02   Ilene:        .h Jane?
       03   Jane:         yes.
       04   Ilene:        ah it's me .h uh:m .h look uhwh-uh-weh: Pat and I
       05                 are just off to Newbury no:w.
       06   Jane:         ah hah
       07   Ilene:        uh: an oo-uh .hh uh a:n:d um:: (0.7) uh:::
       08                 Edgerton's got to go over to: (.) Granny's because
       09                 Molly is: u- ou:t,
       10   Jane:         ah hah
       11   Ilene:        so he's going to have a cup of soup with he:r the:re:
       12        →        so if you come over I'll put the key un:derneath
       13                 the ma:t.
```

In the closing segments of phone calls, offers can be made after a closing move, and these offers are always made with the *Do you want me to X?* format (Curl, 2006, p. 1259):

```
(50)   [Curl, 2006, p. 1267—modified]
       01   Emma:         ...ALRIGHT HONEY WELL .hh good- I:'m SO
       02                 glad you had a wonderful ti:me=
       03   Lottie:  →    =well listen (.) e-uh: do you want me uh come
```

```
04                  down and get you to [morrow or] anyth]ing
05    Emma:                              [n:  :o :  : ] d e a:r]
06                  no[:  I'm] fine  ]
07    Lottie:       [to the ] sto::]re or anyth[i:ng
08    Emma:                              [.hh I've got everything
09                  bought dea:r.
```

Lottie's offer at lines 03–04 and 07 is not addressed to any overtly expressed problem from Emma but to a possibly covert problem. Emma has repeatedly referred earlier in the phone call to the Thanksgiving dinner she has to prepare, which may be construed as her need for help. By placing *Do you want me to X?* some distance from the original talk about trouble, offerers may be showing that they have come to an understanding later on in the talk that their co-participants were "angling for" their assistance (Curl, 2006, p. 1276).

Finally, participants use a variety of constructions other than the *Do you want X?* format when they respond to overt problems during the closing segments of the calls (Curl, 2006, p. 1259):

```
(51)  [Curl, 2006, p. 1271—modified]
      01    Emma:     .hh  [h but I: got ] to get my turkey=I'll go up to uh
      02    Lottie:        [a:nd y'know]
      03          →    I'll take you up Wednesday.
```

```
(52)  [Curl, 2006, p. 1271—modified]
      01    Emma:     a:nd uh: (0.2) cuz I: want to and let me know by
      02                  tomorrow I've got some of the stuff but I haven't
      03                  bought the turkey y'know I'd  [lo:ve]
      04    Bart:   →                               [well ] what can I:
      05                  bring down can bring some pie:s or
      06                  something.
```

RESPONDING TO REJECTION

In the event of potential or actual rejections, the inviter or offerer can either go along with the rejection or further pursue acceptance (Davidson, 1984, 1990).

Accepting rejection   Acceptance of rejection is done with a **rejection finalizer** (Davidson, 1990, p. 163).

Rejection finalizer is a minimal response token (e.g., *oh, oh I see, okay*, or *alright*) designed to accept rejections.

In the following example, A accepts B's rejection with "O:kay" at line 04:

(53) [Davidson, 1990, p. 162—modified]
```
      01   A:         You want me to bring you anything?
      02              (0.4)
      03   B:         No: no: nothing.
      04   A:    →    O:kay.
      05              (.)
      06   B:         Thank you.
      07              (.)
      08   A:         Okay bye bye:
```

Revising invitation and offer   To maximize acceptance, participants routinely revise their initial invitations or offers after potential or actual rejections (Davidson, 1984, 1990). In the instance below, the delay at line 02 foreshadows the dispreferred action, i.e., a potential rejection, after which A revises his/her invitation at line 03:

(54) [Davidson, 1984, p. 105—modified]
```
      01   A:         Come on down he:re,=it's oka:y,
      02              (0.2)
      03   A:    →    I got a lot of stuff,=I got be:er and stuff.
```

In the next instance, an actual rejection emerges at line 03, and the invitation is made more attractive at lines 04–05:

(55) [Davidson, 1984, p. 108—modified]
```
      01   A:         ° Gee I feel like a real nerd ° you can ah come up
                      here,
      02              (0.3)
      03   B:         Nah that's alright will stay down he[re,
      04   A:    →                                        [We've got a
      05              color T. V:,
```

In the third instance, a weak acceptance occurs at line 04, and the inviter proceeds to revise his/her original version to provide a second chance for a response:

(56) [Davidson, 1984, p. 113—modified]
```
      01   B:         So I just want to tell you if you'd come we- we're
      02              inviting the kindergarten teachers too becuz we
      03              think it's a good chance to get to know the mothers.
      04   A:         Uh huh. =
      05   B:    →    =.hh So if you're free:, (.) It's at the youth ho:use.
```

In the above cases, revised invitations are given after an actual rejection, a weak rejection, or a gap. There is an even earlier position for revised invitations called **monitor space** (Davidson, 1984, 1990).

Monitor space refers to a space around the first possible completion point of the invitation or offer during which potential acceptance or rejection may be detected. There are three types:

(1) tag-positioned components;
(2) sound stretch;
(3) sound stretch followed by either a micro-pause or a filled pause (e.g., inbreath, laughter).

The following three extracts are examples of (1)–(3) listed above:

(57)   [Davidson, 1984, p. 117—modified]
   (tag-positioned components)
   01   P: →   Oh I mean uh: you wanna go to the store **or**
   02   **anything** over at the Market Basket or anything?

(58)   [Davidson, 1984, p. 121—modified]
   (sound stretch)
   01   B: →   .hh So if you're **free:,** (.)
   02   It's at the youth ho:use.
   03   (0.2)
   04   A: We:ll? (.) as far as I kno:w, (0.8) I will be.

(59)   [Davidson, 1984, pp. 122–123—modified]
   (sound stretch plus inbreath)
   01   B: I wanted to call to ask you if you'd come up (0.2)
   02   →   and have a piece of strawberry (stuffed) **pi:e,**=.hh=
   03   =And A and W root beer, h=
   04   A: =.h Susan (kih-)=.hh I was going to call you to see
   05   if you wanted to go for a walk with me.

Note that what comes after the monitor space is the revised version of the original invitation or offer (Davidson, 1984, 1990). Just as inviters and offerers can revise their original proposals, rejectors may revise their rejections and do so after monitor spaces as well (see Davidson, 1990 for more examples).

Task 9

> Consider this ESL textbook dialog taken from Bernsten (2002). Rewrite it to incorporate concepts such as pre-invitation, monitor space, and revised invitation.
>
> 01 A: Hello. Is Tomoko there?
> 02 B: This is Tomoko.
> 03 A: Hi! This is Sally. Can you come to my birthday party
> 04   tomorrow?
> 05 B: Sure.

ESL/EFL learners may not be able to hear or use utterances such as *What are you doing?* as a pre-invitation. They also may not be able to detect the subtle signs of potential rejection such as silence or weak acceptance. They are very unlikely to use strategies such as the monitor space to gauge possibilities of acceptance. They are probably rarely taught to revise their invitations to make them more attractive. In short, they need to learn the skill of building an invitation sequence to maximize its acceptance. Explicit instruction on the variety of ways of doing invitation would expand ESL/EFL learners' repertoire of interactional practices and help them navigate the target speech community with greater ease and confidence. (For a sociolinguistic approach to the study of invitations, see Wolfson, 1989.)

Request

Like invitations and offers, requests are also designed to be accepted. The granting of requests is typically done in a preferred format, and the rejection in a dispreferred one. Unlike invitations and offers which benefit the recipients, requests impose upon them. Requests tend to be delayed, mitigated, and accounted for. Although all requests are dispreferred in principle, different requests may be dispreferred to different degrees. The distinction between immediate and deferred requests, for example, reflects such a difference (Schegloff, 2007, p. 94). Requests that can be granted immediately such as *Can you pass the salt?* can receive an immediate response. A deferred request that requires compliance in some future time such as *Please rewrite the conclusion* would be more dispreferred.

The following is an extreme case where the request is delayed to the extent that it never gets articulated:

(60) [Schegloff, 2007, p. 64—modified]
    01 Donny: Guess what.hh
    02 Marcia: What.
    03 Donny: hh My ca:r is sta::lled.
    04   (0.2)

05	Donny:		(and) I'm up here in the Glen?
06	Marcia:		Oh::.
07			(0.4)
08	Donny:		hhh
09	Donny:		A:nd.hh
10			(0.2)
11	Donny:	→	**I don' know if it's po:ssible, but hhh (0.2) see I**
12			**have to open up the ba:nk.hh**
13			(0.3)
14	Donny:		a:t uh: (.) in Brentwood?hh=
15	Marcia:		=Yeah: – and I know you want- (.) and I wou- (.)
16			and I would, but- except I've gotta leave in about
17			five min(h)utes. [(hheh)
18	Donny:		[Okay then I gotta call somebody
19			else.right away.

Donny hints at his need for help ("My car is stalled."), the potential feasibility of the help ("up here in the Glen?"), and the urgency of this need ("I have to open up the bank") before he even begins to edge towards launching the request at lines 11–12. The sequence is also littered with mitigation markers such as pauses, fillers, and the uncertainty preface "I don't know if it's possible but . . ."

Because a request is a dispreferred first pair-part, its pre-sequence works differently from, for example, those of invitations and offers. Recall that in pre-invitations and pre-offers, the preferred second pair-part is a go-ahead. If someone says, *Are you doing anything Saturday night?*, the preferred response is *Oh nothing*, which allows the inviter to go forward with his/her invitation. By contrast, the preferred second pair-part of a pre-request is not a go-ahead. If someone says, *Are you going to eat that banana?* as a pre-request to take the banana, the go-ahead "no." is less preferred than the offer *Please take it*. Ideally, the potential requester would not have to explicitly state the request at all.

Author's story (HW): The students in my CA class frequently commented on learners' inability to request appropriately. In a role-play with a noisy neighbor, for example, one learner would begin with "Can you please be quiet?" In parent–teacher conferences, some Japanese parents would start with "Can you pay more attention to my son in class please?"

Thus, helping learners understand that a speech act such as a request is dispreferred and needs to be produced with delay, accounts, and mitigation would go a long way to enhancing their interactional competence.

In terms of the request format, Schegloff (1988b) cautions against the speech act approach of assigning the function of "request information" to a structure such as "Do you know who's going to that meeting?" In the following extract, Mother's question at line 01 is initially understood as a pre-announcement, to which Russ gives a go-ahead at line 02. Only after line 03 does Russ come to understand Mother's question as an information request:

(61)   [Schegloff, 1988b, p. 57–58—modified]
    01   Mother: →   **Do you know who's going to that meeting?**
    02   Russ: Who.
    03   Mother: I don't kno:w.
    04   Russ: Oh::. Probably Mrs. McOwen and
    05   probably Mrs. Cadry and some of the teachers.

Based on ordinary telephone calls between family and friends and out-of-hours calls to the doctor, Curl and Drew (2008) consider the use of two different request formats: *Can/could/will/would you . . .* vs. *I wonder if.* They found that the modal format tends to occur in ordinary calls and *I wonder if* in calls to the doctors. However, rather than being constrained by the two different contexts, they found that by using the modal form of the request, speakers treat the request as unproblematic, and by using the *I wonder if* form, they display uncertainty as to whether the request can be granted (Curl & Drew, 2008, p. 147). In the following segment, the urgency of the situation as well as the patient's entitlement warrants the use of the *Could you* format:

(62)   [Curl & Drew, 2008, p. 139—modified]
    01   Doc: Hello:,
    02   Client: Hello, is that the- doctor?
    03   Doc: Yes, Doctor ((omitted)) speaki:ng,
    04   Client: →   **i: i: Yeah could you just call and see my wife**
    05   **please,**
    06   .h   [h
    07   Doc: [Yes:.
    08   Client: She's breathless. She can't .hh get her breath .hh

By contrast, Kat's cautiously formatted request (i.e., "Would it be possible . . .") suggests the difficulty of its granting. Although *Would it be possible . . .* is not exactly the same as *I wonder if . . .*, it displays a similar sentiment towards the possible impediments to granting the request:

(63)   [Curl & Drew, 2008, p. 146—modified]
    01   Lesley: Anyway when d'you think you'd like to come home
    02   ↓ love.
    03   (.)
    04   Kat: Uh:m (.) we:ll Brad's going down on Monday.
    05   (0.7)
    06   Lesley: Monday we:ll ah- :hh .hh w: ↑Monday we can't
    07   manage because (.) Granny's ↓coming Monday.
    08   (0.4)
    09   Kat: Oh:,
    10   (0.5)

11		Could- (0.3) Dad ↑couldn't pick me up from:: (.)
12		ee- even from Wesbury could be
13	Lesley:	.hh I ↑CAN'T HEAR you very well cuz of this darn
14		machine that's attached to this telephone ↑say it
15		again,
16	Kat: →	**Would it be possible: for Dad to pick me up from**
17		**Wesbury on [Monday.**
18	Lesley:	[Ye:s yes ↑THAT would be ↓alright.

Task 10

The following information is taken from the ESL textbook *New Interchange*. Based on what you have read so far about requests, discuss the advantages and disadvantages of using this list to teach requests.

Less formal	Can I borrow your pencil?
	Could you please lend me a suit?
	It is okay if I use your phone?
	Do you mind if I use your CD player?
	Would it be okay if I borrowed your video camera?
	Would you mind if I borrowed your video camera?
	Would you mind letting me borrow your laptop?
	I wonder if I could borrow $100.
Formal	I was wondering if you'd mind lending me your car.

Response Tokens

Besides the generic and type-specific sequences, another important collection of practices central to sequencing is response tokens. These are lexical items used to perform a range of functions:

(1) acknowledge prior talk;
(2) invite continuation;
(3) offer assessments;
(4) indicate unnecessary persistence of prior speaker(s);
(5) signal incipient speakership.

Items (1)–(5) may be roughly viewed as a continuum that suggests increasing engagement: from simply receiving prior talk to taking up a position, and finally, to gearing up to speak. One of the functions of response tokens not listed here is also treating prior talk as news (see section on announcement response earlier).

Acknowledge Prior Talk

As a listener, the most basic activity is claiming "hearing-understanding" with acknowledgment tokens (Jefferson, 2002, p. 1353). *Okay* is a typical acknowledgment token, as shown below:

(64)   [C. Goodwin in Beach, 1993, p. 329]
    01   Don: I'll go get some more water. ((leaves with pitcher))
    02   John: →   **Okay.**

Although *mm hm* can be used as an acknowledgment token as well, *okay* is more likely to be used when prior talk is more complete, and *mm hm* when prior talk is more likely to continue (Guthrie, 1997).

Invite Continuation

In fact, tokens such as *mm, mm hm, uh huh* and *ah hah* delivered in a slightly rising intonation work as continuers, i.e., to invite continuation (Schegloff, 1982). In the following segment, Speaker A projects a multi-unit turn at line 04, and B the recipient utters continuers at possible completion points (lines 07 and 09) until the announced action is completed:.

(65)   [Schegloff, 1982, p. 82—modified]
    01   A: I've listened to all the things that you've said,
    02   and I agree with you <u>so</u> much.
    03   Now,
    04   I wanna ask you something.
    05   I wrote a letter.
    06   (pause)
    07   B: →   **Mh hm,**
    08   to the governor.
    09   →   **Mh hm::,**
    10   telling him what I thought about him!
    11   Will I get an answer d'you think,
    12   A: Ye:s

By not taking a full turn at the possible completion points, B shows the specific understanding that an extended unit of talk is under way, thereby inviting A to continue. Both *Yeah* and *Okay* can work as continuers as well:

(66)   [Drummond & Hopper, 1993, p. 205]
    01   M: So- the next day I was out playing tennis and oh my
    02   gosh we were out in the clu:b eating?
    03   E: →   **Yeah.**
    04   M: And I about hh (0.2) threw up all over the table
    05   because . . .

(67) [Guthrie, 1997, p. 405]
```
        01    A:              .hh so what we're talking about i::s (1.2)
        02                    tch=removing (1.6) a minus?=ten point eight,
        03    S:      →       ° Okay, °=
        04    A:              =deficit, (1.0) .hh by::: spring ninety two, (0.4) by
        05                    the end, (0.3) alright?=of spring ninety two. .h
        06                    a::::nd (1.3) do not increase deficit.
```

Offer Assessments

An equally or even more engaged way of responding to prior talk is to offer assessments. Assessments can be brief or extended. Typical assessments are agreement or disagreement turns (see the section earlier). Here we limit our discussion to minimal assessments specifically designed as response tokens (e.g., *great*). Compared to continuers, assessments index one's heightened involvement in the ongoing activity (Goodwin, 1986). Nancy's turn at line 06 below is in fact a combination of a news receipt and an assessment:

(68) [Goodwin, 1986, p. 206—modified]
```
        01    Hyla:           One time I remember, .hh this girl wrote and
        02                    her, .hh she was like (.) fifteen or six[teen and ] her=
        03    Nancy:                                                  [Uh hu:h,]
        04    Hyla:           =mother doesn't let her wear.hh nail polish or short
        05                    skir:::ts or: [:: .hhhhhhh ]=
        06    Nancy:  →                     [Oh: wo(h)w]
        07    Hyla:           =O::h no I remember what yesterday was.
```

Assessments have a closing quality that is in keeping with their role as sequence-closing thirds (Schegloff, 2007):

(69) [Schegloff, 2007, p. 125—modified]
```
        01    Don:            I:s this ai:med accurate enou:gh?
        02                    (0.5)
        03    John:           Yes it's aimed at the table.
        04    Don:    →       Grea:t.
```

Indicate Unnecessary Persistence of Prior Speaker(s)

One type of response tokens is multiple sayings (e.g., *no no no, alright alright alright*) (Stivers, 2004). Multiple sayings are used to suggest that the prior speaker has persisted unnecessarily. This may be illustrated in the following segment, which concerns a discussion on the meaning "collocations." At line 15, Libby moves to halt the group's repeated explanation despite her clearly claimed understanding at line 05:

(70)   [Waring, 2005b, p. 5]
    01   Libby: =<u>W</u>hat're collocations.
    02   Prof: What're collocations.
    03   Ellen: It's like- a tall building you will never say a high
    04   building?
    05   Libby: >Oh oh< O::H >okay thanks.<
    06   °(Very go[o d.]°
    07   Prof: [It's-] it's <u>ways</u> that [<u>w</u> o:::r d s] tend to=
    08   Libby: [>°Yeah.°<]
    09   Prof: =be used together.
    10   Libby: >°Ye[ah.]°<
    11   Prof: [<u>C</u>]   <u>O</u>:::::<u>llo</u>:<u>ca</u>:<u>tion.</u>
    12   Libby: °Yeah.°=
    13   Tamar: =Rather than- <u>s</u>:et the table rather than a<u>rra</u>::nge
    14   [°the table or something like that.°]
    15   Libby: →   [Y e a h. y e a h.   ] °yeah. yeah.°
    16   (°I know.°)
    17   Prof: and you know things like com<u>mit</u>, where you
    18   com<u>mit</u> (0.1)

Signal Incipient Speakership

Finally, compared to *mm hm* or *mm*, which tends to be used for passive recipi-
ency, *yeah* is more likely to signal incipient speakership (i.e., readiness to take
the floor) (Gardner, 2007b, p. 321; Jefferson, 1985, 1993). This distinction is
elegantly showcased in the following segment:

(71)   [Jefferson, 1985, p. 7—modified]
    01   Lottie: <u>I</u> didn't have <u>five</u> m<u>i</u>nutes yesterday.
    02   Emma: I don't know how you <u>do</u> i:t.
    03   (0.3)
    04   Lottie: I don't <u>kno</u>:w. nh hnh
    05   Emma: You wor: work all day to<u>da</u>:y.
    06   (0.3)
    07   Lottie: <u>Ye</u>:ah.
    08   (0.2)
    09   Just get W<u>ell</u> I'm (.) b<u>y</u> mys<u>e</u>lf I'm k<u>i</u>nd of cl<u>ea</u>ning
    10   <u>up</u> from y<u>e</u>sterday.
    11   Emma: →   **Mm: hm,**
    12   (0.2)
    13   t hhh [hh<u>h</u>
    14   Lottie: [° A- and ° (.) ° <u>I</u> was just g- <u>washing</u> the
                            dishes, °
    15   Emma: →   **Yeah** w<u>e</u>'re just (.) cl<u>ea</u>ning up h<u>e</u>re to<u>o</u>:.

Jefferson also speculates that in responding to an extended turn, the recipient may move from *mm hmm* to *uh huh* and to *yeah* as s/he gets closer to becoming the next speaker. Similar to *yeah*, *okay* can also preface further talk:

(72)   [Beach, 1993, p. 340]
    01   C: I guess the ba:nd <u>st</u>arts at <u>ni</u>:ne.
    02   D: Oh really?
    03   C: Ya from what Jill told me.
    04   D: →   **Okay** when's Jill gonna go.
    05   C: Same time (0.2) we're gonna meet her there.

It is important to keep in mind that the use of response tokens may vary cross-culturally. An obvious variation is that different languages have different linguistic forms for the same function.

> **Author's story (HW):** As a newly arrived international student working as an assistant in my professor's office, I would frequently respond to her remarks with "<u>mm</u>," and she would ask "<u>mm</u> yes or <u>mm</u> no?" I was using the Chinese version of *mm hm?* to acknowledge, accept, and agree to what she said!

Different languages can also vary by the specific placement of response tokens. English speakers tend to use response tokens at points of grammatical completion with or without intonational completion, Mandarin speakers at points of *both* grammatical and intonational completion, and Japanese speakers at points lacking either grammatical or intonational completion (Clancy, Thompson, Suzuki, & Tao, 1996, p. 375). In other words, of the three languages, in Mandarin speakers would wait the longest to produce a response token, and in Japanese the shortest. In fact, Japanese speakers orient to smaller interactional units such as particular noun phrases to facilitate collaborative participation inside a TCU (Iwasaki, 2009; Morita, 2008). Korean speakers also tend to place response tokens at intra-turn units to offer overt support for an ongoing turn, and these tokens tend to have longer duration and can be elicited via sound stretch as well as continuing intonation by the prior speaker (Young & Lee, 2004). Not understanding these differences can lead to cross-cultural misunderstandings.

> **Author's story (HW):** After my Intercultural Communication class where we discussed Clancy et al.'s (1996) work on response tokens, a male American student came up to me and said, "When I first went to Japan and I was talking to these Japanese women, they made me feel as if I were the most interesting person to listen to [with all the response tokens]. I thought they were trying to seduce me!"

These tiny bits of language behavior such as *mm hm*, *okay*, or *yeah* are what we rely on in daily conversation to ensure ongoing mutual understanding. ESL/EFL students need to learn the importance of using response tokens to fully participate in a conversation. They also need to learn to place these tokens at the grammatical completion points of prior talk to avoid sounding overly interested or uninterested. For instance, Japanese learners can benefit from learning not to overuse response tokens. In addition, ESL/EFL learners need to be made aware that using the same token such as *mm hm* repeatedly can give the impression of boredom when they don't intend to. Being able to use a variety of tokens and do so for different purposes is an important part of one's interactional competence. Using *oh really?* regardless of the content of prior talk, for example, can be puzzling for others.

Teaching Sequencing Practices

In contrast to the lack of materials on teaching turn-taking, CA findings on sequencing practices have attracted a great deal more attention from language teaching professionals. In what follows, we introduce a few activities on teaching adjacency pairs, preference organization, invitation, and response tokens. Our intent is to provide some triggers for teachers to develop their own materials based on the CA findings we have introduced in this chapter.

Adjacency Pairs

Awareness-raising Activity: *Finding Responses*

(1) The following exchanges are based on the data from this chapter. Make cards for all the initiation turns or first pair-parts. Distribute them to pairs (or small groups): one for each pair. Note that depending on the specific level of your learners, you may choose to focus on a smaller number of exchanges or a specific action sequence (I = Initiation; R = Response).

(a)
I: Do you agree with the Bush Doctrine?
R: With respect to what, Charlie?
(b)
I: You can't bring the dog on the bus.
R: But I'm carrying him.
(c)
I: Go through all these. Add periods. Use double space.
R: Oh yeah I will.
(d)
I: You need to rephrase the questions.
     ((pause)) if that's what you want to do.
R: I'll think about it. ((laughs)) because . . .

(e)

I: It's a beautiful day out isn't it?

R: Yeah it's just gorgeous.

(f)

I: She was a nice lady. I liked her.

R: I liked her too.

(g)

I: She's stunning!

R: Yeah, she's a pretty girl.

(h)

I: But you admit you think he's funny.

R: I think it's funny, yeah. But it's ridiculous funny.

(i)

I: You've both basically gone your separate ways.

R: Essentially, except we've had a good relationship at home.

(j)

I: I forgot to tell you the two best things that happened to me today.

R: Oh super. What were they?

(k)

I: .hh And I got an athletic award.

R: REALLY?!?

(l)

I: Hey we've got good news.

R: What's the good news?

(m)

I: Hey that was the same spot we took off for Honolulu.

R: Oh really?

(n)

I: You didn't get an icecream sandwich.

R: I know. I decided that my body didn't need it.

(o)

I: Good shot.

R: Not very solid though.

(p)

I: You're looking good.

R: Great. So are you.

(2) Have the pairs go around the room to collect responses to the first pair-parts on their cards. Record the results:

Responses   Initiating Turn:_____

1   _____

2   _____

3   _____

4   _____

(3) The pairs decide which response is most likely to be said by a native speaker.

(4) Have each pair present to the class what responses they have received and what they have decided to be the most native-like response. Have them give reasons for their choices. Elicit opinions from other learners in the class.

(5) The teacher reveals the actual responses. Explain that these are not the only possible native speaker responses.

(6) Discuss possible cross-cultural variations.

Variations

(i)   Have pairs tape their response sheets to newsprints around the room, and every pair goes around to take their pick of the most native-like response by putting a check next to the response. The teacher calculates the number of checks and announces the "winner" response for each initiating turn. Return to item (5) above.

(ii) Make the same cards for both initiations and responses. Give half the class the initiation turns and the other half the response turns. Have everyone go around the room to find their matches. Display and discuss the matched pairs as a class.

(iii) Based on the results of Step (ii) above, along with the actual responses from the transcripts, develop a multiple choice exercise for pairs or groups to work on. Whichever pair or group gets the largest number of "correct" answers wins. Discuss the various choices in class.

Practicing Activity: *Initiating and Responding*

(1) Each learner gets a card for either the initiating or the responding turn listed above. Have everyone sit in a circle and take turns clockwise to reveal their cards one at a time.

(2) Each time a card is revealed, the one sitting to the right of the "revealer" is to think of and say an appropriate initiating or responding turn for that card.

(3) If the appropriate utterance (as decided by the teacher) is not provided, the responder keeps the revealed card. Whoever collects the most cards in the end loses. The teacher decides when the game is finished.

Variation

Have each learner write their own initiating turn and one response to that initiation on separate strips of paper. Collect all the strips in one bag. Ask learners to pick one strip each from the bag. The task is to go around the room and find their matches.

Preference Organization

Awareness-raising Activity: *Agree or Disagree I*

(1) Invite learners to consider the differences between the ways in which agreements and disagreements are done. Use the transcripts from this chapter and those from Pomerantz (1984) from the recommended readings if necessary.

(2) Ask the class to consider the following (adapted from an activity developed by Don Carroll):

(a) Which uses more language?	*agreement*	*disagreement*
(b) Which comes after a pause?	*agreement*	*disagreement*
(c) Which uses delaying words like "well"?	*agreement*	*disagreement*
(d) Which includes "excuses"?	*agreement*	*disagreement*
(e) Which repeats words?	*agreement*	*disagreement*
(f) Which uses "softening" words?	*agreement*	*disagreement*

(3) Introduce the concepts of preference and dispreference (but perhaps use alternative terms such as "expected" vs. "less expected") based on a discussion of the answers to the above exercise.

(4) Discuss how preferred and dispreferred responses are formulated in the learners' first languages.

(5) Brainstorm other activities (e.g., request) to which preference and dispreference may apply. Make a list of these activities.

(6) Have learners gather and transcribe naturally occurring responses to requests, invitations, and the like. Discuss the typical ways of producing a dispreferred response in class.

Practicing Activity: *Agree or Disagree II*

(1) The following utterances are adapted from Pomerantz (1984). Put them on individual strips of paper and distribute one strip to each learner.

(a) Judy is such a great girl.
(b) It's a beautiful day out, isn't it?
(c) Oh they sounded so good.
(d) You know he's a good-looking fellow.
(e) I'm so dumb I don't even know it.
(f) Isn't he cute?!
(g) She seems like a nice little lady.
(h) I like our teacher. S/he's terrific.
(i) We've got pretty good schools.
(j) I think Chris has a good sense of humor.
(k) Do you think she would fit in?
(l) I still think taking the subway would be quicker.
(m) You're not bored?

(2) Make stickers of the various dispreferred markers (e.g., pause, delaying words, excuses, softening words), and put one sticker on each person's forehead.

(3) Ask everyone to go around and initiate a conversation with the utterance on their strip and record the responses received. All responses should consist of disagreements. In formulating the responses, one should consult the sticker on the initiator's forehead and include the required feature (e.g., delaying words) in the response. For example, if someone says "Judy is such a great girl," your task is to disagree with this statement and to do so by consulting the sticker on his/her forehead. We give some examples below:

(a) delaying words: *Judy?, Yeah but . . ., Well, uh, . . .*
(b) excuses: *Oh I don't really know her that well.*
(c) softening words: *I guess she's okay.*

(4) Each person is then to guess which dispreferred marker is taped on his/her forehead and discusses the reasons for the guess based on the responses s/he has collected.

(5) The teacher leads a discussion on the appropriateness of the responses.

Variations

(i) Have learners generate statements that they have trouble disagreeing with in real life and use those in lieu of (a)–(m) above.

(ii) Focus on an action sequence (e.g., request or complaint) other than agreement/disagreement. Consult the recommended readings for naturally occurring utterances.

Invitations

Awareness-raising Activity: *Invitation Script*

(1) Have learners write down a short script that involves an invitation scenario on newsprints around the classroom in the form below (They can have more or fewer lines):

A: _____
B: _____
A: _____
B: _____

(2) Conduct a class discussion about each script by focusing on the following two sets of questions:

(a) How does the inviter begin his/her invitation? Does s/he invite directly or start with some prefacing words or questions?

(b) What does the inviter say upon hearing a rejection? Does s/he accept it (if so, how?) or revise his/her invitation?

(3) Show transcripts of actual interaction presented in this chapter as well as in the relevant articles listed in the suggested readings below. Discuss discrepancies between these and the learner scripts.

(4) Highlight the following three points about naturally occurring invitation sequences:

(a) Inviters often try to gauge the likelihood of their initiations being accepted by first querying the invitee's plans (e.g., "What are you doing tonight?") or announcing one's own future activities (e.g., "I'm doing a poetry reading in Soho this Friday."). These queries and announcement are called pre-invitations.

(b) Invitees have three choices when responding to pre-invitations: go-ahead, blocking, and hedging.

(c) Inviters can accept rejections with a rejection finalizer ("Okay.") or revise their invitations to make them sound more attractive.

(5) Learners revise their scripts on the newsprint.

(6) Have pairs go around the room commenting on each others' scripts on the newsprint.

(7) The teacher leads a class discussion to wrap up the activity.

Practicing Activity: *Getting your Invitation Accepted*

Have learners go around the room offering pre-invitations. The goal is to elicit the three types of responses listed in the chart below, strictly following the order from blocking to hedging and finally to go-ahead, as if they were climbing a ladder. As a way to record your progress, write down the name of the person who gives the desired response as you go. The first person who receives the go-ahead response and proceeds to get his/her invitation accepted wins. Write down what exactly you have invited the other person to do in the "Your Winning Invitation" cell in the chart.

Responses	Names	Your Winning Invitation
Go-ahead ↑	_____	_____
Hedging	_____	_____
Blocking	_____	_____

For example, if your pre-invitation is "What are you doing tonight?" the three types of responses you will receive could be "Nothing" (go-ahead), "Why?" (hedging), or "I'm having dinner with Craig." (blocking). The first name you can put down should be someone who gives you a blocking response, and the second name someone who gives you a hedging response, and the third name someone who gives you a go-ahead response.

Response Tokens

Awareness-raising Activity: *Responding with Little Words I*

(adapted from Olsher, forthcoming)

(1) Use the transcripts provided in this chapter that contain response tokens to design a fill-in-the-blank exercise for response tokens. Begin the activity with a class discussion on what they would say in those blanks.

(2) Show the actual transcripts. Highlight discrepancies between learner answers and the actual language use.

(3) For each response token in the actual transcripts, ask: (a) What is the token responding to? (b) How is the token delivered? (c) What does it mean? (d) Would any other tokens fit in this slot?

(4) Return to and redo the original fill-in-the-blank exercises (with multiple answers for each blank).

Practicing Activity: *Responding with Little Words II*

Have learners complete Step (4) above in pairs and role-play the dialogs.

Chapter Summary

While turn-taking practices afford the opportunities for speaking, sequencing practices solve the problems of what to say and how to say what needs to be said. The basic practice of sequencing is adjacency pair (AP), which consists of a first pair-part (FPP) and a second pair-part (SPP). A particular type of first pair-part calls for a particular type of second pair-part. This basic sequence may be built upon with pre-expansions, insert-expansions, and post-expansions. An important organization intrinsic to adjacency pairs is preference, where the alternatives that fit in a certain slot in a sequence are treated as nonequivalent. Preferred actions are often, though not necessarily, done without delay, mitigation, or accounts—characteristics of the production of dispreferred actions. Aside from adjacency pairs and preference organization that are generic to interaction, type-specific sequences (e.g., agreement and disagreement, announcement, complaint, compliment response, invitation and offer, and request) come with their own individual organizational features and linguistic resources. Finally, response tokens are integral to sequencing practices and perform a variety of functions. Taken together, sequencing practices provide learners with the tools to answer the critical question of how to do things with words in a second language. For the second language teacher, understanding the complexities of sequencing practices is an important component of one's pedagogical repertoire. Actual pedagogical decisions on what to teach or how to teach should be tailored to specific learner populations. Specific activities may be designed to target difficult areas such as formulating pre-expansions or producing dispreferred responses. Our suggestions are meant to provide an initial template from which additional or alternative pedagogical visions may be generated.

Key Concepts

- **Adjacency pair (AP):** A sequence of two turns produced by different speakers and ordered as first pair-part (FPP) and second pair-part (SPP), where a particular type of FPP requires a particular type of SPP.
- **Insert-expansion:** An adjacency pair that comes between the first and second pair-parts of the base adjacency pair to either clarify the first pair-part or seek preliminary information before doing the second pair-part.
- **Monitor space:** A space around the first possible completion point of the invitation or offer during which potential acceptance or rejection may be detected. There are three types: (1) tag-positioned components; (2) sound stretch; (3) sound stretch followed by either a micro-pause or a filled pause (e.g., inbreath, laughter).
- **News receipt** is a type of announcement response that discourages elaboration in the following forms: (1) *oh*; (2) *oh really*; (3) uninverted *yes/no* question (*she did?*), or (4) *oh* + assessment.
- **Newsmark** is a type of announcement response that encourages elaboration in the following forms: (1) *oh* + partial repeat; (2) *really?*; (3) *yes/no* questions.
- **Post-expansion:** A turn or an adjacency pair (AP) that comes after and is still tied to the base AP. Post-expansion can be minimal or non-minimal.
- **Pre-expansion:** An adjacency pair positioned before the base adjacency pair designed to ensure its smooth running.
- **Preference:** A structural organization in which the alternatives that fit in a certain slot in a sequence are treated as nonequivalent (i.e., preferred vs. dispreferred).
- **Rejection finalizer:** A minimal response token (e.g., *oh, oh I see, okay,* or *alright*) designed to accept rejections.
- **Sequence-closing third (SCT):** An additional turn (e.g., *oh, okay,* or *great*) beyond the second pair-part designed to terminate the sequence.
- **Sequencing practices:** Ways of initiating and responding to talk while performing actions such as requesting, inviting, story-telling, or topic initiation.
- **Solicit:** The preferred second pair-part of the pre-announcement sequence, where one requests the news with a *wh-*question.

Post-reading Questions

1. What is the basic unit of sequencing in English?
2. What are the three ways of expanding an adjacency pair? Give examples.
3. What does the term "preference" mean in conversation analysis? How is it different from our everyday understanding of "preference"?

4. If you have read the literature on cross-cultural and interlanguage prag-
    matics, do you see any connections to the content of this chapter? How do
    the two approaches complement one another?
5. Did you learn anything from this chapter that you did not get from your
    intuition? Please explain.
6. Based on your experience in teaching or learning a language, could you
    relate to any of the Author's stories? If yes, please share.
7. Select one of the suggested readings listed below and present the article in
    class, summarizing the article's key points and offering your questions and
    concerns. Consider how the points raised in the article might be related to
    issues in language teaching especially if the article does not have a peda-
    gogical orientation.
8. Having read the chapter, what questions or concerns do you still have
    about sequencing?

Suggested Readings

Curl, T. S., & Drew, P. (2008). Contingency and action: A comparison of two forms of
    requesting. *Research on Language and Social Interaction*, *41*(2), 129–153.
Davidson, J. (1990). Modifications of invitations, offers and rejections. In G. Psathas
    (Ed.), *Interaction competence* (pp. 149–179). Washington, DC: University Press of
    America.
Dersley, I., & Wootton, A. (2000). Complaint sequences within antagonistic argument.
    Research on Language and Social Interaction, *33*(4), 375–406.
Drew, P. (1984). Speakers' reporting in invitation sequences. In J. M. Atkinson &
    J. Heritage (Eds.), *Structures of social action: Studies in conversation analysis*
    (pp. 129–151). Cambridge: Cambridge University Press.
Gardner, R. (2007b). The *Right* connections: Acknowledging epistemic progression in
    talk. *Language in Society*, *36*(3), 319–341.
Golato, A. (2002). German compliment response. *Journal of Pragmatics*, *34*(5),
    547–571.
Olsher, D. (forthcoming). Responders. In N. Houck & D. Tatsuki (Eds.), *Pragmatics
    from theory to practice: New directions*, Volume 2. Alexandria, VA: TESOL
    Publications.
Pomerantz, A. (1978). Compliment responses: Notes on the co-operation of multiple
    constraints. In J. Schenkein (Ed.), *Studies in the organization of conversational
    interaction* (pp. 79–112). New York: Academic Press.
Pomerantz, A. (1984). Agreeing and disagreeing with assessments: Some features of
    preferred/dispreferred turn shapes. In M. Akinson & J. Heritage (Eds.), *Structures
    of social action: Studies in conversation analysis* (pp. 57–101). Cambridge:
    Cambridge University Press.
Terasaki, A. K. (2004). Pre-announcement sequences in conversation. In G. Lerner
    (Ed.), *Conversation analysis: Studies from the first generation* (pp. 171–224).
    Amsterdam/ Philadelphia: John Benjamins.

Chapter 4

Sequencing Practices and Language Teaching II

Topic Management and Story-telling

Pre-reading Questions

1. Do you think being able to initiate and shift topics is an important skill for language learners? Why or why not?
2. Are you aware of ESL/EFL textbook materials addressed to issues of topic management in English? If yes, how effective do you think those materials are?
3. What is it about the ability to tell stories (e.g., anecdotes) that is teachable to ESL/EFL students?

Chapter Overview

The sequence types discussed in Chapter 3 are all adjacency pair (AP)-based. In this chapter, we go beyond the AP-based sequences and focus on two larger sequences: topic management and story-telling. Topic management and story-telling are vital interactional practices that enable us to partake, appreciate, and take pleasure in the full experience of a conversation. They are the very resources language learners can profit from in achieving integration into the target speech community. We offer a conversation analytic account of how participants (1) initiate, pursue, shift, and terminate topics, and how they (2) launch, produce, and respond to a story. Transcripts of naturally occurring talk showcasing real-life topic management and story-telling practices are used for illustration. The pedagogical relevance of the various practices is considered throughout the chapter. We conclude by suggesting ways of teaching topic management and story-telling.

Topic Management Practices

Knowing how to participate in conversations effectively includes knowing how to initiate, shift, and exit a topic smoothly. These skills do not necessarily come easily even for proficient speakers. After all, we cannot always initiate a topic with *Let's talk about X*, shift the topic with *Let's change the topic*, and exit the topic with *I'm done with this topic*. There are systematic methods by which participants let each other know that topics are being initiated, shifted, and terminated. These methods are typically not made explicit to language teachers and learners.

> **Author's story (HW):** One of my graduate students who is a very fluent speaker of French talks about her difficulty shifting topics in an ongoing French conversation. She calls the ability to do topic management "one of the final 'hurdles' in feeling like a truly communicatively competent French speaker."

CA work on topic has been generally lacking. Atkinson and Heritage (1984) write that " 'topic' may well prove to be among the most complex conversational phenomena to be investigated and, correspondingly, the most recalcitrant to systematic analysis" (p. 165). In addition, the use of terms such as topic initiation, topic maintenance, topic shift, or topic change has not always been consistent in the CA literature. In this section, we introduce topic management in its four aspects: topic initiation, topic pursuit, topic shift, and topic termination. We define each in specific ways.

Topic Initiation

Task 1

Imagine you are preparing a lesson on teaching ESL/EFL students how to initiate topics in conversation. In groups of three or four, list three topic initiating strategies.

Topic Initiating Strategies:

1. _____
2. _____
3. _____

. . .

> **Topic initiation** refers to practices of starting a new topic (1) at the beginning or closing of a conversation, (2) following a series of silences, or (3) after the closing of a prior topic.

There are four environments in which new topics unrelated to the prior are initiated (cf. "boundaried topic movement" in Sacks, 1992a):

(1) during conversation openings;
(2) after closings have been initiated;
(3) after the shutdown of a prior topic;
(4) following a series of silences.

Topics can be initiated through a variety of methods (Button & Casey, 1984, 1985; Maynard, 1980; Maynard & Zimmerman, 1984):

(1) topic initial elicitor;
(2) itemized news inquiry;
(3) news announcement;
(4) pre-topical sequence;
(5) setting talk.

Topic Initial Elicitor

One way to generate topics is through a three-turn sequence launched by **topic initial elicitors** (Button & Casey, 1984) (also see Chapter 6 on closings):

Topic initial elicitor sequence is a three-turn sequence that consists of:

(1) topic initial elicitor (*What's new?*);
(2) newsworthy event (*I got a raise.*);
(3) topicalizer (*Really?*).

The example below contains these three turns (see complete transcription key at the beginning of the book):

(1)   [Button & Casey, 1984, p. 168—modified]
       01   N: =You'll come abou:t (.) eight. Right?=
       02   H: =Yea::h,=
       03   N: =Okay
       04   (0.2)
       05   N: 1→   **Anything else to report,**
       06   (0.3)
       07   H: 2→   **Uh::::::: m::,**
       08   (0.4)
       09   **Getting my hair cut tomorrow,=**
       10   N: 3→   **Oh really?**

Task 2

Identify the topic initial elicitor, newsworthy event, and topicalizer in the following segments:

(1)   [Button & Casey, 1984, pp. 167–168—modified]

01   A: hello::,

02   B: Good <u>mor</u>ning Olivia,

03   A: How are <u>you</u>::,

04   B: Fine.

05   <u>How</u>'re [you

06   A: [That's good ehheh

07   What do you <u>kno:w</u>.

08   B: .hh just got down last night.

09   A: Oh you <u>di:d</u>,?

(2)   [Button & Casey, 1984, p. 168—modified]

01   S: Y'know I- <u>a</u>nyway it's a hunk of stuff goes on

02   I don' have to <u>t</u>ell you.

03   (0.7)

04   G: .hmhhhh hhhhhh <u>BU</u>:::<u>T</u>? hhh SO HOW'RE

05   YOU:? hh I'm oka::y?

06   S: What's new,

07   G: We::ll? °let me see ° last ni:ght, I had the

08   girls ove[r?

09   S: [Yea:h?=

Topic initial elicitors regularly appear after: (1) closing components such as *okay* or *alright* (see segment above); (2) opening components such as the initial greeting and/or *how-are-you* sequences (see below); (3) topic-bounding turns after another topic has clearly drawn to a close (see below) (Button & Casey, 1984, p. 170):

(2)   [Button & Casey, 1984, p. 172—modified]
      01   J: Hello <u>R</u>edcuh five o'six <u>one</u>?

```
02   M:          Mum?
03               (0.2)
04   J:          Ye:s?
05   M:          Me Mathew,
06   J:     →    Oh hello there what are you ↑doing.
```

(3)   [Button & Casey, 1984, p. 175—modified]
```
01   A:          It was too depre [ssing
02   B:                          [Oh::: it is te::rrible-=
03          →    =What's new.
```

Depending on the environments in which topic initial elicitors occur, their turn designs vary. More specifically, they are marked lexically by *else* (*What else?*) in closing environments, *doing* (*What/how are you doing?*) in opening environments, and *new* (*What's new?*) after topic-bounding turns (Button & Casey, 1984). The following is a list of some topic initial elicitors that ESL/EFL might find useful:

- *What else?*
- *What's new?*
- *What's new with you?*
- *What's going on?*
- *What are you doing?*
- *How are you doing?*
- *How are things going?*
- *Anything else to report?*
- *What do you know?*

The preferred response after the topic initial elicitor is a report of a newsworthy event. This report exhibits two features. First, it is shown as a result of the prior elicitation rather than the speaker's plan all along. Two techniques are deployed in this regard: (1) present the event as being searched for (e.g., "U::::m. . . . getting my hair cut tomorrow"); (2) preface the report with markers such as *Oh* as in "Oh I went to the dentist." (Button & Casey, 1984, p. 178). Second, the report presents a possible topic to be talked about—one yet to be accepted by the co-participant. Both features downgrade the newsworthiness of the report. That is, they are used to show that the speakers themselves do not exactly treat them as news.

The third turn in the topic initial elicitor sequence after a newsworthy event is the **topicalizer**:

(4)   [Button & Casey, 1984, p. 182—modified]
```
01   S:          What's new,
02   G:          We::ll? °let me see° last ni:ght, I had the
03               girls ove [r?
```

```
04   S:   →              [Yea:h?=
05                        ((continues on topic))
```

> **Topicalizer** is the third turn in the topic initial elicitor sequence that
> upgrades the newsworthiness of the report and transforms a possible
> topic into an actual topic (e.g., *yea:h, oh really? did you really?*).

Task 3

What other topicalizers can you think of that people use in conversation to get someone to say more about what s/he just mentioned?

Itemized News Inquiry

While a topic initial elicitor begins a new topic with a general inquiry, an
itemized news inquiry does so by targeting a specific newsworthy item
related to the recipient (Button & Casey, 1985, pp. 5–6):

(1) "Did you talk to Dana this week?"
(2) "When are you getting your ↑dining room suite."
(3) "Have yo::u heard yet."

> **Itemized news inquiry** is a topic initiation method that targets a specific
> newsworthy item related to the recipient.

The following segment provides the extended context for (3) above:

```
(5)  [Button & Casey, 1985, p. 6]
     01      Sheila:        Hello:?
     02      John:          Hi: Sheila?
     03      Sheila:        Ye:ah.
     04      John:          How are you.
     05                     (0.2)
     06      Sheila:    →   Have yo::u heard yet.
```

Itemized news inquiries take three forms (Button & Casey, 1985, pp. 8–11):

(1) requests to be brought up-to-date on a recipient-related event (e.g., "When are you getting your ↑di̲ni̲ng room suite.");
(2) solicitous inquiries into recipient troubles (e.g., "How's your fo̲o̲t.");
(3) inquiries into a recipient-related activity that can possibly generate news (e.g., "How's everything at the restaurant?").

In Russian, similar other-attentive topic initiations (e.g., "Did you buy the chicken?") that appear in conversation closings tend to be introduced with the particle *to* (Bolden, 2008).

News Announcement

Unlike itemized news inquiries that target a recipient-related event, **news announcements** report on speaker-related activities (see Chapter 3 on announce sequences).

> **News announcement** is a topic initiation method that reports on speaker-related activities.

Although the activity is not necessarily *about* the speaker, it is the speaker who has the first-hand knowledge (Button & Casey, 1985):

(1) "Uh:m your m̲other met M̲ichael last night.
(2) "Now l̲ook (.) im-uh Il̲ene has just pushed a n̲ote in front of my fa̲ːce."
(3) "A̲ni̲ːta ca̲me: u oh̲: they a̲ll came o̲ver a̲ll of them."

The segment below provides the extended context for (1) above:

(6)   [Button & Casey, 1985, p. 21—modified]
       01   Geri: How are you do̲ing.
       02   Shirley: Ok̲ay how're you.
       03   Geri: O̲h alriː: [ːg̲ht,
       04   Shirley: [(ːhhhhh)
       05   →   **Uh:m your m̲other met M̲ichael last night.**

News announcements are typically produced as partial reports. They only "headline" the news for the other to prompt further telling (Button & Casey, 1985, p. 24).

With regard to the distribution of the various topic initiation methods, topic initial elicitors are distinctly featured in conversation closings, where the general tendency is to avoid raising new topics (see Chapter 6 on closings). Since news announcement is a "strong" move to introduce a topic, it is not used in conversation closing sections (Button & Casey, 1985, p. 45).

Announcements relying on common backgrounds (e.g., "Joe came by the other day.") are also used to initiate topics (Maynard, 1980):

(7)   [Maynard, 1980, p. 283]
    01   Melissa: →   **But uh hah Dr. Buttram. Today he gave us a**
    02   **lecture on Freud? And it's the most interesting**
    03   **lecture on Freud I have ever**
    04   **[had.]**
    05   Warren: [Oh] good.

Both itemized news inquiries and news announcements are considered topic nomination practices (Button & Casey, 1985; cf. "topic proffering sequences" in Schegloff, 2007).

Pre-topical Sequence

Another topic initiating method is **pre-topical sequence** (Maynard & Zimmerman, 1984).

Pre-topical sequence is a topic initiation method used to get acquainted with one another with personal questions about the recipient's identity or activity.

Some examples of personal questions are "Are you a freshman?," "Do you live here on campus?," and "What's your major?," as shown below:

(8)   [Maynard & Zimmerman, 1984, p. 306—modified]
    01   A1:   →   **What's your major?**
    02   A2:   Well my major's physics but I haven't really taken
    03   a physics class yet so I have a good chance to
    04   change it. Probably to anthropology if I change it.
    05   A1:   I've heard it's a good major.

Author's story (HW): I recently observed a wonderful ESL class, where students were simulating giving their "elevator pitch" (i.e., a mini-"speech" given within the span of an elevator ride) to rotating partners to promote themselves during a networking event. One Japanese student begins each time with "Hi, my name is Moto. Nice to meet you. I'm an engineer . . ." I remember thinking that Moto could really benefit from learning some topic initiating strategies to avoid sounding pushy and inappropriate.

Setting Talk

Referencing the setting can also be used for initiating a topic (Maynard & Zimmerman, 1984).

Setting talk is a topic initiation method that points to the immediate environment of the interaction.

Some examples of setting talk in ordinary conversation are:

- *Nice day, isn't it?*
- *Do you have the time?*
- *This bus is taking a long time.*
- *That's a cool bag.*

In the following two extracts, the participants are pointing to the experimental setting they are in as a way of initiating topics:

(9)   [Maynard & Zimmerman, 1984, p. 304]
01	Sharon:		Hi there.
02	Judy:	→	**This is no good.**
03	Sharon:		I know.
04	Judy:		There are two-way mirrors one-way mirrors,
05			whatever they're called.

(10)   [Maynard & Zimmerman, 1984, p. 304]
01	Bill:	→	**Hey, I know he's been watching us. They're**
02			**going to leave us in here.**
03	James:		They're not watching me. Oh, it's my moment
04			of glory then.
05			(1.7)
06			Well
07			(3.0)
08			No, actually I was on TV twice.
09	Bill:		Real TV?

Task 4

Identify the topic initiation methods in the following segments.

(1)   [Button & Casey, 1985, p. 11—modified]
01	Lawrence:	Well I'm up to calling you to see if I can

```
02                    see you and have some fun with you again
03                    (maybe)
04      Maggie:       AHhh ha ha ha ha ha
05                    .hh Sounds delightful. How's your sister and
06                    her husband?
```

(2)   [Maynard & Zimmerman, 1984, p. 307—modified]
```
01      A:            Where do you live, IV? Or-
02      B:            Yeah, I live in, uh, at the Tropicana.
03      A:            Ah.
04      B:            Good old Trop.
05      A:            Did you try to get into the dorms or-
06      B:            Mm hmm. I thought I'd meet more people
07                    that way . . .
```

(3)   [Button, 1991, p. 261]
```
01      A:            and I don't think block board would wo::rk there.
02      B:            No::
03      A:            No:::
04                    (0.5)
05      B:            Uhm:::. So, anything new with you.
```

Topic initiation is not yet a standard component in ESL/EFL texts, but material designers have begun to address areas such as using *so* to start a topic (McCarthy, McCarten, & Sandiford, 2006) or using questions to get specific information and carry on a conversation (Reinhart & Fisher, 2000). The strategies presented above can be used to complement the existing materials in helping learners develop a full range of techniques in initiating topics. Being able to initiate topics appropriately is vital to one's interactional competence. It is a basic interpersonal communication skill without which a person can feel a bit like a fish out of water.

> **Author's story (JW):** I felt like a fish out of water when I was part of a Mandarin conversation among physicists. The participants' talk was flying back and forth. As a nonnative speaker of Mandarin, I was trying frantically to keep up with the conversation, and I had no idea when and how to initiate a topic of my own.

Topic Pursuit

> **Topic pursuit** refers to practices of insisting upon developing a topic when its initiation receives less-than-enthusiastic responses.

Just because a topic is initiated does not mean it gets developed. Any topic initiation attempt can receive less than enthusiastic or "curtailed" responses (i.e., those that do not encourage the further development of the topic) (Button & Casey, 1985). When this happens, participants may engage in topic pursuit in a number of ways (Button & Casey, 1985):

(1) recycling of no-news report;
(2) itemized news inquiry;
(3) return topic initial elicitor;
(4) news announcement;
(5) reclaimer.

First, one can recycle a newsreport to pursue a topic, as M does below:

(11)   [Button & Casey, 1984, p. 185—modified]
        01   M: How are things going?
        02   P: Oh-h-h-h nothing doing.
        03   M: →   **Nothing doing huh?**
        04   P: No, how's it with you?

As can be seen, pursuing the topic does not mean the topic necessarily gets taken up. Second, itemized news inquiry can be used to do topic pursuit when topic initial elicitors or news announcements receive curtailed responses:

(12)   [Button & Casey, 1985, p. 27—modified]
        01   Maggie: .h What have you been up to.
        02   (0.5)
        03   Lawrence: We:ll about the same thing. One thing
        04   anoth [er. I should
        05   Maggie: →   [**You're still in the real estate business**
        06   **Lawrence?**

(13)   [Button & Casey, 1985, p. 35—modified]
        01   B: Oh I got hurt a little bit last night.
        02   C: You did.
        03   B: Yeah,
        04   C: →   **What happened to you.**

Third, a return topic initial elicitor is also used to do topic pursuit:

(14) [Button & Casey, 1985, p. 28—modified]
```
01    F:                    What's going o:n.
02    J:        →          Not mu:ch.What do you know.
```

Fourth, a specific form of news announcement, which shows that the speaker knows something that the recipient is not telling, may be used to pursue the topic when itemized news inquiries receive curtailed responses:

(15) [Button & Casey, 1985, p. 41—modified]
```
01    A:                    How's Tina doing.
02                          (.)
03    J:                    Oh she's doing goo:d.
04    A:        →          Is she I heard she got divo:rc:ed.=
```

Finally, following any curtailed reply, the initial questioners may do topic pursuit through a "reclaimer," bringing the focus back to themselves (Maynard & Zimmerman, 1984, p. 308):

(16) [Maynard & Zimmerman, 1984, p. 308]
```
01    B1:                   What are you majoring in?
02    B2:                   Undeclared.
03    B1:       →          heh heh all right! I think that's the first
04                          sophomore that I know that's undeclared.
```

(17) [Maynard & Zimmerman, 1984, p. 308]
```
01    A2:                   What year are you.
02    A1:                   I'm a sophomore I think.
03    A2:       →          Yeah, I'm a junior. I transferred from J.C.
```

Task 5

Identify the topic pursuit methods in the following segments.

(1)   [Button & Casey, 1984, p. 186—modified]
```
01    A:                    What's doing,
02                          (.)
03    B:                    Ah:, noth [i:n:g,      ]
04    A:                              [Y'didn't g]o meet Grahame?=
05    B:                    hhhhahh Well I got ho::me,=
```

(2)   [Button & Casey, 1985, p. 41—modified]
```
01    A:                    How you feeling Marge=
02    B:                    =Oh fi:ne.
03    A:                    Cuz- I think Joanne mentioned that you
04                          weren't so well? A few weeks ago:?
```

```
(3)    [Maynard & Zimmerman, 1984, p. 308]
01     A:            Where'd you come from.
02     B:            Sacramento.
03     A:            Oh yeah? I'm from Concord. It's up north
04                   too.
05     B:            Yeah it's a little bit close.
```

Insofar as "interactive production" is key to developing speaking skills (Lee, 2006b), the various methods of pursuing a topic provide precisely the tools to go beyond a single turn and build sequences of interaction. ESL/EFL textbooks rarely make explicit these methods, without which learners' conversations may grind to a halt, or their interests in certain topics may be underestimated by their native speaker co-participants.

Topic Shift

Besides topic initiation and topic pursuit, another important component of topic management is **topic shift**.

> **Topic shift** refers to practices of (1) shifting emphasis within a topic or (2) moving towards a new topic either with a disjunctive marker or in a stepwise fashion.

"Moving towards a new topic" in the definition above may sound similar to "topic initiation" discussed earlier. The difference is that topic initiation is done in the four environments of openings, closings, after a topic boundary, and after a series of silences. Topic shift, by contrast, is done within a current topic, and it is done in two ways:

(1) disjunctive topic shift;
(2) stepwise topic shift (cf. "topic shading" in Schegloff & Sacks, 1973).

Disjunctive Topic Shift

Topic shifts can be specifically marked as disjunctive.

> **Disjunctive topic shift** is a method of moving into a new aspect of the same topic or a new topic by marking such moves as not tightly fitted to the ongoing talk with utterances such as *actually* or *by the way*.

The following are **disjunctive markers** used to signal topic shifts (Crow, 1983, pp. 141–143):

- *Anyway*
- *Alright*
- *Oh*
- *Speaking of X*
- *That reminds me of*
- *Oh say*
- *I tell you what*
- *One more thing*
- *Listen, there's something I've gotta tell you*
- *You know what?*
- *Before I forget*
- *By the way*
- *Incidentally*

> **Disjunctive marker** is an utterance used to mark the introduction of a new focus or topic as abrupt or unexpected.

These explicit markers for topic shift are an important part of one's interactional competence. Even very advanced nonnative speakers may have trouble using these markers fluently.

> **Author's story (HW):** Once I was talking with my colleague on the phone, and at one point, he started to sound a bit lost. His responses became a bit "noncommittal" as if he had no idea what I was really talking about but wanted to be polite and play along. Then he said, "Oh I didn't realize you already changed the topic!" Well, I never marked my change!

Task 6

Go to some ESL/EFL textbooks and grammar books as well as reference grammars. Do you find any of the utterances below explained in these materials? What utterances did you not find? Of the ones that you found, how are they explained?

- *Anyway*
- *Alright*
- *Oh*
- *Speaking of X*
- *That reminds me of*
- *Oh say*

- *I tell you what*
- *One more thing*
- *Listen, there's something I've gotta tell you*
- *You know what?*
- *Before I forget*
- *By the way*
- *Incidentally*
- *Actually*

In what follows, we provide some examples of four topic-shift markers: *by the way, anyway, alright,* and *actually. By the way* is one of the items used to indicate that an utterance is off-topic (Sacks, 1992b, p. 352). It is also referred to as a "misplacement marker" used to indicate that what follows is not done in its proper place, as shown in the segment below (Schegloff and Sacks, 1973):

(18)   [Schegloff & Sacks, 1973, p. 320]

01	Caller:		You don't know w- uh what that would be, how
02			much it costs.
03	Crandall:		I would think probably, about twenty five
04			dollars.
05	Caller:		Oh boy, hehh hhh!
06			Okay, thank you.
07	Crandall:		Okay dear.
08	Caller:	→	**OH BY THE WAY. I'd just like to say that uh,**
09			**I DO like the news programming. I've been**
10			**listening, it's uh . . .**

In UK general practice *by the way, Doctor* is referred to as the "doorhandle remark" used by patients to initiate new topics as they leave the doctor's office (Campion & Langdon, 2004). Other topic shifting remarks used by the patients are:

(a) "I know it's a separate thing, doctor."
(b) "I do have another little problem."
(c) "Also, Doctor Rod, she's got worms as well."

Anyway is another marker of disjunctive topic shift, and it is typically delivered with "increased amplitude, raised pitch, and hesitancy (inbreaths, pauses, sound stretches)" (Drew, 1997, p. 76). In the following extracts, Lesley and Mum are talking about the death of a mutual acquaintance. Lesley's shift into a new topic is prefaced with "anyway" along with its prosodic emphasis:

(19)   [Drew, 1997, p. 76—modified]
```
01   Lesley:        He had a good innings did [n't he.
02   Mum:                                     [I should say so:
03                  Ye:s.
04                  (O.2)
05   Mum:           Marvelous,
06   Lesley:   →   .hhhh Anyway we had a very good evening on
07                  Saturda:y . . .
```

Unlike *by the way*, which marks what follows as off-topic, *anyway* is used to show that "what it precedes is fitted not to the immediately preceding, but to what preceded that" (Schegloff, 1984, p. 38; also see Sacks, 1992b, pp. 567–568).

Besides *by the way* and *anyway*, *alright* can also be used to mark topic shift (Holt & Drew, 2005):

(20)   [Holt & Drew, 2005, p. 40—modified]
```
01   Nancy:    I'm just not ready for any kind of a battle,=
02             =[.hhhhhh  ]hhh yet at a: [ll
03   Emma:      [°Mm-mm°]                [Well that's ↓good,
04             that your
05             (0.4)
06   Emma:    .hhh you're keeping busy that's good,
07   Nancy:   ↑Well su:re. Worki[ng (        )]
08   Emma:                      [Tha:t's ↓a : ll,]
09             (.)
10   Nancy:   °↑Ri:ght.°=
12   Emma:  → =A::LRI[GHTY I don't know]=
13   Nancy:         [°(Ye::ah          )°]
14   Emma:   =What ti:me is it I- I: WOKE UP at
15             a::↑six ↓this
16             mor:n [ing Go]:d what is it q]uarter=
17   Nancy:         [ O h : ]m y Go::d.   ]
18   Emma:   =after eleven?
19   Nancy:   °Ya:h,°
20             (1.0)
21   Nancy:   °Ya[h well° ]
22   Emma:       [The SU] :N'S COMIN OU:T.
```

Finally, *actually* plays an important role in marking topic shift as well (Clift, 2001). TCU (turn-constructional unit)-initial uses of *actually* serve to mark movement within a topic. In the following segment, Mike has been talking about the practice of eighteenth-century upper-class women to drink hot chocolate in church. At line 15, Alice shifts to another aspect of the topic with a question prefaced by *actually*:

(21)   [Clift, 2001, p. 282—modified]

```
01   Mike:          and some would have their- their servants to (.) rush
02                  into church during the- just before the se:rmon with
03                  their fix of chocolate.
04                  (2.0)
05   Gus:           [that's right and then-
06   Mike:          [[(and nobody seemed) to object.
07   Gus:           then a bit of lau:danum a:fterwards,
08                  (1.5)
09   Gus:           huhhuhhuh
10   Mike:          $that's right, yeah yeah that's [true yes.$
11   Gus:                                          [then the men- the
12                  men had chocolate (1.0) laudanumsnuff::.
13   Harriet:       uhehhhe
14                  (1.0)
15   Alice:  →      ↑Actually why are the ↑la::dies there, cus I- ↑I
16                  (found most) -
17                  (2.0)
18   Mike:          I suppose the men stu- [stuck to b↑ee::r I don't
19                  know,
20   Alice:                                [↑I don't know if this is just
21                  me, but I think girls are more addicted to chocolate
22                  than (.) guys,
```

By contrast, TCU-final *actually* is used to mark movement to a new topic
(Clift, 2001). The following segment is taken from BBC Radio, where Melvin
is the interviewer and Sue a TV producer who produces a drama series in some
science laboratories. She has just explained how the Cavendish laboratory at
Cambridge organizes open days for school pupils. At lines 10–12, Melvin does
a topic change with a TCU-final *actually*.

(22)   [Clift, 2001, pp. 279–280—modified]

```
01   Sue:           [(h)And that's very good because (.) they
02                  do that at the end of summer term so befo:re these
03                  youngsters[in the fourth form have made their=
04   Melvin:                  [mm
05   Sue:           =choi:ce, and the idea is if you turn them on to the
06                  exci:tement of Physics perhaps those girls .h will
07                  then make a decision to do Physics at A:
08                  level. and then go o::n and do it,
09                  (.)
10   Melvin:  →     I'm ↑very touched by your belief in the inpru- in
11                  the impro:ving uh- possibilities of tele- popular
12                  television actual[ly,
13   Sue:                            [..hh well I think the point is that
14                  you ↑CA:n't really
```

| 15 | | do it as a documentary, (I mean) first of all, |
| 16 | | television IS the media isn't it . . . |

Task 7

The following segment contains a topic shift. What is the speaker shifting to and away from? How is the shift done?

[Clift, 2001, p. 277—modified]
((L =Lesley, K=Kevin. Gordon is L's son, Katherine her daughter)

01	L:	Ye:s. Oh: shame. h .hhhh Gordon <u>d</u>idn't pass his
02		<u>t</u>est I'm afraid, h
03	K:	<u>O</u>h dear
04	L:	He's going- (.) W<u>e</u>ll .hh he w<u>a</u>s hoping to get
05		it (0.2) in: uh in the s<u>u</u>mmer but (.) they're g<u>e</u>tting
06		<u>v</u>ery booked <u>u</u>p so I d<u>o</u>n't know if he'll even: get it in
07		th<u>e</u>:n .h
08		(1.1)
09	K:	Y<u>e</u>s I: ah: no doubt he's back at uh
10		(0.5)
11	L:	.hhhh Y<u>e</u>s. We're going up- (.) we:ll- (.) we're get (0.2)
12		<u>a</u>ctually it's gonna be a ↑rather busy Ju:ne, Katherine's
13		home for three week<u>e</u>:n:ds. As it h<u>a</u>ppens people're coming
14		do:wn and can bring her d<u>o</u>wn which is rather nice,
15		(1.2)
16	L:	which yea::: so we're rather looking <u>for</u>ward to that,

---

Stepwise Topic Shift

Besides disjunctive topic shift, one can also move from one topic or one aspect of a topic to the next in a stepwise (i.e., gradual) fashion. In fact, **stepwise topic shift** is considered "the best way to move from topic to topic" (Sacks, 1992b, p. 566).

Stepwise topic shift is a method of gradually moving into a new focus or a new topic with the following devices:

(1) pivot + new focus/topic;
(2) invoking semantic relationships between items;
(3) summary of prior topic → ancillary matters → new topic.

PIVOT + NEW FOCUS/TOPIC

The first way of doing a stepwise topic shift is by using a pivot: if what you want to talk about is not connected to what is currently being talked about, find something that connects to both and use that to introduce the new topic (Sacks, 1992b, p. 300). This "something that connects to both" is a "pivot," which can take four forms:

(1) acknowledgment;
(2) assessment;
(3) commentary;
(4) figurative expression.

Jefferson (1993), for example, describes how one could attend to another's talk while shifting the topic to matters of his/her own interest with acknowledgments (e.g. "yes" or "yeah"), assessments (e.g., "well that's good."), and commentaries (e.g., "Oh really they are casual aren't they."), showing increasing degrees of engagement with the prior speaker's talk. In the following extract, "yes" serves as the pivot:

```
(23)   [Jefferson, 1993, p. 4—modified]
       01   J:        It en:ded with a great big ↓bang=
       02             =ehh he[h  I jum  ]ped=
       03   V:               [°Oh-huh::°]
       04   J:        =out of the seat I jumped.
       05             (.)
       06   J:        [shot about three feet in]the air I think=
       07   V:        [°Oh:::::::::::::::::::::::° ]
       08   J:        =he[h heh]      [hhhh
       09   V:   →       [Y e s ]::.hh[Eh:m, we didn't go to have our
       10             hair done by the wa:y,=
       11   J:        =.h No well I gathered not.
```

Okay may also be used both responsively and transitionally, allowing the speaker to be both on topic and usher in "next-positioned matters (topics/activities)" (Beach, 1993, p. 329):

```
(24)   [Beach, 1993, p. 340—modified]
       01   C:        I guess the ba:nd starts at ni:ne.
       02   D:        Oh really?
       03   C:        Yah from what Jill told me.
       04   D:   →    Okay when's Jill gonna go.
       05   C:        Same time (0.2) we're gonna meet her there.
       06   D:   →    Okay um (0.5) so you wa:nt to take your car
       07   C:        We can take your car if you wa:nt.
       08   D:        .hhh hhh I meant you want- you wanna have your
```

```
09                    car there so you can le:ave.
10     C:             Yeah I think that'd be a better idea.
11                    Okay.
12                    (0.5)
13     D:    →        Okay hhhh well what what time is it now °I don't
14                    have my watch on.
15     C:             Six o'clock.
```

In the next extract, the assessment "well, that's good" serves as the pivot:

```
(25)   [Jefferson, 1993, pp. 9–10—modified]
       01    A:       and I really felt te:rribly ba:d about the way she (.)
       02             treated her [bef°ore. °
       03    P:                   [Ye:ah,
       04             (0.2)
       05    A:       And she jus:t gr:abbed her by the ha:nd when she
       06             got through with it It was:: (0.4) it=
       07             =[was rea:lly ↑Oh it](   )
       08    P:        [↑Oh:::   t h a t's:]
       09             (0.3)
       10    A:       one of the most thri:lling. programs I know I've
       11             ever (0.6) been to [(        )
       12    P:                          [Well it had a ni:ce writ:e up in
       13             the paper  [too
       14    A:                  [Yeh I noticed [that
       15    P:    →                            [Well that's good .hhh
       16             Well ↑LI:STEN uh- ↑↑Tuesday ni:ght we're starting
       17             that Mother's Club bit again at the church.
```

The commentary "No, she wasn't saying anything too much, was she." serves as the pivot below:

```
(26)   [Jefferson, 1993, pp. 9–10—modified]
       01    K:       I mean I was: (.) one that was grea:tly at
       02             fault. .hhhh And I: don't ↓think ↑Elva appreciates
       03             anything like that <No:t that she said anything
       04             but (.) you (.) you just don't (.) pla:y Bridge
       05             that wa[y Claire.      ]
       06    C:    →        [No uh she w]asn't saying anythin:g too
       07             much was ↓she. .hhh .hhhh I was just wondering if
       08             we had that other ta:ble (0.2) in the dining room=
       09    K:       =to [me that w]ould-
       10    C:          [Yah I::   ] Now if I: had been Teresa:.
       11    K:       I: wou:ld have (0.2) I don't know she could shorten
       12             her table but . . .
```

Finally, figurative expressions also work as pivotal utterances in stepwise topic shift (Holt & Drew, 2005). In the extract below, the topic shifts from D's account of his meeting with someone he went to high school with to M's tale about his friend's son. The figurative expression "late bloomer" serves as a pivot for this shift although M's story is not at all about a later bloomer, but someone who was initially successful but failed later:

```
(27)   [Holt & Drew, 2005, p 44—modified]
       01   D:      .hhh hhh And I- You know it- for some
       02                   reason he struck me as never even being
       03                   able to get out of high school well I was
       04                   talking to him well he's go- he's got a year
       05                   left at SMU in law school.
       06   M:      hh [h huh huh] huh [huh .hhh].hhh=
       07   D:         [hh h      ]    [ h h h h  ]
       08   D:      =and he's rea:l cute now.
       09   M:  →   .hhh We:ll see that just goes to show you
       10                   he's a late bloomer.
       11   D:      Yeah he was re:al handsome.
       12              (1.0)
       13   M:      You know (0.4) sometimes the late bloomers
       14                   will fool you
       15              (0.6)
       16   D:      Yeah that's true.
       17   M:      I told you about my friend whose son
       18                   graduated from .hhh A and [M:]
       19   D:                                        [ye:]ah and he went
       20                   straight to law schoo:l and
       21              (0.5)
       22   M:      all that kind of [stuff and now he's     ]
       23   D:                       [and now he's working]  as a
       24                   painter.
       25              (0.6)
       26   M:      driving a trailer or something
```

INVOKING SEMANTIC RELATIONSHIPS

A second way of doing stepwise topic shift is to invoke the semantic relationships between two items. One such relationship is "co-class membership": if A talks about cigars, B can talk about pipes (i.e., cigars and pipes belong to the same class of smoking) (Sacks, 1992a, p. 757). In the following example, "resting for a day" (lines 04 and 06) and "playing around" (line 09) belong to the same class of "getting way behind" activities:

```
(28)   [Maynard, 1980, p. 271—modified]
       01   Jenny:      It's really pressur[ing    ]
```

```
02  Lisa:                        [They ]move so: fast=
03  Jenny:        =um hmm=
04  Lisa:    →   =You just- you kno:w GOD [you jus   ]rest=
05  Jenny:                                 [Oh Ye::ah]
06  Lisa:    →   =for a DA::Y and you're w- way- behind
07               [ it seems like ]
08  Jenny:   →   [Oh ye::ah      ] An I been
09               PLAY:in aroun' too much
10  Lisa:        Rea:lly?
11  Jenny:       Cuz I'm USE to PLAY:in' . . .
```

Another semantic relationship in this extract involves moving from a categorical to a particularized statement, where Lisa's "You" at line 04 is an abstract "you," and Jenny subsequently conducts a shift to "I" herself (Maynard, 1980).

SUMMARY OF PRIOR TOPIC→ANCILLARY MATTERS→NEW TOPIC

Finally, stepwise topic shifts can involve multiple stages. The following segment starts with L saying, "It's terrible to keep people alive" and somehow ends with E saying, "We just had a beautiful time."

```
(29)  [Jefferson, 1984, pp. 200–201—modified]
      01  L:   1→   But eh-it's-it's terrible to keep people ali:ve and
      02               [you know and just let them suffer [day in and=
      03  E:           [Right.                            [R:ight.
      04  L:           = day out, [it's-
      05  E:                      [They don't do that with an animal.
      06               (0.5)
      07  E:           you kno[:w,
      08  L:                  [Yeah.
      09  E:           Oh well [bless his heart Well, we don't know what=
      10  L:                   [((sniff))
      11  E:           =it's all about I g- I- ((sniff)) Don't get yourself=
      12  L:           [Oh I'm not. I just- you know I wish        ]
      13  E:           =[Honey you've got to get ho:ld of your- I know]
      14  L:   2→   =I'd- I'd kind of liked to gone out there but I was
      15               afraid of the fog I was gonna drive him in:: I- .hh
      16               last [ni:ght. But,
      17  E:   3→        [.hh Oh it was terrible coming down ev[en=
      18  L:                                                    [But-
      19  E:           = this morning. ((sniff))
      20  L:           But San Diego? I c- I couldn't believe it last night.
      21               We left there about, .hh eleven thirty (.) and it w-
      22               it was clear all the way up until we hit, (1.0) uh::
      23               the uh Fashion Square here in Balboa.
      24               [I couldn't believe it [and we went into,=
```

```
25   E:        [((sniff))              [(   )
26   L:        =you couldn't even see:.
27   E:    4→  Oh God it's terrible. ((sniff)) That's why well we
28             didn't get home till two o'clo:ck. God it's-
29             (0.2)
30             [beautiful-]
31   L:        [It was ter ]rible in to:wn?
32   E:        .h Oh we just got into bed at two:. I wasn't gonna (.)
33             go down, wait let me turn this fa- uh:
34             (0.5)
35        5→   You know we w-this par:ty and then we went to
36             another little party a:fterwards and oh I met so
37             many f: fa::bulous pees- (.) people and danced
38             with my poor old toes with no t(h)oenails
39             and I was in- .hhhh hh(h)igh (h)h(h)eels
40             and .hahh and oh:we (.) just had a (.) beautiful
41             time.
```

Jefferson (1984) describes the stepwise transition in the above segment from troubles talk to a next topic as consisting of five moves shown at the five arrowed turns in the transcript:

(1) troubles teller sums up the heart of the trouble;
(2) troubles teller turns to other matters that are on topic but ancillary;
(3) troubles recipient topically stabilizes the ancillary matters;
(4) troubles recipient produces a pivotal utterance that has independent topical potential;
(5) participants arrive at the matters that constitute the target of a series of moves.

Task 8

Think of a way to teach stepwise topic shift using the information we have provided above. How would you convey the concepts in ways that your learners would understand? Would you use any of the transcripts above? If so, how?

The ability to shift topics is an indispensable resource for avoiding answering too personal a question, averting an argument, getting out of a topic that we are not interested in, and so on. This applies to all talk-in-interaction. Developing the finesse to manage topic shifts can pose great challenges for ESL/EFL learners. In order to keep up with a conversation, ESL/EFL learners need to be able to both recognize and do topic shifts. Little words and phrases such as *actually, anyway,* or *by the way* carry nuanced interactional meanings. Learners can easily get lost in a conversation if they don't recognize the subtle topic shifts marked by a word such as *actually*. Using the wrong marker (e.g., *by the way* instead of *anyway*) can cause confusion for one's co-participants. Teaching learners the techniques of moving more gradually on to the next focus or topic with simple utterances such as *okay, yeah*, or *that's good* can further enhance their ability to keep a conversation going. Finally, a systematic understanding of all these subtleties involved in topic shifts is a pre-requisite for language teachers who are interested in helping their learners master the domain of topic management.

Topic Termination

In addition to topic initiation, pursuit, and shift, the last stage in topic management is **topic termination** (for a wide range of practices for closing a conversation, see Chapter 6).

Topic termination refers to practices of closing down a topic.

Topic termination can, but does not necessarily, coincide with conversation closing. According to Schegloff and Sacks (1973), for example, utterances such as "well" or "okay" work as possible pre-closings when placed at the end of a topic (p. 303). Assessment tokens regularly occur at topical boundaries. These include utterances such as *great, good, that's good, oh splendid, oh great, oh good, lovely, very good*, or the like (Antaki, 2002; Heritage, 1984b; Waring, 2008; Wong & Waring, 2009). In the following extract, the speaker closes down the topic with the assessment "lovely," after which the conversation ends:

```
(30)   [Antaki, 2002, p. 10—modified]
       01   Ed:       I think she'd like to.
       02             (0.2)
       03   Les:      Hm: hn- [Okay then. [Right [well
       04   Ed:               [So-        [(yes) I ['ll see you on-
       05             on Thursday at six thirty then.
       06   Les:   →  Lovely.
       07   Ed:       [(   )
       08   Les:      [(Bye bye then,
       09   Ed:       Bye:,
```

In the extract below, "oh: splendid" signals the end of a prior topic:

```
(31)   [Wright, 2004—modified]
       01   Bod:      It might be mo:re I don't [know.]
       02   Les:                               [Yes:  ] I was going
       03             to bring Mrs. La:mp,
```

```
04                (0.2)
05    Les:        from North Cadbury
06                (.)
07    Les:        but she can't come becuz her husband's
08                unexpectedly .hhh had to go away so she's
09                comin::g to the f:irst one
10                after Christmas.
11    Bod:   →    Oh: splendid.
12    Les:        Yahp. Okay the[n
13    Bod:                       [Righ[t, well I shall] see you
14    Les:                            [See you later]
15                (.)
15    Les:        B[ye bye:
16    Bod:         [Bye
```

Story-telling Practices

Much of life is about story-telling. We tell each other anecdotes about what happened in our daily lives—things that are happy, sad, moving, surprising, exhilarating, and sometimes shocking. They are the fabric of social interaction. Through stories, we build families, get to know our co-workers, and get things done. Teaching second language learners the skill of story-telling is an important step towards socializing them into the target speech community. However, the teaching of story-telling is often tied to the elements of a story such as setting, plot, character(s), conflict, climax, and ending. Students are taught what goes into a story, but not how the story gets to be told during a conversation in the first place. Story-telling as observed in ESL classrooms sometimes turns out to be a series of monologs. Although stories can be elicited as those shown in Labov and Waletsky's (1967) sociolinguistic interviews, in everyday interaction, stories tend to be introduced by tellers themselves. In addition, compared to Labov and Waletsky's (1967) famous model of narratives (i.e., abstract, orientation, complication, resolution, and coda), CA work on story-telling foregrounds how stories get told as a natural part of a conversation and as a joint accomplishment between the teller and the recipient. Story-telling is composed of three types of sequences addressed respectively to (1) launching the story; (2) telling the story; (3) responding to the story. These sequences suspend the normal alternation of turns, which resumes after the completion of the story-telling sequences.

Launching the Story

Stories may be launched with a single turn or a sequence (Jefferson, 1978; Lerner, 1992; Sacks, 1974).

Launching with a Single Turn

When stories are launched in a single turn, they are often triggered by prior talk. The methods for initiating a triggered story in a single turn include (Jefferson, 1978):

(1) disjunctive marker and/or embedded repetition;
(2) conventional story-prefixed phrase as topically coherent next utterance.

The next extract includes an example of disjunctive marker with embedded repetition:

```
(32)   [Jefferson, 1978, p.220—modified]
       01   Ken:          The cops, over the hill. There's a place up in
       02                 Mulholland where they've- where they're building
       03                 those hous[ing projects?
       04   Roger:   →              [Oh have you ever taken them
       05                 Mulhollan' time trials?
       06                 .hh You go up there with a girl. A bunch of guys're
       07                 up there an [STORY]
```

Other disjunctive markers are expressions such as *incidentally, that reminds me of,* or *speaking of X* (see "Disjunctive topic shift" above).
   Stories can also be produced as a topically coherent next utterance with a conventional story-prefixed phrase such as:

- *One day*
- *As a matter of fact*
- *I heard X.*

These entry devices are often surrounded by the presence of "perturbation" such as "uh one-" in the segment below (Jefferson, 1978):

```
(33)   [Jefferson, 1978, p. 225—modified]
       01   Holly:       Well he must've known what she was like before he
       02                married her.
       03   Fran:        I guess. And-
       04   Holly:   →   He can be a (   ) too, he uh one- one day we
       05                [STORY]
```

Launching with a Sequence

Besides a single turn, three types of sequences can also be used to launch a story (Lerner, 1992; Mandelbaum, 1987; Sacks, 1974):

(1) preface sequence;

(2) assisted story preface;
(3) three-part series of turns.

PREFACE SEQUENCE

> **Preface sequence** is a sequence of minimally two turns, where a teller projects a forthcoming story with a story preface and the recipient aligns as a potential recipient.

(34) [Sacks, 1974, p. 338]
```
        01   Ken:    →   You wanna hear muh-eh my sister told me a
        02                story last night.
        03   Roger:  →   I don't wanna hear it. But if you must,
```

As discussed in Chapter 2, a story preface (e.g., lines 01–02 above) is designed to establish that the recipient does not already know the story, and it is characterized by three features (Sacks, 1974, p. 340):

(1) offer or request to tell;
(2) initial characterization of the story;
(3) reference to time or source of the story.

These features allow the recipients to assess whether this is a story they have already heard. The initial characterization of the story as, for example, "incredible" also makes it possible for recipients to recognize its completion. You will have to wait until you hear something "incredible" to know that the story is complete.

> **Author's story (JW):** My daughter called, and I was in a rush to get back to my writing. She began with "Well, this is incredible." That told me she was launching into a story. I thought, "Oh no, how do I get out of this one? When does the 'incredible' part come? I need to get back to my writing."

Story prefaces such as "Well, this is incredible." may not be recognized by second language learners, since different story launching methods may be used by speakers of different languages. In a study of story initiation by Japanese and Australian speakers, Fujii (2007) found that, instead of using a story preface, Japanese adopt a more subtle approach, starting with a summary statement of the forthcoming story (e.g., "But there was a time when I failed a test, you know."), gauging the recipient's reaction, while the recipient promotes the telling by asking questions (e.g., "A test to see who could keep raising their neck the longest?") (p. 204).

ASSISTED STORY PREFACE

Story initiation can also be brought off with an **assisted story preface** (Lerner, 1992, pp. 250–254).

Assisted story preface is a way of launching a story collaboratively by using:

(1) story prompt;
(2) story provocation;
(3) reminiscent solicit + recognition.

In the following extract, Leni prompts Jim to tell the story:

(35)   [Lerner, 1992, p. 251—modified]
       (story prompt)
       01   Leni: →   **Oh you have to tell them about your typewriter**
       02   **honey.**
       03   Jim: oh yes.
       04   Edith: Yeah did you hear from them?

In the instance below, David is provoked by Allan's teasing into telling the story:

(36)   [Lerner, 1992, p. 254—modified]
       (story provocation)
       01   Allan: →   **Of course then this irreverent fellow was going**
       02   **(.) ↑Max see these Terracotta horses down at**
       03   **(Falli's) I wonder if it's a real one,=**
       04   Sally: =ah [hah hah hah
       05   David: [I didn'- no I didn't I didn't say that it was just
       06   (.) [STORY]

A third type of assisted story preface is a "reminiscent solicit (lines 01–02) + recognition (line 03)" sequence:

(37)   [Lerner, 1992, p. 255—modified]
       (reminiscent solicit + recognition)
       01   B: →   **Dave remember when we used to wear the same**
       02   **size shoes?**
       03   (.)

```
04   D:   →   [ye(hh)ah
05   A:       [ahahh
06   D:       and we bought a pair of shoes at the s[ame time?
07   B:                                             [at the same
08            day ((continues))
```

THREE-PART SERIES OF TURNS

Two potential co-tellers can also begin a story by employing a three-part series of turns: a "remote" approach gets "forwarded" by the co-participant, which is in turn ratified by the first person who began with the remote approach (Mandelbaum, 1987). In the following extract, Shawn is talking about having to start going to church as a remedy for his feeling "tense":

```
(38)   [Mandelbaum, 1987, p. 149—modified]
01   Shawn:    →   I have to start goin'. (0.8) cuz I'm getting really
02                 tense.
03                 (0.4)
04   Matthew:      Yeah.
05   Shawn:        and that really ca::lms you.
06                 (0.3)
07   Nina:         Yeah: it does. and its- like medica:[tion
08   Shawn:    →                                       [I was going
09                 cra:zy today. On the- on the roa:d.
10                 (0.4)
11   Vicki:    →   Well you know what he di:d?=
12   Shawn:    →   =Went out of my ((curse)) mi:nd.=
13   Vicki:        =He made a right-
14                 ((story continues))
```

Shawn begins at lines 01–02 by remotely suggesting he has a story to tell, with "have to" signaling the possibility of something unusual. He becomes more specific (i.e., less remote) at lines 08–09, where "tense" is rephrased as "crazy," and the event is presented as a recent one, i.e., tied to "today . . . on the road." At line 11, Vicki forwards the telling by strongly projecting a possible story with "Well, you know what he di:d?." At line 12, Shawn shows that he understands what Vicki is referring to by intensifying the unusualness of the event, which begins the collaborative telling. In other words, he ratifies Vicki's forwarding.

Task 9

Collect as many story-launching utterances as you can over the course of one to two weeks from the media and your daily interaction.

Do these utterances fit into the categories discussed above? Please explain.

Telling the Story

After launching the story, the telling of the story can be done by (1) a single party in a single or multiple turn(s) (Sacks, 1974) or (2) multiple parties jointly (Lerner, 1992; Mandelbaum, 1987).

Single-party Telling

In single-party telling, the teller is the only one that has the story. Beyond the preface sequence (lines 01–03 below), the main story segments may include background, parenthesis, and climax (Goodwin, 1984). In the segment below, the climax of the story is Don's reported utterance "Did they make you take this wallpaper or did you pick it out?" at lines 11–13. Ann begins the story with its background, i.e., Karen has a new house with unusual wallpaper (lines 04–05):

```
(39)   [Goodwin, 1984, pp. 225–226—modified]
       01   Ann:          Well- ((throat clear)) (0.4) We could've used a little,
       02                 marijuana. to get through the weekend.
       03   Beth:         What h[appened.
       04   Ann:    →          [Karen has this new hou:se. and it's got
       05                 all this like- (0.2) silvery:: g-go:ld wa:llpaper, .hh
       06           →     and Don say(h)s, y'know this is the first time
       07                 we've seen this house.=Fifty thousand dollars in
       08                 Cherry Hill.=Right?
       09                 (0.4)
       10   Beth:         Uh hu:h?
       11   Ann:    →     Do(h)n said. (0.3) dih- did they ma:ke you take
       12                 this wa(h)ll pa(h)p(h)er? or(h)
       13                 di [dju pi(h)ck i(h)t ou(h)t.
       14   Beth:            [Ahh huh huh huh huh huh [huh
       15   Don:                                       [Uhh hih huh
```

At line 06, Karen is about to begin the climax utterance with "Don say(h)s," but stops to offer more information (i.e., "y'know this is the first time we've seen this house.=Fifty thousand dollars in Cherry Hill.=Right?"). Goodwin (1984) calls this inserted information "parenthesis." At line 11, Ann returns to what Don says—something incredibly inappropriate and hilarious for that reason. Don's utterance is what makes this story interesting. It is the climax of the story. As can be seen, the laugh tokens serve to distinguish the climax segment from its adjacent background segment and parenthesis segment (Goodwin, 1984).

Oh (2006) also shows how zero anaphora (i.e., pronoun drop indicated by Ø below) is used in the climax segment of the story to create a sense of tight continuity between actions, and thereby excitement:

```
(40)   [Oh, 2006, p. 833—modified]
       01   Mike:          So, boy when Keegan come in he- y'know how he's
       02                  gotta temper anyway, he jus::: screamed his ((curse
       03                  word)) e:ngine y'know,
       04                  (0.5)
       05   →             Ø sitting there and he takes his helmet off and
       06                  clunk it goes on top of the car he gets out and Ø
       07                  goes up to the trailer and Ø gets a °God ((curse
       08                  word)) iron ba:r ·hhh Ø raps that trailer
       09                  and away he starts to go and everybody says hey
       10                  you don't need that y'know, Ø say yea:h you're
       11                  right and he throws   [that down-
       12   Curt:                               [°Mhm hm
       13   Mike:          So they all  [go dow[n
       14   Gary:                       [A:ll   [All show.
```

Another story-telling technique is the format of "first saying + insertion + second saying" used to inform the recipient that "what I'm saying now is what I was saying before" (Wong, 2000a, p. 418). In the following segment, Bee recounts how she spotted Adele's husband one day while she was out shopping for glasses:

```
(41)   [Wong, 2000a, pp. 410–411—modified]
       01   Bee:           =You must have a heart attack with   [him
       02   Adele:                                              [Ugh:: .h oh::
       03                  he ordered new glasses today he's getting wire
       04                  [(fram::es) his mother's buying him (for [(him)
       05   Bee:    →      [Oh yeah                                 [I
       06                  thou::ght I saw:: him=it was frea::ky .h I was
       07                  driving around my- y'know school trying to get
       08                  parked=I don't know if it was today:: or
       09                  yesterday=
       10   Adele:         =°yeah°
       11   Bee:    →      and I THOUGHT I SAW HIM in uh mov-
       12                  I'm STA:::RING at this GUY::  [hih hih .h
       13   Adele:                                       [(  ) hih::
       14   Bee:           [I said GEE:: that looks like my girlfriend's
       15                  husband I said no can':: be.
```

At lines 05–06 and 11, there is a first and second saying of "I thought I saw him." The inserted information between these sayings provides background for understanding Bee's surprise at seeing Adele's husband. Interestingly,

Wong (2000a) found that the nonnative speakers in her data do not use this story-telling technique. Learners' ability to use this technique is perhaps a sign of their developing mastery of the target language.

Multi-party Telling

In multi-party telling, more than one person has the story, and the story is jointly told (Lerner, 1992; Mandelbaum, 1987). Those who know the story participate in both its delivery and its response. Their response is distinctly marked by "anticipatory laughter" or confirming continuers addressed to the recipient (Lerner, 1992, p. 259). Five collaborative telling techniques have been identified:

(1) verify details;
(2) monitor for errors;
(3) repair trouble;
(4) render own part;
(5) engage in complementary telling.

In the segment below, Nina verifies for Matthew that they were not loaded:

```
(42)   [Mandelbaum, 1987, p. 158—modified]
       (verify details)
       01   Matthew:          Fir:st of a:ll, (1.1)
       02                     we were (.) w- were loaded? ((looks up at Nina))
       03                     (1.1)
       04                     I don't  [know if we were   [loa:ded] or no:t.
       05   Nina:      →      [I don't think we [loaded]
       06                     (1.0)
       07   Matthew:          But
       08                     (1.1)
       09                     First of all we see this car, going down the
       10                     street si:deways ((story continues))
```

At line 05 in the following segment, Shawn corrects Vicki's mention of "made a right":

```
(43)   [Mandelbaum, 1987, p. 156—modified]
       (monitor for errors)
       01   Vicki:           He made a right- It was:: in Santa
       02                    Monica. You know ha:ve- the ha:ve
       03   Shawn:           [Oh: ((curse word))]
       04   Vicki:           [all those       ] (b)ri:ght
       05   Shawn:    →      I made a left- left-
       06   Vicki:           They ha:ve (.) m one-way stree:ts
       07                    and everythi::ng? (0.4) and then two-way streets?
```

08	he ma:de (0.4) a left turn from a one-way
09	street. (0.8) into a two-way street, (0.5)

In the next segment, the participants are talking about a chain letter. Tim begins by reporting what he said, but Melenie at line 03 corrects him with "Well FIRST he didn't say anything for a long time":

(44) [Lerner, 1992, p. 261—modified]
      (repair trouble)
      01 Tim: so I said (I said y'know) and what do you think I
      02   ought to do?
      03 Melenie: → **Well FIRST he didn't**
      04   **[say anything for a long time**
      05 J: [(boy ya better send that o(h)ne)

In the next segment, Tim quotes himself as it happened in the story:

(45) [Lerner, 1992, p. 266—modified]
      (render own part)
      01 Melenie: so don't break the chain and see what happens to
      02   you in four days
      03 Tim: → **so I said (I said y'know) and what do you think**
      04   **I ought to do?**

The fifth collaborative telling technique is complementary telling, which is done when (1) one narrates while the other dramatizes, (2) both tellers provide own details simultaneously, and (3) one tells, and the other indicates how recipients might react to the telling (Mandelbaum, 1987, p. 159). In the following segment, Vicki narrates while Shawn dramatizes:

(46) [Mandelbaum, 1987, p. 159]
      (complementary telling)
      01 Vicki: → **he's tra:veling [dow:n   ]**
      02 Matthew: [Wrong way?]
      03   (0.5)
      04 Vicki: **The wrong: way:**
      05 Shawn: → **All of a sudden this guy goes**
      06   **[AAAAAAHHH][AAAAAAH-]**
      06 Vicki: → **[(and how much)][(   )]**
      07   **cro:ss the blo::ck.**

Responding to the Story

The recipient plays an important role in the midst of the telling by offering continuers (see Chapter 3) (Schegloff, 1982) or even redirecting the story

(Mandelbaum, 1989). Upon the completion of a story, three tasks become relevant for the recipient (Jefferson, 1978; Sacks, 1974: Schegloff, 1992a):

(1) display understanding of the completion;
(2) show appreciation of the point of the story;
(3) demonstrate the story's potential to generate subsequent talk.

Joint tellers participate in these activities as well (Lerner, 1992), and one way to demonstrate a story's potential to generate subsequent talk is by providing a second story (Ryave, 1978). In the absence of any story response upon its completion, the teller may add various expansions to seek recipient responses (Jefferson, 1978):

```
(47)  [Jefferson, 1978, p. 232—modified]
      01  Maggie:      [STORY] A::n uh: I guess once was enough.
      02  Gene:        Yeah. (.) Yeah.
      03               (1.0)
      04  Maggie: 1→   But as far as I'm concerned he [ex-husband] he
      05               has, shown his color::s to the point where:: .hhh
      06               n:obody in his right mi:nd who's even got a:
      07               decent breath left in them. .hhh wou:ld think
      08               that he was acceptable.
      09  Gene:        Yeah.
      10               (0.7)
      11  Maggie: 2→   and it's a sure ((curse word)) thing that
      12               whenever:: this kid ((her son)) grows up he'll
      13               have n:obuddy to thank for anything. .hh uh: of
      14               that family ((ex-husband's)).
      15  Gene:        Yeah. (.) Yeah.
      16               (1.0)
      17  Maggie: 3→   I wouldn't spit on the best side of him and I've
      18               yet to see the best si:de.
      19  Gene:     →  hhhehh heh-heh-heh .hhhh Well how about the
      20               rest of the family . . .
```

Maggie's initial story completion at line 01 is expanded upon three times (see arrows 1–3) until Gene at line 19 displays his appreciation through laughter followed by more talk related to the story.

Task 10

Consider the following modified list of story-telling ingredients taken from an ESL textbook (Carter & McCarthy, 1997, p. 23). Given your understanding of the CA work on story-telling so far, how can this list be improved? What aspects of story-telling still need to be addressed in CA based on this list?

1. References to times, places, and settings
2. Characters involved in the events
3. Plot of events
4. Outcome or conclusion
5. Embellishments via exaggeration, amusing details, etc.
6. Features that add to the vividness of the story, such as dialogs
7. Comments on the events
8. Relevance to the ongoing conversation
9. Appropriate beginning and ending

Teaching Topic Management and Story-telling

In what follows, we introduce a few activities on teaching topic initiation, topic shift, and story-telling. Again, our intent is to provide some triggers for teachers to develop their own materials based on the CA findings we have introduced in this chapter.

Topic Initiation

Awareness-raising Activity: *What Comes after Hello?*

(1) Have learners work in pairs on the following task: You ran into your American friend in the street. What would you say after exchanging greetings? Make a list of the things you would say.

(2) Share and discuss the lists as a class. Categorize the lists into various "strategies" if possible. Introduce the concept of topic initiation. Explain that there are specific topic initiation strategies used by native speakers of English.

(3) To discover these strategies, have learners work in groups of three and discuss how topics are initiated in the following modified transcripts. Explain that the underlining, colons, and brackets indicate emphasis, sound stretch, and overlap in delivery.

> (a) [Button & Casey, 1985, p. 21]
> 01 Geri: How are you doing Shirley?
> 02 Shirley: Okay how're you.
> 03 Geri: Oh alri:::ght,
> 04   Uh:m your mother met Michael last
> 05   night.
>
> (b) [Button & Casey, 1984, p. 182—modified]
> 01 S: What's new,
> 02 G: We::ll? Let me see last ni:ght, I had
> 03   the girls ove[r?

04   S: [Yea:h ?=
05   ((continues on topic))

(c)   [Maynard & Zimmerman, 1984, p. 306]
01   A1:   What's your major?
02   A2:   um, well my major's physics but I
03   haven't really taken a physics class
04   yet so I have a good chance to
05   change it. Probably to anthro if I
06   change it.
07   A1:   I've heard it's a good major.

(d)   [Button, 1991, p. 263]
01   E: Life's a drag.
02   B: Yeah isn't it?
03   E: Yeah,
04   B: Uhm
05   E: So, are you going Thursday?
06   B: No.

(4) Share the discussion results as a class. The learners may come up with conclusions such as "You can ask a question to start a topic." Push the discussion by asking "What kind of questions?" Point out that they may be general "fishing" questions such as "What's new?" or "Anything new?" or questions related to a specific newsworthy aspect of the listener's life such as "Did you finally finish that paper?" In the case of meeting someone new, one can ask personal questions about the listener's identity or activity such as "What do you do?" Finally, add that besides questions about the listener's life, one can also tell something about one's own such as "I got a raise!"

(5) Compare the native speaker strategies of topic initiation with those generated earlier by the learners. Discuss similarities and differences.

Variation

Ask learners to work in pairs to supply at least four or more turns in the following conversation. Two friends saw each other in the cafeteria:

A: Hi
B: Hi

———
———

. . .

Repeat (2)–(5) above.

Practicing Activity: *Exchanging Pleasantries*

(1) Have learners work in pairs role-playing meeting someone new or running into a friend in the street using the newly learned topic initiation strategies.

(2) Have each pair perform their role-plays while others write down the topic initiation utterances they used.

(3) Discuss each performance as a class.

Disjunctive Topic Shift

Awareness-raising Activity: *Oh by the Way*

(1) Have learners work in pairs on the following transcript. Explain that a topic shift occurs in the turns beginning with the blanks. What is the speaker shifting away from and shifting to? What can be placed in the blanks to mark the shift?

> (a) [Crow, 1983, p. 143]
> 01 M: And there was something so incredibly strange
> 02   about that place,
> 03   you know.
> 04 F: [Uh huh
> 05 M: [Here's some guy singing "Tiny bubbles, in the
> 06   water" you know. It was just so incredibly strange
> 07   sitting out there in the middle of the water.
> 08 F: _____ I heard a strange song today
> 09   that I haven't heard since I was a little kid, and I
> 10   used to listen to Arthur
> 11   Godfrey on the radio with my mother.
> ((Answer based on the actual transcript: *Speaking of that*))

> (b) [Schegloff & Sacks, 1973, pp. 320—modified]
> 01 Caller: You don't know what that would be, how
> 02   much it costs.
> 03 Crandall: I would think probably about twenty-five
> 04   dollars.
> 05 Caller: Oh boy, hehh hhh!
> 06   Okay, thank you.
> 07 Crandall: Okay dear.
> 08 Caller: _____ I'd just like to say that uh, I DO
> 09   like the news programming. I've been
> 10   listening, it's uh . . .
> ((Answer based on the actual transcript: *OH BY THE WAY*))

(2) Have learners consider the following questions:

(a) Would the conversations stay intact without the topic-shifting phrases?

(b) What other topic-shifting remarks might fit in the two blanks? (see the list of phrases for marking topic shift in the chapter)

(c) Can *anyway* be used in the same transcript? If yes, would the nature of shift change?

(3) Conduct a discussion in groups of three on three cultural differences between the US and the learners' home countries.

(4) As a wrap-up, create a list as a class of things to say to mark disjunctive topic shifts.

Variations

(i) For a lower-level class, simplify the transcripts above or compose your own.

(ii) For an advanced class, have learners watch a taped segment of a talk show (e.g., *The View, Larry King Live*) and discuss how topic shifts are explicitly marked by both the hosts and the guests.

Practicing Activity: *Around and Around*

Divide the class into two groups, asking one group to form a circle facing out, and another facing in. Ask the learners to start a conversation on cross-cultural differences with someone they are facing. The conversation will be timed by the teacher (e.g., 40 seconds), during which at least one disjunctive topic shift needs to be done by at least one person. When the time is up, the outer group moves one spot to their right and starts the conversation again. Keep the activity going as long as necessary.

Stepwise Topic Shift

Awareness-raising Activity: *Gradual Shifts*

(1) Have learners consider the following transcripts in pairs or groups. Explain that at each arrowed turn, the speaker does a topic shift. Have learners write down exactly what can be said to shift to that topic. The transcripts may be presented in various degrees of details depending on your class.

(a) [Jefferson, 1993, pp. 9–10—modified]
```
01   A:          That's one of the most thrilling programs I
02               know I've ever been to.
03   P:          Well it had a nice write up in the paper too.
04   A:          Yeah I noticed that.
05   P:    →     ((Make an announcement about starting the
                 Mother's club Tuesday night.))
```

(Answer based on actual transcript : *Well that's good. Well LIS-TEN uh- Tuesday night we're starting that Mother's Club bit again at the church.*)

(b) [Beach, 1993, p. 340—modified]
01 C: I guess the band starts at ni:ne
02 D: Oh really
03 C: Yeah from what Jill told me
04 D: →   ((Ask when Jill is going.))

(Answer based on transcript: *Okay when's Jill gonna go?*)

05 C: Same time (0.2) we're gonna meet her there
06 D: →   ((Asks if C wants to take his/her car.))

(Answer based on transcript: *Okay um so you want to take your car?*)

07 C: We can take your car if you wa:nt.
08 D: I meant you want- you wanna have your car
09   there so you can leave?
10 C: Yeah I think that'd be a better idea.
11   Okay.
12   (0.5)
13 D: →   ((Asks what time it is now.))

(Answer: *Okay well what what time is it now . . .*)

15 C: Six o'clock

(2) Assuming that your learners have learned to mark topic shifts explicitly first, they would most likely come up with answers such as *speaking of X* or *by the way*. This would serve as a good review for disjunctive topic shifts. Following this review, show the answers based on the actual transcripts. Have learners discuss how these shifts are done differently from disjunctive topic shifts.

(3) Introduce the concept of stepwise topic shifts as follows:

Pivot	+	New Topic/Focus
Acknowledgment		
Assessment		
Commentary		

(4) Assign as homework: Collect three instances of stepwise topic shifts from daily conversations or TV programs to be shared in the next class.

Variations

(i)   Start by presenting the above transcripts without the topic shifting practices. Ask learners what appears to be wrong or awkward about these conversations and what can be done to improve them.
(ii) Create multiple choices for each blank above.

Practicing Activity: *Cross-cultural Shifts*

(1) As a follow-up to the above awareness-raising activity, for the next class: In groups of three, conduct a 5-minute discussion on cross-cultural differences in managing topic shifts. Record the discussion.
(2) Have learners listen to their recordings and identify topic shifting strategies and how topic shifts may be better managed.
(3) Redo the discussion to accomplish better topic shifts. Repeat the above procedures as many times as necessary.

Launching a Story

Awareness-raising Activity: *How do I Begin to Tell you?*

(1) Have learners work in groups and write down the first thing they would say in a conversation when they want to tell a story.
(2) Share the results in class and compare them with the list below, taken from transcripts of actual interaction:

(a) You wanna hear a story?
(b) My sister told me a story last night.
(c) Oh that reminds me of what happened last week.
(d) Yesterday my roommate Sarah . . .
(e) Oh you have to tell them about the present.
(f) Remember when we used to wear the same size shoes?
(g) I was going crazy today on the road.

(3) Categorize the above utterances into three groups:

(a) When you have a story to tell:
(e.g., *You want to hear X? That reminds me of X.*)
(b) When you want someone to tell a story:
(e.g., *You have to tell them about X.*)
(c) When you want to tell a story jointly with someone:
(e.g., *Remember when . . .?*)

(4) Discuss possible cross-cultural differences in launching stories.
(5) Have learners collect authentic examples of story launching outside of class and report back.

Practicing Activity: *I Have a Story to Tell you*

(1) Role-play the three situations under (3) above.
(2) Have learners try out the story launching techniques outside of class and report back.

Chapter Summary

Sequencing practices in our model of interactional practices are divided into basic sequences (i.e., adjacency pair-based) and larger sequences such as topic management and story-telling. In this chapter, we discussed the latter two. Topic management involves initiating, pursuing, shifting, and terminating a topic. Topic initiation can be done with a variety of techniques such as topic initial elicitors, itemized news inquiries, and news announcements. Topics may also be pursued using techniques such as itemized news inquiries and news announcements. A key component of topic management is topic shifting; such shifts may be done disjunctively or in a stepwise fashion. Topic termination is often marked by assessment tokens. Like topic management, story-telling sequences are not entirely adjacency pair-based. The three main components of a story-telling sequence include launching the story, telling the story, and responding to the story. Stories may be launched with a single turn or a sequence such as a preface sequence or an assisted story preface. The telling of the story may include background, climax, and parenthesis along with the use of techniques such as zero anaphora and "first and second sayings." Stories may be told jointly with a range of techniques such as verifying details, rendering own part, and engaging in complementary telling. Finally, upon the story's completion, it is the recipient's responsibility to display understanding of its completion, show appreciation of its significance, and demonstrate the story's potential to generate further talk. For the language teacher, understanding the complexities of topic management and story-telling is an important component of one's pedagogical repertoire. We gave some suggestions for teaching topic management and story-telling. Actual pedagogical decisions on what to teach or how to teach should be tailored to specific learner populations.

Key Concepts

- **Assisted story preface:** A way of launching a story collaboratively by using: (1) story prompt; (2) story provocation; (3) reminiscent solicit + recognition.
- **Disjunctive marker:** An utterance used to mark the introduction of a new focus or topic as abrupt or unexpected.
- **Disjunctive topic shift:** A method of moving into a new aspect of the same topic or a new topic by marking such moves as not tightly fitted to the ongoing talk with utterances such as *actually* or *by the way*.
- **Itemized news inquiry:** A topic initiation method that targets a specific newsworthy item related to the recipient.

- **News announcement:** A topic initiation method that reports on speaker-related activities.
- **Pre-topical sequence:** A topic initiation method used to get acquainted with one another with personal questions about the recipient's identity or activity.
- **Preface sequence:** A sequence of minimally two turns, where a teller projects a forthcoming story and the recipient aligns as a potential recipient.
- **Setting talk:** A topic initiation method that points to the immediate environment of the interaction.
- **Stepwise topic shift:** A method of gradually moving into a new focus or a new topic with the following devices: (1) pivot + new focus/topic; (2) invoking semantic relationships between items; (3) summary of prior topic → ancillary matters → new topic.
- **Topic initial elicitor sequence:** A three-turn sequence that consists of: (1) topic initial elicitor (e.g., *What's new?*); (2) newsworthy event (e.g., *I got a raise.*); (3) topicalizer (e.g., *Really?*).
- **Topic initiation:** Practices of starting a new topic (1) at the beginning or closing of a conversation, (2) following a series of silences, or (3) after the closing of a prior topic.
- **Topic pursuit:** Practices of insisting upon developing a topic when its initiation receives less-than-enthusiastic responses.
- **Topic shift:** Practices of (1) shifting emphasis within a topic or (2) moving towards a new topic either with a disjunctive marker or in a stepwise fashion.
- **Topic termination:** Practices of closing down a topic.
- **Topicalizer:** The third turn in the topic initial elicitor sequence that upgrades the newsworthiness of the report and transforms a possible topic into an actual topic (e.g., *Really?*).

Post-reading Questions

1. Name three methods of topic initiation. Give examples.
2. What is the difference between disjunctive and stepwise topic shift? Give an example of each.
3. What is a story preface? What are the other methods for launching a story beyond using the story preface? Give examples.
4. As a second language instructor, what are the pros and cons of using CA findings in teaching topic management and story-telling?
5. What other activities can you think of to teach topic management and story-telling?
6. Select one of the suggested readings listed below and present the article in class, summarizing the article's key points and offering your questions and concerns. Consider how the points raised in the article might be related to issues in language teaching especially if the article does not have a pedagogical orientation.

7. Having read the chapter, what questions or concerns do you still have about sequencing?

Suggested Readings

Button, G., & Casey, N. (1984). Generating topic: The use of topic initial elicitors. In M. Atkinson & J. Heritage (Eds.), *Structures of social actions: Studies in conversation analysis* (pp. 167–190). Cambridge: Cambridge University Press.

Button, G., & Casey, N. (1985). Topic nomination and pursuit. *Human Studies, 8*(3), 3–55.

Button, G., & Casey, N. (1988/1989). Topic initiation: Business-at-hand. *Research on Language and Social Interaction, 22,* 61–92.

Clift, R. (2001). Meaning in interaction: the case of "actually". *Language, 77*(2), 245–291.

Holt, E., & Drew, P. (2005). Figurative pivots: The use of figurative expressions in pivotal topic transitions. *Research on Language and Social Interaction, 38*(1), 35–62.

Jefferson, G. (1993). Caveat speaker: Preliminary notes on recipient topic-shift implicature. *Research on Language and Social Interaction, 26*(1), 1–30.

Mandelbaum, J. (1987). Couples sharing stories. *Communication Quarterly, 35*(2), 144–170.

Maynard, D. W. (1980). Placement of topic changes in conversation. *Semiotica, 3/4,* 263–290.

Sacks, H. (1974). An analysis of the course of a joke's telling in conversation. In R. Bauman & J. Sherzer (Eds.), *Explorations in the ethnography of speaking* (pp. 337–353). Cambridge: Cambridge University Press.

West, C., & Garcia, A. (1988). Conversational shift work: A study of topical transitions between women and men. *Social Problems, 35*(5), 551–575.

Chapter 5

Overall Structuring Practices and Language Teaching I

Conversation Openings

Pre-reading Questions

1. How important is it for second language learners to have the skills needed for talking on the telephone in the overall goal of learning conversation?
2. What language structures and vocabulary do second language learners need to know so that they can engage in an ordinary telephone conversation?
3. Why is learning to talk on the telephone more difficult in a second language than it is in a first language?
4. How is a telephone conversation different from a face-to-face conversation?

Chapter Overview

This chapter covers the topic of overall structuring practices with a focus on conversation openings. The ability to talk on the phone is an important part of one's interactional competence and a daily challenge for many second language learners. Telephone openings are more subtle than we might initially think; its complexities are not easily captured by our intuitions. As Wong (1984, 2002) shows, ESL/EFL textbook dialogs sometimes do not represent telephone openings as they actually occur in real life. In order to make this particular phone skill teachable, language instructors need to develop a solid understanding of the structure of telephone conversation openings. To that end, we offer a conversation analytic account of the basic sequences that make up a telephone opening. Transcripts of actual landline and cellular phone calls are used for illustration, and we note the pedagogical relevance of these sequences throughout the chapter. In addition, we briefly consider cultural variations in telephone openings. Finally, we offer suggestions of how telephone openings can be taught in the language classroom.

Overall Structuring Practices: Openings

As discussed in Chapter 1, **overall structuring practices** are a key component in our model of interactional practices.

> **Overall structuring practices** are ways of organizing a conversation as a whole, as in openings and closings.

The most generic sorts of overall structuring practices are conversational openings and closings, which are treated in this and the next chapter. As stated in Chapter 1, native speakers of a language breeze through openings and closings with the greatest of ease, not necessarily aware of their important structuring role in the interaction. If you have ever studied another language and didn't quite know how to begin a conversation or exit one, i.e., feeling like a fish out of water, you get a sense of what speakers take for granted and do seemingly effortlessly when engaging in ordinary interactions. In this chapter, we focus on telephone openings. This emphasis in part reflects a dearth of CA literature on face-to-face openings, the data for which are nearly impossible to collect.

Task 1

1. Write down the opening turns in a typical telephone conversation in English. Feel free to go beyond the initial four lines.

    01 _____

    02 _____

    03 _____

    04 _____

2. Would you change any of the sample turns above if you were calling the people listed below? Jot down any changes and note why they would be needed.

    a) your boss
    b) your colleague or co-worker
    c) your mother, father, or guardian
    d) your boyfriend, girlfriend, or partner
    e) your teacher or professor

Here we take a detailed look at telephone conversation openings, mainly relying on classic CA research (Schegloff, 1968, 1979b, 1986, 2004). Although the insights about telephone openings may seem obvious, native speakers are not necessarily able to articulate their features and patterns, at least not at the level of being able to explain them to second language learners. As you read about telephone openings in the following sections, ask yourself whether you would have known about the findings if they were not pointed out.

Why is engaging in telephone openings an important skill? Ask yourself: How much do I rely on the phone to manage various aspects of my daily life? Could I live without my phone? Clearly, given the global world in which we live today and people's reliance on the phone as a major, if not primary mode of communication, for handling professional and personal matters, being able to talk on the telephone is of utmost importance. It is one of the most useful survival skills that a second language learner must have in order to succeed. This cannot be overstated.

Language learners who are unable to engage in fluent telephone conversations will be severely hampered in their dealings in the real world. If teachers take the time to find out how language learners feel about talking on the telephone, they will find that many second language learners shy away from interactions on the phone or keep their phone conversations to a minimum. This is not surprising. Phone conversations can be difficult for second language learners particularly because participants do not have access to nonverbal cues. It is vital for language teachers to provide instruction about how to talk on the telephone, but before this instruction, teachers' own awareness and understanding of the structure of telephone openings need to be raised.

> **Author's story (JW):** My parents, immigrants from China, hardly ever answered the phone, because they were nervous, given their limited command of English. Once, when the phone rang, my father answered it but immediately handed the phone to me, saying that he could not understand because the person was speaking in Mandarin-Chinese (my father only spoke Toisanese-Chinese; I had studied Mandarin in college). After speaking with the person on the phone, I said to my father, "*Baba* [Dad], the person wasn't speaking Mandarin. He was speaking English!"

Task 2

List some questions that you might ask to find out what your learners know about telephone talk and the kinds of problems or difficulties that they have.

The opening of a phone conversation does not happen effortlessly despite its seemingly routine nature (Schegloff, 1986). Participants work through the opening to arrive at the **anchor point**, where a **first topic** can be raised (Schegloff, 1968). The first topic may, but need not, be the reason for the call. An instance from actual telephone talk is given shortly.

> **Anchor point** refers to the place in the phone opening where the first topic or reason for the call is introduced.

> **First topic** refers to what is initially talked about in a telephone conversation, which may but need not be the same as the reason for the call.

Telephone openings are typically composed of four stages, i.e., four kinds of sequences. Learners need to be able to engage in these sequences when talking on the telephone. These four sequences are listed below and occur in the order shown when they are all present:

(1) summons–answer;
(2) identification–recognition;
(3) greeting;
(4) *how are you.*

The example below is from a landline phone call (A = answer; C = caller; see complete transcription key at the beginning of this book):

(1) [Schegloff, 1986, p. 115—modified]

01		((ring))	summons–answer
02	A:	Hello,	
03	C:	Hello, Jim?	identification–recognition
04	A:	Yeah,	
05	C:	It's Bonnie.	identification–recognition
06	A:	Hi,	greeting
07	C:	Hi, how <u>a</u>re yuh.	greeting + first *how are you*
08	A:	Fine, how're you,	second *how are you*
09	C:	Oh, okay I guess.	
10	A:	Oh okay,	
11	C:	Uhm, (0.2) what are you	anchor point
12		<u>d</u>oing New Year's Eve.	

We can ask whether the four kinds of opening sequences apply to cell phone conversations. Hutchby and Barnett (2005) claim that there are more similarities than differences between cellular and landline openings. Based on their analysis of a database of 20 recorded mobile phone conversations, they note that "if the communicative affordances of mobile phones are indeed modifying the terms under which conversations are initiated and pursued, the modifications are not pervasive, or not immediately obvious" (Hutchby & Barnett, 2005, p. 157). In the next example, the cell phone opening shows the four sequences:

(2)   [Hutchby & Barnett, 2005, pp. 155–156—modified]
```
01              ((ring))                    summons–answer
02  SB:        Hello?
03  Tasha:     Hi Sim Simma.  greeting+identification–recognition
04  SB:        How are you.                    how are you
05  Tasha:     I'm doing >quite< fi:ne=
06  SB:        Yeah you settled in?    anchor point/first topic
```

In what follows, we discuss the four sequences in more detail.

Summons–Answer Sequence

Just as one speaker can call out to another to get his/her attention in face-to-face interaction (e.g., *Hey, Michael!*), the phone ring is a summons, and the answering of the phone displays the other party's availability for interaction. In a **summons–answer sequence**, the summons is the first pair-part (FPP) of an adjacency pair while the answer is the second pair-part (SPP) (see Chapter 3 on adjacency pairs).

> **Summons–answer** is a sequence of two turns in which participants check and display their availability to talk.

A summons is incomplete without an answer (Schegloff, 2007). Interestingly, of the 30 textbook telephone dialogs Wong (2002) analyzed, only 3 contained complete summons–answer sequences; the other dialogs contained either half of the sequence or none at all.

Phone Ring

That the phone ring counts as a turn is not a trivial matter. Sometimes answerers even wait until the end of a ring or the start of a new one before picking up the phone (Schegloff, 1968, 1986). And the number of times a phone rings before it is answered can have a strong impact on what gets talked about in the opening. For instance, the caller might say that the phone was picked up very quickly, and the answerer might say that s/he was sitting by the phone:

(3)   [Schegloff, 1986, p. 119]
```
01                 →    ri- ((stands for cut off phone ring))
02    Joan:              Hello?
03    Cheryl:            Hello:,
04    Joan:              Hi:,
05    Cheryl:   →        .hh You were sitting by the pho:ne?
06    Joan:     →        No, I'm (0.3) I'm in the kitchen, but I was
07                       talking to a friend of mine earlier. I was
08                       just putting (0.2) my fried rice on my
09                       plate to go each lunch.
```

Joan picks up the phone before it has rung once, and her quickness becomes the first topic of the conversation (lines 05–09), pre-empting other opening sequences such as an exchange of *how are you* (*how are you* sequences are discussed shortly).

The interactional function of a phone ring noted above is not always captured in textbook dialogs, as shown in the case below ("T-1" stands for textbook dialog number one):

(T-1)   [Boyd & Boyd, 1981, p. 75]
```
01    Jenny:    Hello. Why Tom Miller—I never want to speak to
02              you again. You're over two hours late and we've
03              missed the concert.
04    Tom:      I'm sorry, Jenny, but I can explain.
05    Jenny:    O.K., explain! But it'd better be good.
```

There is much to say about the unnaturalness of this phone dialog, but for our purposes, note that without the line of the phone ring in the dialog, one cannot teach when Jenny is saying her *hello*, how that timing can affect subsequent talk, and for what purpose that *hello* is used.

Answers

As obvious as it may seem, in ordinary telephone conversations it is the answerer who speaks first. This practice is referred to as the **distribution rule** (Schegloff, 1968).

Distribution rule states that in telephone conversations the answerer speaks first.

This rule may be suspended for those with caller ID (identification). For ESL/EFL learners, answering the phone is often a frustrating, nerve-wracking, or even frightful experience because they do not know what to say and often have difficulty understanding the other party.

> **Author's story (JW):** My uncle originally from China answered very few phone calls, given his very limited command of English. If I called him, he would pick up the phone and wait for me to talk first. I would hear silence. Then, I would say, "*San bak* [i.e., "third uncle"], it's Su Jen [Sue Jean]," and he would reply "Oh, Su Jen!" In fact, before calling him, my mother would always remind me, "You have to talk first or else he won't know that it's you, and he won't say anything."

Regular ways for answering the phone are:

(1) self-identification;
(2) *hello*;
(3) *yeah* or *hi*;

SELF-IDENTIFICATION

One type of answer to the phone ring is self-identification. In fact, if someone does not produce a self-identification in answering a business call, that is often a tip-off that one has reached the wrong number:

(4)   [Schegloff, 1986, p. 122—modified]
```
01              ((ring))
02   A:   →    Hello?
03   C:        HeLLO!?
04   A:        Yeah. Hello.
05   C:        Wh- Is this 657–6850?
06   A:        No, this is 657–6855.
07   C:        Oh. Well, you have a very lovely voice.
08   A:        Why thank you. Am I supposed to be a business
09              firm?
10   C:        Yes that's right, that's exactly right. I'm calling my
11              office.
12              They never answer with hello.
```

Although self-identification can be used in personal calls (e.g., *Zoe speaking*) in American English, it occurs far less frequently. By contrast, it is much more common in ordinary Dutch telephone conversation:

(5)   [Houtkoop-Steenstra, 1991, p. 235–modified]
```
01              ((ring))
02   A:   →    It's Reina de Wind?
                Met Reina de Wind?
03   C:        Hello:, it's Bren.
                Hallo:, met Bren.
```

In the case below, following the answerer's use of "*Hallo*" ("Hello") is a long gap of silence, which signifies the caller's puzzlement (Houtkoop-Steenstra, 1991). But the caller resolves the problem by offering the name of the person she thinks she has reached at line 04 ("*Rene?*"), to which the answerer confirms with "*Ja*" ("Yah") at line 05:

```
(6)   [Houtkoop-Steenstra, 1991, p. 239—modified]
      01                   ((ringing))
      02   A:     →        Hello:,
                           Hallo:.
      03                   (0.9)
      04   C:     →        Rene:?=
                           Rene:?=
      05   A:     →        =Yah.=
                           =Ja,=
      06   C:              =Karl Ko:nings.=
                           =Karl Ko:nings.=
      06   A:              =Hi.=
                           =Hai.=
      07   C:              =Hello.
                           =Hallo.
```

Houtkoop-Steenstra (1991) suggests that these differences between Dutch and American telephone openings relate to issues of formality and social status. She claims that in Dutch people who do not identify themselves by name on the telephone are considered to be rude or uneducated.

Self-identification by name (first and/or last name) is also the most common way of answering a ringing phone in Swedish calls; answering by stating the recipient's phone number is the second most common method (Lindstrom, 1994). Lindstrom (1994) hypothesizes that some of the cultural variation that she found in her Swedish data may speak to the issue of trust. That is, if we take it that the "American way" of not providing self-identification is an indirect way of screening the call, it could be argued that Dutch and Swedish participants are more initially trusting of one another on the phone than Americans are (Lindstrom, 1994). Learners of English whose native language is Dutch or Swedish can benefit from knowing the different ways of answering the phone between these languages and English to avoid sounding overly formal in personal calls.

Hello

Hello is the most common way of answering the phone in English, especially in personal calls. When an answerer says *hello* in taking a call, s/he provides the caller with a minimal **voice sample**.

> **Voice sample** is an utterance in the opening of a phone conversation that gives a clue as to the identity of the speaker based on the sound of his/her voice.

Related to the notion of voice sample is the **signature *hello*.**

> **Signature *hello*** is a way of answering the phone that is distinctive for that speaker.

We recognize the signature *hellos* of someone with whom we speak regularly on the phone. If the person doesn't sound the same on a particular occasion, this can even become the first topic of the conversation beginning with an apology such as *Oh sorry, I didn't recognize your voice*. In the case below, because Mei Fang's signature *hello* does not come across when answering the phone, Joan the caller turns this into the first topic of the conversation.

```
(7)  [Schegloff, 1986, p. 125—modified]
     01  A:  →  Hello,
     02  C:     Hi, Mei Fang?
     03  A:     (Hmm?)
     04  C:     This is Joan Wright.
     05  A:     Hi [How are you.
     06  C:  →     [Did I wake you up?
     07            (0.4)
     08  A:     No.
     09  C:  →  Oh: you soun:ded as if [you might have=
     10  A:                           [(no really)
     11  C:     =been (0.2) resting.
     12            (0.2)
     13  A:  →  I have a cold.
     14  C:     Oh:::
```

The issue of signature *hello* may seem trivial or irrelevant to language teachers. But if textbook writers present dialogs related to the signature *hello*, second language learners will be able to develop more real-life phone skills.

Yeah or hi

When the answerer responds to a summons with *yeah* or *hi*, s/he often displays pre-knowledge of who is calling, as is the case with caller ID. This is in contrast with the answerer's use of *hello*, which does not claim knowledge of who is calling. In answers such as *yeah* or *hi*, speakers display that they know who is calling or at least the type of person who is calling, i.e., someone from a certain organization, institution, business, or the like. Speakers on intercom calls also tend to use *yeah* or *hi* more than they use *hello*.

Yeah or *hi* also is used in immediately returned calls. In the following example, E has asked J to call a mutual friend to check on something. J calls back after a few minutes:

(8)   [Schegloff, 2004, p. 69]
      01   ((ring))
      02   E: →   **Yah?**
      03   J: Well, she doesn't <u>know</u>.

If the answerer were to respond to a call-back with *hello* and not with *yeah* or *hi*, the caller might say *Oh, it's me* (Schegloff, 1968). Using *yeah* or *hi* is the answerer's way of showing pre-knowledge of the caller. Thus, *yeah* and *hi* are not alternative or informal forms of *hello* (Schegloff, 1968).

Answering the phone with *yeah* or *hi* is integral to one's telephone skills, but interestingly, of the three textbook dialogs that Wong (2002) found that actually contained complete summons–answer sequences, none included *yeah* or *hi*. With this absence, ESL learners are not exposed to the variable answers to a phone ring or the specific sociolinguistic function each answer performs in its specific context. With the prevalence of cell phones and caller ID, a recipient is more likely to use *yeah* or *hi* in answering a call from a friend, in which case using *hello* may even be inappropriate. Teachers need to focus on these differing ways of answering the phone, helping learners to realize their (subtle) interactional functions.

Task 3

What is your signature hello? Do you have more than one? Has your signature hello ever been mistaken for someone else's? What other ways are there to answer the phone besides *hello*, *yeah*, or self-identification?

Identification–Recognition Sequence

How participants answer the phone is very much connected to the issue of **identification–recognition**. Think of the times when you did not recognize someone's voice on the telephone. Imagine calling your supervisor and mistaking him/her for someone else.

> **Identification–recognition** is a sequence in which participants in a telephone conversation negotiate the recognition of one another by name or voice sample.

As mentioned earlier, when a recipient answers the phone with *hello*, *hi*, or *yeah*, s/he offers a minimal voice sample that gives the caller an initial hint as to his/her identity. In American English, this hint often eliminates the need for callers to self-identify explicitly. This is the practice of "oversupposing and undertelling" (Schegloff, 1979b, p. 50). That is, participants provide the least amount of information they consider necessary for the other party to recognize who they are:

(9) [Schegloff, 1986, p. 114]
```
     01                    ((ring))
     02   Nancy:    →   H'llo:?
     03   Hyla:     →   Hi:,
     04   Nancy:    →   ↑Hi::.
     05   Hyla:         How are yuh=
     06   Nancy:        =Fi:ne how're you,
     07   Hyla:         Okay: [y,
     08   Nancy:              [Goo:d,
```

At line 03, Hyla recognizes Nancy by her voice sample ("H'llo:?") as displayed by her greeting ("Hi:,"). This greeting offers a minimal voice sample for Nancy, who shows recognition of Hyla at line 04 by returning the greeting. Neither party exchanges names. The interactional jobs of greeting one another and doing identification and recognition are bundled up in three minimal turns that last only a few seconds. In doing the talk in this way, Nancy and Hyla also display the closeness of their relationship. On the other hand, in the next extract, the relationship between the participants is more distant:

(10) [Schegloff, 1986, p. 115—modified]
```
     01                    ((ring))
     02   A:           Hello?
     03   C:     →   Hello, Jim?
     04   A:     →   Yeah.
     05   C:     →   It's Bonnie.
     06   A:           Hi,
     07   C:           Hi, how are you.
     08   A:           Fine, how're you,
     09   C:           Oh, okay I guess.
     10   A:           Oh, okay,
     11   C:           Um (0.2) what are you doing New Year's Eve?
```

At line 03, Bonnie produces a greeting followed by what she presumes to be the name of the answerer ("Hello, Jim?"). When Jim replies with "yeah," he claims not to recognize Bonnie by her voice only. He would have otherwise responded with a turn such as *Hi Bonnie*. Subsequently, Bonnie gives her first name, and this is shown to be enough for Jim to know who she is.

Jim and Bonnie's exchange of identification and recognition speaks to the intimacy of their relationship. That is, if Jim were not able to recognize Bonnie by first name only, that would bear serious consequences for their relationship. For people who know one another on a first-name basis, using both first and last name would come across as odd or inappropriate. The specific form of identification that participants use is based upon their relationship to one another. For instance, *My name is X* is more likely to be used with strangers in a phone opening, while *This is X* is more likely to be used with acquaintances or friends.

This kind of relationship-based variation in managing the identification–recognition sequence is underrepresented or even misrepresented in scripted dialogs. In the textbook dialog below, Kim and Matt do not recognize each another by voice sample when they should have because as the conversation continues, we realize that they are dating and making arrangements to go to a movie (later lines of the dialog not given):

(T-2) [Earle-Carlin & Proctor, 1995, p. 49]
01 Kim: ((phone rings)) Hello?
02 Matt: →   **Hi. Is Kim there?**
03 Kim: →   **This is Kim.**
04 Matt: →   **Hi, this is Matt. What's up?**
05 Kim: Not much. What are you doing?

It appears as if Kim didn't give her signature *hello*, which prevented Matt from recognizing her voice. In real telephone conversations, however, the malfunction of a signature *hello* becomes something to talk about in its immediate aftermath. In addition, what would be the reason for Matt not to recognize Kim's voice sample? And, why didn't that become a topic of conversation later on?

Based on (T-2) above, ESL/EFL learners may think that the first opening line in a phone call for the caller is invariably: *Is X there?* or *May I speak with X?* They may also think that the reply to this question is invariably: *This is X.* In real life, Kim might have said to Matt, "Why didn't you recognize me?" This textbook dialog can mislead learners and create "phone monsters" that sound unintentionally distant or even socially inept.

Author's story (JW): My colleague recently answered this phone call from a foreign student:

                ((phone ring))
Professor: Nancy Armstrong.

> Student: ((silence))
> Professor: Hello? Hello?
> Student: Hello.
> Professor: Hi. How can I help you?
> Student: Hi.
>
> The dialog continues for another 14 turns before it became clear that the student wanted an appointment. My colleague writes, "I get lots of these calls, and they are pretty painful."

The student in the anecdote above did not say anything in her first turn; she didn't say who she was or offer a greeting. As a matter of fact, these essential elements of a phone opening did not come out until later when the professor explicitly asked, "Who are you?"

Task 4

Consider the following real phone openings (A=answerer; C=caller). Label the summons–answer and identification–recognition sequences: (a) How is identification–recognition accomplished? (b) Do the parties use voice samples and/or self-identification? (c) Do the parties recognize each other readily?

(1)   [Schegloff, 1986, p. 135—modified]
01   ((ring))
02   A: Hello?
03   C: Hi Marcia,
04   A: Yeah?
05   C: This is Tony.
06   A: HI Tony.
07   C: How are you,
08   A: Oh I've got a paper (0.2) the yearly paper due tomorrow
09   C: heheheh I can tell you a lot about that.

(2)   [Schegloff, 1986, p. 145—modified]
01   ((ring))
02   A: Hello?
03   C: Are you awake?
04   A: YEAH. I [just got up.
05   C: [I-
06   Oh did you?
07   A: Yeah.
08   C: Well good. I'm alone.
09   (0.4)

```
10   A:   [my-
11   C:   [Guy left me last night.
```

(3)   [Schegloff, 1986, p. 115—modified]
```
01        ((ring))
02   A:   Hello,
03   C:   Hi, Susan?
04   A:   Ye:s,
05   C:   This's Janet. Weinstein.
06   A:   Janet!
07   C:   heh Susan.
08   A:   How are you.
09   C:   I'm fine. How're you.
10   A:   Fi:ne. Back from the wilds of Colombia.
11   C:   Yeah. heh
```

Callers have nine ways of producing their first turn in a phone conversation, and these are tied to doing identification and recognition of one another. The nine types of caller's first turns are listed below (Schegloff, 1979b, pp. 28–32):

(1) greeting term:

A: H'llo?
C: →   **Hi.**

(2) answerer's name (with rising intonation):

A: Hello.
C: →   **Sally?**

(3) answerer's name (with assertive, exclamatory, or falling intonation):

A: Hello?
C: →   **David.**

(4) question about answerer's state of being:

A: Hello.
C: →   **Are you awake?**

(5) first topic or reason for the call:

A: Hello.
C: →   **Hi, is Zoe there?**

(6) request to speak with another person (switchboard request):

A: Hello.
C: →   **Is Marika there?**

(7) self-identification:

A: Hello?
C: →   **Hi Zeynep. This is Faridun.**

(8) question about identity of answerer;

A: Hello.
C: →   **Hello. Is this Shu Ping?**

(9) joke or joke version (1)–(8) above:

A: Hello?
C: →   **Is this the Communist Party Headquarters?**

With type (6) above, i.e., the switchboard request, the relationship between the answerer and caller is typically distant or neutral. For the other types, it is probably the case that the caller knows the answerer and may even have a (very) close relationship with the answerer. Of the nine types of caller's first turns, six types or their combinations occur more frequently than others. They are listed below from the most common to the least common (Schegloff, 1979b):

(1) switchboard request (e.g., *Is Nate there?*);
(2) greetings (e.g., *Hi*);
(3) other's name in rising intonation (e.g., *Nate?*);
(4) other's name in falling intonation (e.g., *Nate!*)
(5) combination of greeting + other's name in rising intonation (e.g., *Hi Nate?*);
(6) combination of greeting + other's name in falling intonation (e.g., *Hi Nate!*).

With the increasing presence of caller ID, this list may need to be revised based on further research. The most frequent caller's first turn is not always the most appropriate in all situations. To become interactionally competent in handling telephone calls, ESL/EFL learners need explicit instruction on the various ways of doing a caller's first turn, including information on what is appropriate based on the relationships between the caller and the answerer.

Author's story (JW): My son Nate had a friend, an ESL learner, who would call the house and ask for him. When I answered the phone, he would always say, "May I speak with Nate Link?" I found that somewhat strange because the friend visited the house often, and I got to know him fairly well. I wondered why he was referring to my son by first and last name when asking to speak with him. Also, in saying "May I

> speak with Nate Link?," he was bypassing me, not saying *hello* or even acknowledging who I was. I was being treated like a switchboard operator.

Thus, sometimes a "correct" utterance such as *May I speak with X?* is not necessarily the most appropriate one. Second language learners may not be aware of these practices, just as textbook writers can overlook the social relationships between the participants when creating dialogs.

In institutional talk, the social relationships may be different, which affects the caller's first turn. In the following service call to a bookstore, the caller gets to his/her reason for the call in the very first turn (Bowles, 2006):

(11)   [Bowles, 2006, p. 335—modified]
    01   ((ring))
    02   R: good afternoon xxxxxx bookshop.
    03   C: →   **hello there .h ehm I'm looking for the book of**
    04   **the story of Pinocchio.**

Korean callers do not always produce self-identification in their first turn; they sometimes produce a second summons, i.e., another "*yeposeyyou*" (i.e., *hello*) (Lee, 2006a):

(12)   [Lee, 2006a, p. 261—modified]
    01   ((2 rings))
    02   A: Hello::
                    yeposeyyou::
    03   C: →   **Hello:**
                    yeposeyyo:
    04   (.)
    05   A: →   **Yes::?=**
                    ney::?=
    06   C: =Yes ma'am it's ((first name))
                    =ey samonim ce ((first name))

The second summons functions to invite the answerer to recognize who the caller is by voice sample. In other words, Korean callers, like Americans, "prefer" to be recognized by voice sample, except that it is the caller that invites this recognition (Lee, 2006a).

> **Author's story (JW):** When my friend Shuping, who is a fluent speaker of English, calls me, she sometimes says "hello?" after I answered the phone with "hello?" Her echo of my "hello?" threw me off a bit. Then I realized that she was providing me with a voice sample.

Task 5

> Do you currently teach caller's first turns? Examine some ESL/EFL textbook phone dialogs. Of the nine types of caller's first turns, which ones occur more often in these dialogs? Which ones need supplemental instruction?

Despite the critical role of the caller's first turns, their representation in textbooks can be incompatible with what actually takes place in real telephone conversations. Take the following first turn from a textbook phone opening. The highly compact and multi-tasking first turn leaves no room for recognition of the parties:

(T-3)   [Boyd & Boyd, 1981, p. 87]
    01   Mrs. H: →   **Hello, Mr. Rossini, this is Mrs. Harvey. Could**
    02   **you tell me if somebody has moved into that**
    03   **vacant house next door?**
    04   Mr. R: I don't think so.

Mrs. Harvey could have ended her turn after saying, "Hello, Mr. Rossini, this is Mrs. Harvey," providing Mr. Rossini with the opportunity to say "hello" to her and recognize who she is (e.g., Mr. Rossini: "Hi, Mrs. Harvey"). Notice that when Mrs. Harvey immediately proceeds from self-identification to her reason for the call ("Could you tell me if somebody has moved into that vacant house next door?"), Mr. Rossini has no interactional space to offer a greeting and return the recognition.

Of course, with the advent of caller ID and mobile phones, the task of identification–recognition sometimes is managed a bit differently (Hutchby & Barnett, 2005; Arminen & Leinonen, 2006). Hutchby and Barnett (2005), for example, note the phenomenon of **pre-voice sample identification** (Hutchby & Barnett, 2005, p. 159).

> **Pre-voice sample identification** refers to instances where the caller or answerer is able to identify the other party prior to the offer of a voice sample. Two types of this identification are: (1) pre-voice sample caller

identification (when answerer pre-identifies caller); (2) pre-voice sample answerer identification (when caller pre-identifies answerer).

The following is an example of both the caller (SB) and answerer (Michelle) pre-identifying each other simultaneously:

(13) [Hutchby & Barnett, 2005, p. 161—modified]
```
01                    ((ring))
02   SB:       →   [Michelle!
03   Michelle: →   [Simone.
04   SB:           [Yeah.
05   Michelle:     [Yeah what's happening girl you alright?
```

This may seem like an extreme case. With the caller ID function on, Michelle the answerer is able to guess with some certainty Simone's identity. And perhaps because the cell phone often has a single owner, in this particular case SB the caller exhibits a similar or even stronger level of certainty (see exclamation mark) in her recognition of Michelle.

Greeting Sequence

The third type of sequence in the telephone opening is greeting. Greeting exchanges typically interlock with the doing of identification and recognition, as shown in Extract (9) above reproduced below:

(14) [Schegloff, 1986, p. 114]
```
01                    ((ring))
02   Nancy:  →   H'llo:?
03   Hyla:   →   Hi:,
04   Nancy:  →   ↑Hi::.
05   Hyla:       How are yuh=
06   Nancy:      =Fi:ne how're you,
07   Hyla:       Okay: [y,
08   Nancy:            [Goo:d,
```

Hyla offers a **greeting** at line 03, which Nancy returns at line 04. With this exchange of *hi*, they also accomplish identification–recognition.

Greeting is a sequence of two or more turns in which participants say *hi*, *hey*, *hello*, or the like to each other upon initial contact on the phone.

When participants produce a greeting exchange, they reveal something about the formality, informality, or intimacy of their relationship. For friends and acquaintances, *hi* may be an appropriate greeting term, and it serves to both exchange greetings and show recognition as illustrated in the extract above in which Nancy and Hyla exchange *hi*. For strangers, however, *hi* may be an inappropriate greeting. For example, when one party says *hi* to another, and possibly even a big *hi* (or big *hello*) but then realizes that the person is not someone that s/he knows, the *hi* often comes across as misdirected.

Task 6

Think about the ways in which you greet the various people on the phone. How do your greetings vary, if at all? Include mention of any non-verbal behavior.

When participants do not recognize the other party, they sometimes withhold return greetings, even if momentarily, to avoid having it mistaken for recognition:

(15)   [Schegloff, 1986, p. 115—modified]
```
01                     ((ring))
02   Susan:            Hello,
03   Janet:            Hi Susan?
04   Susan:    →       Yes,
05   Janet:    →       This is Janet. Weinstein.
06   Susan:            Janet!
```

In the example above, Susan says "Yes" instead of a return greeting, thereby delaying her recognition of Janet momentarily. After Janet's self identification at line 05, Susan still does not recognize her. Note that Janet's self-identification is done in two parts. She has to add her last name for Susan to recognize her with a "big *hello*" ("Janet!") at line 06.

In the following example, at line 04 Alice says *hi* back, which is later shown to be a false greeting:

(16)   [Schegloff, 2002, p. 292—modified]
```
01                     ((ring))
02   Alice:            Hello?
03   Robin:            Hi:
04   Alice:    →       Hi:
05                     (0.3)
06   Alice:    →       Oh Hi Robin.
```

At line 05, there is a slight gap of silence, after which Alice recognizes who the caller is (e.g., "Oh"). Armed with this new awareness, Alice redelivers her greeting, this time adding the caller's name: "Oh Hi Robin." (line 06).

In American English, *hello* can be used both as an answer to the phone and as a greeting later on, as shown in the extract below:

(17) [Schegloff, 1986, p. 119—modified]
```
01                  ((ring))
02   Jerry:   →     (Hello?)
03   Irene:         u- Jerry?
04   Jerry:         Yeah,
05   Irene:         Irene.
06   Jerry:   →     Oh=hello Irene.
07   Irene:         Hi:. I j [us-
08   Jerry:                  [I was just thinking about you. Just this
09                   moment.
10   Irene:         Uh huh. Thee- the phone rang so lo:ng. I uh was
11                   worried.
12   Jerry:         Oh?
13   Irene:         Mm hmm,
14   Jerry:         .hh Well I jus- I just got i:n oh: not five minutes
15                   ago. From the hospital.
16   Irene:         mm hmm
```

In Korean telephone openings, participants rarely produce greeting sequences (Lee, 2006a). Samoans rarely use *halao* (*hello*) as a greeting even though it is regularly used to answer the phone; greetings are extremely rare in close relationships (Liddicoat, 2000, p. 98). In Swedish, *halla* (*hello*) is not used as a form of greeting. In fact, using *halla* as a form of greeting is rude, i.e., the equivalent of saying *hey you* in American English (Lindstrom, 1994).

How are you Sequences

After greeting sequences come *how are you* sequences.

How are you is a sequence in which participants in a telephone conversation inquire about each others' well-being.

How are you sequences (e.g., *How are you doing? How are things going?*) are different from greeting sequences in that a first exchange of *how are you* often is followed by a second although the latter is not required. Extract (10), reproduced below, illustrates first and second *how are you* sequences:

(18) [Schegloff, 1986, p. 115—modified]
```
01                  ((ring))
02   A:             Hello?
03   C:             Hello, Jim?
```

```
04   A:            Yeah.
05   C:            It's Bonnie.
06   A:            Hi,
07   C      →      Hi, how are you              first how are you
08   A      →      Fine, how're you,            second how are you
09   C      →      Oh, okay I guess.
10   A:            Oh, okay,
11   C:            Um (0.2) what are you doing New Year's Eve?
```

The intonational contour in a speaker's saying of *how are you* may vary slightly. That is, *how are you*, with the main stress on the final word, may be used in first or second *how are you* sequence. But *how are you*, with the main stress on the second word, is more likely to be used in the first *how are you* sequence or when a speaker is doing a "big *hello*," somehow marking the specialness of the occasion, i.e., it has been a long time since the last get-together (Schegloff, 2007).

There are other ways of saying *how are you* that mark it as a second or reciprocal sequence, such as "How're you doing." in Extract (19) below and "How about you." in Extract (20) below:

```
(19)  [Schegloff, 2007, p. 196—modified]
      01                    ((ring))
      02   Karl:            Hello:
      03   Claire:          Hi: Karl:
      04   Karl:            Yeah hey Claire? How're you.
      05   Claire:   →      Good: How're you doing.
      06   Karl:     →      I'm alright.
      07   Claire:          Good?
      08   Karl:            What's up.=

(20)  [Schegloff, 2007, p. 197—modified]
      01                    ((ring))
      02   Ida:             Hello,
      03   Carla:           Hi Ida.
      04   Ida:             Yeah.
      05   Carla:           Hi, =This is Carla.
      06   Ida:             Hi Carla.
      07   Carla:    →      How are you.
      08   Ida:      →      Okay:.
      09   Carla:           Good.=
      10   Ida:      →      =How about you.
      11   Carla:    →      Fine. Don wants to know . . .
```

How do people answer a *how are you* question? There are three types of answers (Sacks, 1975):

(1) neutral (e.g., *good*, *okay*, or *fine*);

(2) plus (e.g., *great, terrific, wonderful, super*);
(3) minus (e.g., *depressed, awful, lousy*).

Neutral type answers typically lead to shutting down the sequence and do not generate more talk about the recipient's state of being. Plus or minus type answers tend to keep the *how are you* sequence open and may lead to talk about why the recipient is feeling unusually good or bad. The selection of an answer to *how are you* comprises two steps:

(1) selecting the category of answer (i.e., neutral, minus, or plus);
(2) selecting an appropriate lexical term from within the category chosen (e.g., *lousy, terrible, great, fine*).

The *how are you* sequence is closely related to the first topic of the conversation, which is usually initiated by the caller. In this regard, callers often position themselves to ask the first *how are you* so that they can be the recipient of the second *how are you*. From the vantage of being the recipient of the second *how are you*, the caller has the opportunity to convert the answer into the first topic of the conversation or the reason for the call (Schegloff, 1986). Unfortunately, these various types of responses to *how are you* and their potentials to close or expand a conversation are rarely made explicit to language learners.

Some answers to *how are you* are preceded by the word *Oh* as in *Oh pretty good, Oh fine, Oh okay,* or the like:

(21) [Schegloff, 1986, p. 135—modified]
    01   ((ring))
    02   Agnes: ((Hello?))
    03   Portia: ((Hello?))
    04   Agnes: <u>Hi</u> honey, how are [yuh.
    05   Portia: [Fine, how're you.
    06   Agnes: → **.hhhhhOh, I'm pretty goo::d, I had a little**
    07   **operation on my <u>toe</u> this week, I had to have-**
    08   **<u>toe</u>nail taken off.**

(22) [Schegloff, 1986, p. 135—modified]
    01   ((ring))
    02   Marcia: Hello,
    03   Tony: Hi <u>M</u>arcia,
    04   Marcia: yeah?
    05   Tony: This is Tony.
    06   Marcia: HI Tony.
    07   Tony: How are you,
    08   Marcia: → **Ohhhh hh I've got a paper (0.2) the**
    09   **yearly paper due.**

```
10   Tony:        How about that. heheheh hh I can tell you a
11                lot about that.
```

In the above two cases, the turn initial marker *Oh* is produced and treated as a preface to upcoming troubles talk (Jefferson, 1988).

That the *how are you* sequence is an important component of openings is in part supported by the fact that if it is missing, it can be resurrected in the closing:

```
(23)   [Schegloff, 2002, p. 260—modified]
       01   S:        Oh well, nah I don't really like to go into
       02             Hollywood (it's)
       03             hard to pa:rk,
       04             (1.0)
       05   J:        [Mm,
       06   S:        [.hhhh We:ll okay: that's about all I wanted to (0.7)
       07             bug you with. (tod [ay).
       08   J:                           [uhhahhahh .hh Okay Stan:
       09   S:   →    So are ↑you okay?
       10   J:        Yeah, (0.4) um: (0.2) what are you doing like: late
       11             Saturday afternoon.
```

How are you sequences are found in phone openings across languages, with some variations in distribution. In Swedish and German telephone openings, participants very rarely exchange *how are you* sequences (Lindstrom, 1994; Taleghani-Nikazm, 2002). When Germans do use *how are you*, they only use the first one and mean it as a sincere question about the recipient's well-being (Taleghani-Nikazm, 2002). In Hong Kong Cantonese phone calls, participants use *how are you* sequences but not with close friends or family members (Luke, 2002). By contrast, Iranians produce elaborate *how are you* sequences because it is considered polite to inquire about the well-being not only of the addressee but also of his/her family (Taleghani-Nikazm, 2002). Koreans also use *how are you* sequences, but in a dataset of 70 Korean telephone openings, there was not a single instance of the plus type response to *how are you* (Lee, 2006a). In Samoan, participants say *what are you doing?* instead of *how are you* in phone openings, and only the callers do so; when the callers do say *how are you*, it is a genuine inquiry about someone's health and is treated by the recipients as such (Liddicoat, 2000).

It is important for second language teachers to know that in some languages people may not use *how are you* sequences as much as Americans do. Thus, ESL learners may need explicit focus on *how are you* sequences, which may seem obvious to an instructor.

Task 7

For each of the real phone openings below, do a line-by-line analysis
(A = answerer; C = caller):

(a) label the types of the opening sequences: summons—answer,
    identification—recognition, greeting, *how are you*;
(b) explain your labeling;
(c) specify the type of caller's first turn;
(d) identify the anchor point, i.e., first topic and/or reason for the
    call, if it appears in the transcript. Is it somehow connected with
    the *how are you* sequence?

(1)   [Schegloff, 1986, p. 115—modified]
01   ((ring))
02   A: Hello,
03   C: Hi Ida?
04   A: Yeah,
05   C: Hi,=This is Carla
06   A: <u>Hi</u> Carla.
07   C: How are you.
08   A: Okay:,
09   C: Good.=
10   A: =How about you,
11   C: Fine, Don wants to know . . .

(2)   [Schegloff, 1986, p. 135—modified]
01   ((ring))
02   A: Hello?
03   C: Hi Marcia,
04   A: Yeah?
05   C: This is Tony.
06   A: HI Tony.
07   C: How are you,
08   A: Oh I've got a paper (0.2) the yearly paper due
09   tomorrow.
10   C: heheheh I can tell you a lot about that.

(3)   [Schegloff, 1986, p. 143—modified]
01   ((ring))
02   A: Hello?
03   C: Are you awake?
04   A: YEAH. I [just got up.
05   C: [I-
06   Oh did you?

```
07   A:   Yeah.
08   C:   Well good. I'm alone.
09        (0.4)
10   A:   [my-
11   C:   [Guy left me last night.
```

Textbook dialogs often do not consider these complexities of the *how are you* sequences, especially its critical role in ushering in the caller's first topic. In Wong's (2002) study of textbook dialogs, only 4 out of 30 phone openings contained *how are you* sequences. Moreover, all of the answers to *how are you* were of the neutral type (e.g., *good, okay, fine*), which, as we know, are less likely to be shaped into the first topic of the conversation. In the textbook dialog opening below, Mom's *how are you* never receives its response and Robert's "first topic" looks out of place (later lines in the dialog reveal that Rob is asking for money):

(T–4)   [*English Language Center*, 1991, p. 82]
```
01   Robert:          Hi Mom. It's me.
02   Mom:      →      Robert! How are you?
03   Robert:          I need to ask . . .
```

Task 8

Analyze the following ESL/EFL scripted dialog openings in terms of the four basic sequences found in real telephone talk. If these dialogs need revising, what would you change and how?

(1)   [*Comfort*, 1996, p. 74]
```
01   A:   Adrienne Lambert speaking.
02   B:   Hello, Adrienne. This is George here. I've
03        been thinking. There are three things we
04        need to think about. Firstly, the salary
05        structure . . .
06   A:   Salary structure . . .
07   B:   Yes, we certainly need that on the agenda . . .
08   A:   Oh I see, this is the agenda for . . .
09   B:   Yes, yes. Um, we should include pensions . . .
```

(2)   [*Boyd & Boyd*, 1981, p. 7]
```
01   Mike:   Hello, Tom. This is Mike.
02   Tom:    Mike, how are you?
03   Mike:   I'm O.K. Listen, Tom, I've got a favor to ask you.
04   Tom:    Yeah, what is it?
05   Mike:   First of all, are you busy Saturday?
```

06	Tom:	This Saturday?
07	Mike:	Yeah, this Saturday, the eighteenth, for about three
08		or four hours in the morning?

(3) [*Boyd & Boyd*, 1981, p. 13]
01	Joe:	Hello.
02	Lopez:	This is Carlos Lopez, from next door. Can I speak
03		to Mr. or Mrs. Riley?
04	Joe:	Oh, hi Mr. Lopez. My parents aren't home right
05		now. I don't think they plan to be back until
06		sometime tomorrow.
07	Lopez:	Is that you, Jim?
08	Joe:	No, this isn't Jim. My brother's not home either,
09		Mr. Lopez. This is Joe.

(4) [*Castro & Kimbrough*, 1980, (book 2), p. 59]
01	Paula:	Hello. Could I speak to Grace, please?
02	Mr. R:	Sure, just a minute.
03	Grace:	Hello?
04	Paula:	Hi, Grace. This is Paula.
05	Grace:	Oh, hi, Paula.
06	Paula:	Listen, do you have an ice bucket?
07	Grace:	Uh-huh.
08	Paula:	Could I borrow it Saturday night?
09	Grace:	Of course. Oh no, wait. I forgot. I gave it to my
10		daughter. Oh. Well, does Ruth have one?

(5) [*Castro & Kimbrough*, 1980, (book 2), p. 81]
01	Tony:	Hello?
02	Tomiko:	Hello. Is Tony there?
03	Tony:	This is Tony.
04	Tomiko:	Oh, hi, Tony. This is Tomiko.
05	Tony:	Hi. What are you doing?
06	Tomiko:	I'm at the ballet. I'm waiting for Paula. Listen, what
07		are you going to do later?
08	Tony:	Nothing special. Why?
09	Tomiko:	Would you like to meet us for dinner?
10	Tony:	Sure. What time? Oh, no, I forgot! I can't I'm going
11		to see *Superman* with Ali.

It is important to note that in institutional phone calls, the opening sequences are much more compact (Bowles, 2006). Typically, the answerer's first turn is greeting plus self-identification of the business or office, and self-identification in the caller's first turn is not an issue. The caller's first turn may contain a return greeting followed by the reason for the call. *How are you* sequences are not regularly exchanged.

Teachers can help learners attend to cultural variations in telephone openings by discussing the similarities and differences between how opening sequences are done in English and in other languages (Barraja-Rohan, 2003). Heightening learners' metalinguistic and pragmatic awareness is a crucial component in the second language acquisition process (van Lier, 1998). Areas of similarities are less likely to pose problems for the ESL/EFL learner, but areas of differences may prove to be difficult. Learners might erroneously transfer patterns from their native language when doing telephone conversation openings in English. For example, if a Korean learner were to produce *hello?* in the caller's first turn, as they do in Korean, that would be inappropriate in English. If a Dutch learner were to self-identify in answering a personal call, that could pose problems as well. The more teachers know about how openings are done in other languages, the more prepared they would be to help learners avoid errors or social blunders. Getting learners to notice and to use the regular routines or fixed chunks that comprise openings is an important part of language teaching.

Teaching Telephone Openings

Increasingly, analyses of scripted telephone dialogs have shown that more connections with naturally occurring talk are needed in language instruction. Here we offer some suggested activities that serve as initial guidelines. Teachers are encouraged to adapt them to meet their learners' needs or to develop other activities that connect CA and second language pedagogy in ways that expose learners to the interactional practices of real telephone openings.

Talking on the Phone

Awareness-raising Activity: *Beginning at the Beginning I*

(1) Generate class discussion using the following questions:

    (a) How much do you talk on the phone in English?

    (b) What are some opening lines that one might say in a telephone conversation in English?

    (c) What questions or concerns do you have about talking on the phone in English?

    (d) How are telephone openings done in your native language?

(2) Ask learners to compose the first 6–10 lines of a telephone opening. They may compare and discuss their sample openings.

(3) Show and discuss examples of real telephone openings, using those presented in this chapter. Explain the four typical sequences found in openings.

(4) Juxtapose the real phone openings against the ones the learners write down in item (2) above. Ask learners to note similarities and differences.

Variations

(i) For item (3) above, gather your own examples by going to CA research (e.g., Schegloff, 1986) or doing your own recordings. Secure permission of the participants before making any phone recordings.

(ii) For item (3) above, cover up some of the turns in the openings and ask learners to generate appropriate ones.

Practicing Activity: *Beginning at the Beginning II*

(1) Groups learners in pairs. Have them sit back-to-back and pretend to engage in a phone conversation. Use the ones that they made up in item (2) above.

(2) Learners role-play the real phone openings, sitting back-to-back. Use the real openings in item (3) above.

Identification and Recognition

Awareness-raising Activity: *May I speak to X?*

(1) Generate class discussion on how people go about identifying and recognizing one another on the phone. Be sure to get across the idea that we often recognize people by voice sample on the phone, and we often give a voice sample rather than our name.

(2) Discuss and show examples of the nine types of caller's first turn (see pp. 159–160).

(3) Give learners examples of real phone openings like those shown below (A = answer; C = caller). Their task is to explain how the answerers and callers identify and recognize one another. One of the main points to emphasize is that *May I speak to X?* is not always the most appropriate caller's first turn. Help learners understand that it is the relationship between the answerer and the caller that influences the type of caller's first turn.

(a) [Button & Casey, 1988/1989, p. 73—modified]
01   ((ring))
02 A: Hello?
03 C: Hi, Liz?
04 A: Yeah?
05 C: John.

(b) [Schegloff, 1986, p. 115—modified]
01   ((ring))

```
02   A:   Hello,
03   C:   Hi, Susan?
04   A:   Yes,
05   C:   This is Janet. Weinstein.
06   A:   Janet!
07   C:   heh Susan.
08   A:   How are you?
09   C:   I'm fine. How're you?
10   A:   Fine. Back from the wilds of Colombia.
11   C:   Yeah. heh
```

(c)   [Button & Casey, 1984, p. 172—modified]
```
01        ((ring))
02   A:   Hello Redka five o'six one?
03   C:   Mum?
04        (0.2)
05   A:   Yes?
06   C:   Matthew,
07   A:   Oh hello there what are you doing.
```

(d)   [Schegloff, 1986, p. 135—modified]
```
01        ((ring))
02   A:   Hello?
03   C:   Are you awake?
04   A:   Yeah, I just got up.
05   C:   Oh did you?
07   A:   Yeah.
08   C:   Well good. I'm alone.
```

(e)   [Schegloff, 1986, p. 115—modified]
```
01        ((ring))
02   A:   Hello,
03   C:   Hi Ida?
04   A:   Yeah.
05   C:   Hi, this is Carla.
06   A:   Hi Carla.
07   C:   How are you?
08   A:   Okay,
09   C:   Good.
10   A:   How about you?
11   C:   Fine, Don wants to know . . .
```

Variations

(i)   Cover up some of the lines in the above examples in item (3) and see if learners can guess what goes in those slots.

(ii) Give learners phone openings from ESL/EFL textbook dialogs to compare with a set of real openings such as those shown in item (3) above or collect your own to suit your learners' needs.

(iii) For more advanced learners, show real openings such as those in the chapter (i.e., complete with transcription symbols). This is important so that learners hear sound stretches, cut offs, intonation, and so on.

Practicing Activity: *Hello? HI!*

(1) Ask learner to make 1–3 phone calls as a homework assignment. If they don't have anyone to call and speak with in English, ask them to call you or one of your colleagues. Ask them to engage in a short conversation, paying particular attention to the opening lines of the conversation.

(2) After the learners have made the phone calls, ask them to jot down any problems or concerns that they had. These can be discussed in class.

The Four Opening Sequences

Awareness-raising Activity: *Wong's Phono-logical Phone Game (WPPG)* (also see Wong, forthcoming a for another version of this activity)

(1) Have learners work individually, in pairs, or groups on completing the blank gameboard in Appendix A with a set of scrambled openings created from Appendix B (i.e., cut out the individual cells in Appendix B and mix).

(2) Ask learners to move about the classroom and compare results with each other.

(3) Discuss the real answers.

(4) Discuss alternative answers.

(5) Ask learners to think about how telephone openings are done differently in their native languages.

Variations

(i) For lower level learners, use fewer openings or provide hints by filling in some of the cells on the gameboard.

(ii) For lower level learners, modify the spelling to more standard forms.

(iii) Separate the five openings. Write each turn on a separate strip; scramble the strips. Ask learners to recreate the dialog.

(iv) Combine these five real openings with five from ESL/EFL textbook dialog openings. The learners' task is to sort the real openings from the textbook ones.

Practicing Activity: *Making a Round of Calls*

(1) Have pairs of learners sit back-to-back and pretend to have a phone conversation. Practice role-playing the following four scenarios:

    (a) You are calling your girlfriend/boyfriend/partner to break off the relationship.

    (b) You are calling your brother to let him know that you got the job and will have to move overseas.

    (c) You are calling your classmate whom you don't know very well to borrow his/her notes for chemistry lab because you were sick.

    (d) You are calling your local pizza restaurant to order some takeout.

(2) Have each pair perform the same scenario in front of the class while the rest of the class takes notes and votes on the most true-to-life dialog.

(3) Wrap up the activity by focusing on problem areas in the dialogs presented as well as areas of strength.

Variations

    (i) Ask learners to rehearse and videotape the four scenarios as homework. Watch and discuss the videos in the next class.

    (ii) Find movie or TV clips that involve phone conversations. Familiarize the learners with the characters and plots. Play the clip and stop immediately after the phone rings, have learners role-play the phone conversations. Play the actual clip for comparison. Or, play the clip first without the sound and have learners role-play. Then play the clip with the sound for comparison.

Chapter Summary

An important component of interactional practices is overall structuring practices such as openings. There are four basic sequences which comprise phone openings: (1) summon–answer; (2) identification–recognition; (3) greeting; (4) *how are you*. The actual words and delivery used in each turn within each sequence can vary widely depending on the relationships between the caller and the answerer as well as whether it is a personal or business call. Although the core sequences and interactional concerns cut across languages, there are some slight variations in distribution. Telephone openings in institutional talk tend to be more compact than they are in personal phone calls. The interactional complexities of telephone openings are not necessarily captured in textbooks or explicitly taught in the second language classroom. For second language educators, understanding the complexities and nuances of openings provides a new lens for critiquing existing materials, developing authentic ones, and delivering useful instruction in helping ESL/EFL learners master the basic survival skill of opening a conversation. CA provides a way to begin at the beginning.

Key Concepts

- **Anchor point:** The place in the phone opening where the first topic or reason for the call is introduced.
- **Distribution rule:** In telephone conversations the answerer speaks first.
- **First topic:** What is initially talked about in a telephone conversation, which may but need not be the same as the reason for the call.
- **Greeting**: A sequence of two or more turns in which participants say *hi, hey, hello*, or the like upon initial contact on the phone.
- *How are you*: A sequence in which participants in a telephone conversation inquire about each others' well-being.
- **Identification–recognition:** A sequence in which participants in a telephone conversation negotiate the recognition of one another by name or voice sample.
- **Overall structuring practices**: Ways of organizing a conversation as a whole, as in openings and closings.
- **Pre-voice sample identification**: Instances where the caller or answerer is able to identify the other party prior to the offer of a voice sample. Two types of this identification are: (1) pre-voice sample caller identification (when answerer pre-identifies caller); (2) pre-voice sample answerer identification (when caller pre-identifies answerer).
- **Signature *hello*:** A way of answering the phone that is distinctive for that speaker.
- **Summons–answer**: A sequence of two turns in which participants check and display their availability to talk.
- **Voice sample**: An utterance in the opening of a phone conversation that gives a clue as to the identity of the speaker based on the sound of his/her voice.

Post-reading Questions

1. What are the sequence types that occur in telephone openings? How are they ordered?
2. What are the nine types of caller's first turns?
3. How does the identification and recognition sequence display participants' identities and relationships?
4. How is the initiation of the first topic or reason for the call in a telephone conversation tied to *how are you* sequences?
5. How are openings in business calls different from those in personal calls?
6. What aspects of openings in other languages were not addressed?
7. In which areas of openings is more research needed, and how could the research project be designed?
8. Would you approach the teaching of openings differently from how you would have before reading the chapter? Explain.
9. Select one of the suggested readings listed below and present the article in class, summarizing the article's key points and offering your questions

or concerns. Consider how the points raised in the article might be related to issues in language teaching especially if the article does not have a pedagogical orientation.

Suggested Readings

Barraja-Rohan, A.-M., & Pritchard, C. R. (1997). *Beyond talk: A course in communication and conversation for intermediate adult learners of English.* Melbourne, Australia: Western Melbourne Institute of TAFE (now Victoria University of Technology).

Bowles, H. (2006). Bridging the gap between conversation analysis and ESP: An applied study of the opening sequences of NS and NNS service telephone calls. *English for Specific Purposes, 25,* 332–357.

Liddicoat, A. (2000). Telephone openings in Samoan. *Australian Review of Applied Linguistics, 23*(1), 95–107.

Luke, K. K., &. Pavlidou, T.-S. (Eds.) (2002). *Telephone calls: Unity and diversity in conversational structures across languages and cultures.* Amsterdam: John Benjamins.

Schegloff, E. (1979b). Identification and recognition in telephone conversation openings. In G. Psathas (Ed.), *Everyday language studies in ethnomethodology* (pp. 23–78), New York: Irvington Publishers.

Schegloff, E. (1986). The routine as achievement. *Human Studies, 9,* 111–151.

Schegloff, E. (2004). Answering the phone. In G. Lerner (Ed.), *Conversation analysis: Studies from the first generation* (pp. 63–107). Amsterdam: John Benjamins.

Wong, J. (2002). "Applying" conversation analysis in applied linguistics: Evaluating dialog in English as a second language textbooks. *International Review of Applied Linguistics (IRAL), 40,* 37–60.

Wong, J. (forthcoming a). Telephone talk: Pragmatic competency in conversational openings. In N. Houck & D. Tatsuki (Eds.), *Pragmatics from theory to practice: New directions.* Volume 2. Alexandria, VA: TESOL Publications.

Appendix A Wong's Phono-logical Phone Game (WPPG)

	Conversation A	Conversation B	Conversation C	Conversation D	Conversation E
1	phone ring	phone ring	phone ring	phone ring	phone ring
2					
3					
4					
5					
6					

Appendix B Wong's Phono-logical Phone Game (WPPG)

	Conversation A	Conversation B	Conversation C	Conversation D	Conversation E
1	phone ring	phone ring	phone ring	phone ring	phone ring
2	Hello?	'ello	Hello	Hallo	H'llo
3	Hi	Hi Monica	Um Nate?	Hello Joan?	Hi
4	Hi, how are you?	(0.3 pause)	Yeh.	Yeah	Hi
5	Okay. What's new?	Your company there?	Is Laura there?	It's Craig.	Hawar yuh
6	Oh nothing	Yeah	No she went to the concert …	Hi	Fine, how 'r you

Chapter 6

Overall Structuring Practices and Language Teaching II

Conversation Closings

Pre-reading Questions

1. How difficult or easy do you think it is for language learners to close a conversation? Explain.
2. Have you ever taught language learners about conversation closings? If so, what did you teach and how did you do it?
3. Are you aware of any cross-cultural differences in closing a conversation?

Chapter Overview

This chapter covers the topic of conversation closings as part of overall structuring practices. The mundane practices of closings are more complex and subtle than we might initially think. It is a vital component of interactional competence. It is a social and linguistic skill that is more challenging for second language learners. Studies have revealed that some scripted dialog closings lack authenticity (Bardovi-Harlig, Hartford, Mahan-Taylor, Morgan, & Reynolds, 1991; Grant & Starks, 2001; Wong, 2007). In this chapter, we provide an overview of CA research on closings. Most of this research uses data from telephone conversations, but clearly some of the same issues and concerns are germane to face-to-face encounters (LeBaron and Jones, 2002; Robinson, 2001). We use transcripts of actual conversations for illustration, noting the pedagogical relevance of closings throughout the chapter. As with Chapter 5, we juxtapose our discussion with what is found in ESL/EFL textbook dialogs. We also include discussions on closings in other languages whenever relevant. We conclude with suggestions for instruction on closings in the ESL/EFL classrooms.

Overall Structuring Practices: Closings

Overall structuring practices are a key component of our model of interactional practices.

> **Overall structuring practices** are ways of organizing a conversation as a whole, as in openings and closings.

The importance of conversation closings is succinctly captured in this excerpt:

> Closings are a delicate matter both technically, in the sense that they must be so placed that no party is forced to exit while still having compelling things to say, and socially in the sense that both over-hasty and over-slow terminations can carry unwelcome inferences about the social relationships between the participants.
>
> (Levinson, 1983, p. 316)

Closings are more complex than openings because the number of turns involved is not as constrained as it is for openings. For example, in telephone openings, there are four core sequences (see Chapter 5). Although there are regular sequences that occur in closings, unlike openings, closings are vulnerable to being opened up, resulting in the never-ending *goodbyes* that we all experience. One reason why participants open up closings is because they need ways of introducing particular topics before the end of a conversation. They need to make room for a last topic, i.e., a **mentionable** (Bolden, 2008; Liddicoat, 2007; Schegloff & Sacks, 1973).

> **Mentionable** is a "last topic" that a participant raises at or near the end of a conversation.

Moreover, closings may be understood by reference to openings. For example, when a *how are you* inquiry occurs in a closing segment, this can reveal that it was missing from the opening (Schegloff, 2002). Most of the early CA research on closings has relied on telephone conversation data between friends or intimates (Button, 1987, 1990, 1991; Schegloff & Sacks, 1973). More research is needed to explore face-to-face leave-takings in ordinary conversation and institutional settings (LeBaron and Jones, 2002; Robinson, 2001).

Task 1

1. Make a list of five words and expressions that regularly occur in conversation closings in English. Share your list with someone in class. Was there anything that was missing on your list that was on your partner's, or vice versa?

    Vocabulary of closings:

(a) _____

(b) _____

(c) _____

(d) _____

(e) _____

Expressions found in closings:

(a) _____

(b) _____

(c) _____

(d) _____

(e) _____

2. Write down a typical telephone closing that you might have with:

   (a) a good friend

   (b) a family member

   (c) a co-worker

   (d) your boss

   (e) a stranger

CA insights on closings may seem transparent, but bear in mind that language teachers may not have explicit knowledge of the features and patterns of closings, at least not at the level of being able to articulate them to ESL/EFL learners. Even native speakers are not necessarily aware of the turns that make up closings. Not surprisingly, for less proficient speakers, closings can be problematic.

> **Author's story (JW):** My daughter Monica lives with Kim, who is originally from South Korea. One day, Kim was coming down the stairs and met Monica going up. She asked Monica whether she could have a ride that evening and Monica replied, "Yes." Kim then said, "Goodbye, Monica," and went back up. Monica was amused. She said, "Kim didn't have to say 'Goodbye.' She's not leaving the house, and I'm not leaving the house!"

That Kim's closing struck Monica as inappropriate is supported by this remark:

> persons in such a continuing state of incipient talk need not begin new segments of conversation with exchanges of greeting, and need not close segments with closing sections and terminal exchanges.
>
> (Schegloff & Sacks, 1973, pp. 324–325)

To close a conversation is an interactional achievement. It takes *doing* to terminate a conversation. Closing does not happen on its own. If a conversation closes, it is because participants have negotiated the talk to its very dying end, dealing with the closing problem: How do participants stop the ongoing turn-taking to reach a closing (Schegloff & Sacks, 1973)? Simply to stop talking does not necessarily close the conversation. If one party were to do so, s/he may be regarded as abrupt, ill-mannered, or angry. For ESL/EFL learners, these issues may be compounded or loom even larger. In the next sections, we first introduce the basic closing, which consists of a preclosing sequence and a terminal exchange. We then show how this basic closing may be expanded with different types of preclosing sequences. We conclude with suggestions for instruction.

A Basic Closing

Extract (1) is a basic telephone closing between friends or acquaintances. It is composed of two sets of adjacency pairs (see Chapter 3 on adjacency pairs and see complete transcription key at the beginning of the book):

(1)   [Schegloff & Sacks, 1973, p. 317—modified]
```
01    A:   OK.          ⎫
                        ⎬   preclosing sequence
02    B:   OK.          ⎭
03    A:   Bye-bye.     ⎫
                        ⎬   terminal exchange
04    B:   Bye.         ⎭
```

The first adjacency pair comprises the **preclosing sequence**, and the second pair the **terminal exchange** (Schegloff & Sacks, 1973).

Preclosing sequence is one or more adjacency pairs where participants initiate closure before the terminal exchange.

Terminal exchange is an adjacency pair where participants exchange *goodbye* and end a conversation.

In the following sections, we elaborate on the terminal exchange and preclosing signals, highlighting cross-cultural variations in these areas. Preclosing signals are part of preclosing sequences, which we address more extensively in a later section.

Terminal Exchange

Other examples of terminal exchanges may include:

(2)   [Schegloff & Sacks, 1973, p. 307]
    01   A: G'bye
    02   B: Goodnight.

(3)   [Schegloff & Sacks, 1973, p. 298]
    01   A: O.K.
    02   B: See you.

(4)   [Schegloff & Sacks, 1973, p. 298]
    01   A: Thank you.
    02   B: You're welcome.

Task 2

Have you ever said *goodbye* to someone but received no response in return, i.e., no return *goodbye*? What was your reaction? Did you think the recipient didn't hear you? Did you think the recipient was snubbing you or was angry with you?

Wong (2007) reported that, from a dataset of 81 textbook dialog closings, only 18 (22 percent) contained terminal exchanges That is, terminal exchanges are sometimes omitted or incomplete in ESL/EFL scripted dialog closings (A = answerer; C = caller):

(T-1)   [Messec & Kranich, 1982, p. 28]
    01   Lee: Do you have any seats left in the balcony?
    02   I need three.
    03   Operator: Yes. Your name, please?
    04   Lee: It's Wong. W-O-N-G.
    05   Operator: OK, Mr. Wong. I'll put aside three tickets for you.

(T-2)   [Reinhart & Fisher, 2000, p. 28]
    01   A: Hello.
    02   C: Hello, Is Nancy Turner home?
    03   A: Wrong number. ((A hangs up))

In (T-1), are we to assume that the caller and the operator hung up without saying *goodbye*? Not saying *goodbye* on the part of the operator who is selling tickets would reflect bad manners and unwise business etiquette. In (T-2), A the answerer rudely hangs up on C the caller without saying *goodbye* when C might have innocently dialed the wrong number. Other examples from Wong's (2007) textbook analysis revealed incomplete terminal exchanges, i.e. no second pair-parts (also see Bardovi-Harlig et al., 1991; Grant & Starks, 2001).

On the other hand, the exchange of *goodbye* in closing environments is not always a regular component in all languages. In the following phone conversation in Kiswahili, the speakers do not exchange *goodbye*, and the conversation ends with an exchange of *OK* (Omar, 1993):

(5)   [Omar, 1993, p. 106—modified]
      01   D: OK, then, if God wishes if I get time,
                      Haya basi, inshallahnikipata fursa
      02   I'll pass by there.
                      nitakuja huko
      03   L: If God wishes, baba.
                      Inshallah baba
      04   D: →   **OK, thanks.**
                      Haya asante.
      05   L: →   **OK.**
                      OK
                      ((end of conversation))

> **Author's story (JW):** When I was in college, one of my Chinese professors would call me, and we would speak in Mandarin-Chinese. He would end the conversation without saying *goodbye* in Mandarin (*zaijian*). Instead, he would say *hao* (*good*) and hang up. Whenever that happened, I always wondered whether he was being rude or abrupt. Then I realized that, in Chinese, *zaijian* isn't always said as a closing on the phone.

In the next example in Ecuadorian-Spanish, the caller says *goodbye*, but the answerer does not reciprocate (Placencia, 1997):

(6)   [Placencia, 1997, p. 71—modified]
      01   A: Yes just call me.
                      si llamenme no mas . . .
      02   C: Okay okay.
                      ya okay
      03   A: Okay.
                      ya
      04   C: →   **Thank you goodbye.**
                      gracias hasta luego

The omission of a reciprocal *goodbye* points to the asymmetry of the interaction. Speaker A, a service provider, is in a more powerful position than the customer and does not need to return the *goodbye* (Placencia, 1997).

In German, *auf Wiederhoeren* is a formal way of saying *goodbye* on the phone and *tschuess* (also *tschuesschen*, *tschoe*, or *tschoho*) an informal way (Pavlidou,

2008). According to Pavlidou (2008), terminal exchanges in Greek include expressions such as *ja* (*bye*, literally *health*) and its variants, e.g., *ja su* (*health to you*) and *ja xara* (*health joy*). These utterances can be used in both openings and closings. Expressions such as *tschau* (*ciao*), *bai* (*bye*), and *filaca* (*kisses*) are also used with family or intimates. Bolden (2008, forthcoming) shows that the equivalent of *kisses* or *I kiss you* is used with family or intimates in Russian.

> **Author's story (JW):** A friend would sign off his email messages with "Greetings!" followed by his name. It struck me as interesting. I now realize that he may be transferring a form of closing from his native language.

It is important for ESL/EFL teachers to understand the complexities involved in the terminal exchange across languages. Students might transfer an expression literally from their native language (e.g., *health joy*) and come across as odd. They might not reciprocate a *goodbye* and come across as rude. They might skip the exchange of *goodbye* entirely and come across as abrupt. The more teachers are aware of the cultural differences in managing terminal exchanges, the more equipped they would be to help learners say *goodbye* appropriately in English phone conversations.

Task 3

Consider the following example. How do the speakers signal to each other that they are about to close the conversation?

```
[Wright, 2004]
01   Ski:   It's good evening isn't it.
02   Joy:   Yes I thoroughly enjoy it.
03   Ski:   Ye:s.
05   Joy:   I really look for[ward to (   )]
06   Ski:                    [.hhhhhhhhh] .huh
07          Ye:s:.(.).hhh O::kay the[n: (.) See you on:: uh (0.5)
08   Joy:                           [(okay)
09   Ski:   on Sunday night then.
10   Joy:   Yes.
11   Ski:   Ri[ght.
12   Joy:     [Oka:y, right you are S[kip      than]ks a million=
13   Ski:                           [Thanks bye-]
14   Joy:   =Bye:
15   Ski:   Bye bye
               ((end of call))
```

Preclosing Signals

One of the problems for second language learners is "the inability . . . to pick up on the closing signals of the interlocutor and/or to respond to these signals accordingly" (Griswold, 2003).

> **Preclosing signal** is a lexical item such as *OK, OK then, alright, alright then, well, so, anyway, yes, yah,* or the like, which neither adds anything new to a current topic nor raises a new one.

These signals can occupy a full turn or occur in combinations. *Okay* in the following extract is a preclosing signal:

```
(7)   [Schegloff & Sacks, 1973, p. 307]
      01   A:   →   Okay boy,
      02   B:   →   Okay
      03   A:       Bye bye.
      04   B:       Good night.
```

Preclosing signals can occur with other items within the same turn, as in the example above (*Okay boy*). The signals (*okay then, alright then, yes,* or the like) are sometimes preceded by a topic-closing token such as *yes* (or a variant of *yes; hm, mm,* or the like), a click (e.g., *tsk* in English) and sometimes an inbreath, and in that order (Wright, 2004):

```
(8)   [Wright, 2004—modified]
      01   Joy:      hhh Oh:: well we don't we're-    [we're very ]=
      02   Les:                                    W [e don't di- ] =
      03   Joy:      = [N O : :
      04   Les:      = [discuss poli[tics do we.]
      05   Joy:                     [N o : no  ]: no
      06   Les:      No.
      07                (0.3)
      08   Joy:      No:
      09                (.)
      10   Les:   →   Yahp. pt .h Okay th[en Jay
[O:kay then]olesley.                     [hh
      12   I[See you
      13                     late[r.
      14   Joy:           [We'll see you y[es.
      15   Les:                          [Yes By[e:
      16   Joy:                                 [Okay bye:,
                  ((end of call))
```

The preclosing signal of "okay then" is preceded by "yahp." (a form of *yes* uttered with falling intonation) + click (transcribed as "pt") + inbreath (transcribed as ".h"). Similar findings, i.e., inbreath plus high pitch onset of preclosing signals, are reported in Bolden's (forthcoming) work using Russian conversation data.

Although preclosing signals like those mentioned above occur in other languages, there are also some culturally specific ones. In Table 6.1 overleaf, we only show the signals in each language that are different from those in English.

The following extract in Ecuadorian-Spanish shows repetitions of preclosing signals (Placencia, 1997):

(9)   [Placencia, 1997, p. 71–72—modified]

01	C:		so uh: I'll be waiting for you at home.
			entonces eh: te espero en la casa
02	A:		very well.
			muy bien
03	C:	→	**okay okay.**
			ya okay
04	A:		okay
			o ka
05	C:		**okay okay okay.**
			ya ya okay
06	A:	→	okay.
			ya
07	C:	→	**okay okay** I'll call her now.
			ya ya le voy a llamar ahora
08	A:		okay.
			ya
09	C:		okay Pato.
			Okay Pato
10	A:		okay.
			okay
11	C:		so we'll see each other at home.
			entonces nos vemos en la casa

Through the technique of reduplication, the "expression of agreement between the two participants [is] reinforced" (Placencia, 1997, p. 72).

In Wong's (2007) study of 81 scripted dialog closings, she found 1 case of *well*, 1 case of *Oh + thanks*, 7 cases of *alright*, and 10 cases of *OK + thank you*. She did not find any cases of *OK*, which is an extremely common preclosing signal in English.

Table 6.1 Preclosing Signals in Other Languages (those dissimilar to English)

Language	Preclosing Signal	English Translation
Ecuadorian-Spanish (Placencia, 1997)	ya okay	okay okay
	muy bien	excellent
German (Pavlidou, 2008)	Also	so then
	gut	good
	bis dann	till then
Greek (Pavlidou, 2008)	lipon	Well, so then
	ejine	Done
	orea	Nicely
	kala	Good
Russian (Bolden, forthcoming)	vse	that's that
	jasna	I see
	ponjatno	I see
	tak shto takie dela	that's how things are
	vot	(a boundary particle)

Author's story (HW): One of my graduate students originally from China writes about her difficulty with closings: "When I worked as a paralegal in a law firm, I used to have difficulty knowing when to end my conversation with my American boss. A couple of times when I was in his office discussing the cases I was working on, at some point, he would sit back and say *O::K::*. I sensed something but was not sure what it was. But I noticed that, after saying this *OK*, he seemed to lose interest in our conversation. It made me feel quite uneasy. It was only after a couple of these encounters that I realized that whenever he said *OK* in a special tone, it was time for me to leave. I thought Americans were direct in their speech and never expected that an *OK* was a signal to close a conversation."

That some ESL/EFL textbook dialogs do not include *okay* as a preclosing signal at all is strong evidence that our intuitions about closings are not entirely reliable. CA work neatly supplements the existing materials by offering a fuller range of possibilities that reflect the actual preclosing signals used in interaction:

- *OK*
- *OK, then*
- *alright*
- *OK, alright*
- *alright, then*
- *well*
- *well, alright*

- *well, then*
- *so*
- *anyway*
- *yes (yah, yep), OK*
- *yes (yah, yep), OK then*
- *yes (yah, yep), alright*
- *yes (yah, yep), alright then*

Preclosing signals are rarely taught explicitly in second language instruction, and learners are often left to fend for themselves. With the knowledge offered by CA findings, teachers can help learners develop more flexibility in exiting a phone conversation in English by making use of the range of preclosing signals found in everyday conversation. By drawing specific attention to the preclosing signals that learners might inappropriately transfer from their native languages (e.g., *done*), teachers can help learners avoid sounding out of place. Teachers can also ask learners to compare and contrast preclosing signals across languages to heighten their metalinguistic awareness. Students will become more interested in preclosings the more they can connect them with their home languages.

Task 4

Consider the following textbook phone dialog. How would you modify it to better reflect a real phone conversation?

[Mosteller & Paul (1994) (Book 3), p. 96]

01	A:	Hello.
02	B:	Hi. This is Lee. Is Kim there?
03	A:	Kim? Kim who?
04	B:	Kim Perez.
05	A:	No, sorry. I think you have the wrong
06		number.
07	B:	Is this 555–2149?
08	A:	No, it isn't.
09	B:	Oh, sorry to bother you.
10	A:	That's O.K.

Types of Preclosing Sequences

That one speaker offers a preclosing signal in a first turn does not guarantee that a conversation closes in a second turn. For example, a mentionable or last topic can open up closings in minimal or drastic ways (Button, 1987, 1990, 1991; Schegloff & Sacks, 1973). Should a mentionable get added, the preclosing signal is tantamount to a fishing expedition with no catch. A mentionable or last topic is sometimes prefaced by a misplacement marker (e.g., *by the way* or *incidentally*) (Goldberg, 2004; Schegloff & Sacks, 1973). In Wong's (2007) study of ESL/EFL scripted dialogs, there was not a single case of *by the way* used as a misplacement marker in closings. Second language learners may not catch on to the kind of nuance that *by the way* signals.

Author's story (JW): Once Yoon, an international student originally from South Korea, was with my daughter Monica and two of her friends. At one point, she said, "by the way." When all eyes and heads turned toward her, Yoon looked puzzled. Then, the others realized that Yoon had nothing more to say. They told her that when she said "by the way" instead of "anyway," they thought she was going to change the topic. And she said, "There are so many words and expressions in English that sound the same!"

Reaching a point of closure may be easier said than done. Sometimes, one party is intent on ending the conversation, but another has the opposite inclination. Participants do preclosings in a variety of ways. Language teachers may not necessarily be aware of these methods.

Task 5

Besides preclosing signals, what are the other things that often get said towards the end of a conversation?

There are nine preclosing sequence types used in telephone conversations, and they can co-occur (Button, 1987, 1990, 1991; Schegloff & Sacks, 1973):

(1) arrangement sequence;
(2) appreciation sequence;
(3) solicitude sequence;
(4) reason-for-the call sequence;
(5) back-reference sequence;
(6) in-conversation object sequence;
(7) topic-initial elicitor sequence;
(8) announced closing sequence;
(9) moral or lesson sequence.

Each type of preclosing sequence leads to a particular trajectory of the talk, leading to "minimal" or "drastic" movement out of closings (Button, 1987, 1990, 1991). ESL/EFL textbook dialog closings display a very limited range of preclosing sequence types, most of which are "arrangements" and "appreciation" described below (Wong, 2007). It is striking that none of the 76 preclosing sequences in Wong's (2007) textbook analysis led to opened up closings, which provides further evidence for the problems of relying on native-speaker intuitions as well as the importance of examining real talk.

Arrangement Sequence

Among the different preclosing sequence types, the **arrangement sequence** has a special status as a last topic. Arrangements emphasize the relationship between participants and make it easier to close the conversation *now*.

Arrangement sequence is a preclosing sequence in which participants make or restate plans to contact one another or get together.

Two examples of the arrangement sequence follow:

(10) [Button, 1990, pp. 97–98—modified]
   01   Emma: um [sleep good tonight swee[tie,
   02   Lottie: →   [Okay-   [**Okay well I'll- I'll**
   03   **see you in the mor[ning**
   04   Emma: →   [**Al:right,**
   05   Lottie: Alright,
   06   Emma: B'ye bye de[ar.
   07   Lottie: [Bye bye, ((end of call))

(11) [Button, 1990, p. 99—modified]
   01   Wilbur: Okay,
   02   Wilbur: →   **Well- well maybe we will see each other uh:::**
   03   **maybe not <u>Thurs</u>day but as soon as you can get**
   04   **<u>do</u>:wn.**
   05   Lila: →   [**Yes,**
   06   Wilbur: →   [**I'm <u>free</u> in the <u>eve</u>nings,**
   07   Lila: →   **Yeah I'll call you= an' bec- I'll ( ) something**
   08   **I've experienced that I- I must tell you, I- I tried**
   09   **to get home before five o'clock since the fog . . .**
                       ((continues))

In Extract (10), Lottie initiates closure by saying she will see Emma tomorrow, which begins an arrangement sequence. Emma accepts with a minimal response ("Al:right") that neither opens up the current topic nor starts a new one. The conversation shuts down at the terminal exchange (lines 06–07) (Button, 1990). Thus, the arrangement sequence leads to minimal movement from closing. By contrast, in Extract (11) above, Wilbur's initiation of arrangements (lines 02–04) touches off another topic of discussion for Lila (lines 07–09). Here, the arrangement sequence leads to drastic movement from closing.

The arrangements in these sequences can be non-specific in the sense that they may or may not be fulfilled:

(12)   [Button, G., 1991, p. 268—modified]
        01   N: He's paranoid.=
        02   D: =He's definitely paranoid.
        03   N: Yeah well hhh
        04   D: Hm:::.
        05   (0.5)
        06   N: →   **We::ll, look, I'll talk to you later.**
        07   D: →   **Yeah, see you.**
        08   N: Okay, bye.
        09   D: Okay,
        10   N: Bye.

German closings also make reference to future plans regardless of whether they will occur or not (Pavlidou, 2008), but in general, using arrangements as a preclosing often poses problems for ESL/EFL learners.

> **Author's story (HW):** One of my graduate students relates the following story about her friend: "When Etty, a native of Israel, first moved to New York, she was really eager to meet people in her building. One day, she ran into an American neighbor in the stairwell, and they chatted a bit. The neighbor said, 'Great, well, we'll have to have coffee!' Etty replied, 'That would be great!' Happy that the neighbor wanted to get to know her better, Etty went back to her apartment, put the kettle on the stove and a plate of cookies on the table, and sat waiting for her neighbor to come for coffee. The neighbor never came. She had only meant, of course, to end the conversation and to indicate that she would be chatting with Etty in the future."

Wong (2007) shows that, even though ESL texts include arrangements-making, it is typically not presented as a practice for doing preclosing.

Appreciation Sequence

Another common way of signaling closing is to use the **appreciation sequence**.

> **Appreciation sequence** is a preclosing sequence in which participants express or repeat thanks to one another.

In the example below, Emma expresses appreciation at line 02:

(13) [Button, 1990, p. 101—modified]
    01   Marian: And you call me at nine tomorrow mor [ning.
    02   Emma: [Alright
    03   →   darling **I appreciate it.**
    04   Marian: →   **Okay,**
    05   Emma: Bye bye.
    06   Marian: Bye-bye. ((end of call))

Emma's appreciation, which is prefaced by the preclosing signal, "Alright darling," functions as an offer to close, which is accepted by Marian with "Okay" at line 04. They end the conversation at lines 05–06.

Solicitude Sequence

As preclosing offers, **solicitude sequences** are probably the most familiar.

> **Solicitude sequence** is a preclosing sequence in which participants express concerns, well-wishes, regards to third parties, holiday greetings, or the like.

(14) [Button, 1990, p. 101—modified]
    01   Sam: Nice talking to you honey maybe I'll see you
    02   [Thursday.
    03   Marge: [uh: [Oh: alright
    04   →   love to see you . . .hh **A:n' uh tell uh: your little**
    05   **gi:rlfrie:nd or other little girlfrie:nd hello and**
    06   **everything like that.**=
    07   Sam: →   =**I will dear.**
    08   Marge: O:kay.=
    09   Sam: =Thank you,
    10   Marge: Bye= [bye,
    11   Sam: [Bye bye. ((end of call))

(15) [Button, 1987, p. 103—modified]
    01   Mark: . . . and uh .hh I'll be talking to you Friday .h
    02   (0.2)
    03   Bob: Oka:y.=
    04   Mark: →   =**Have a happy Thanksgiving:: a:nd uh (.) m-**
    05   **may all your dreams come true.**=
    06   Bob: →   =**Well thank you:. Thank you.**
    07   (.)

```
08   Mark:      [Ah-
09   Bob:       [What are you doing tomorrow [night anything
10   Mark:                                   [.hhhhhhhhhhhh
11              Oh::::.uh
12              Well uh ((continues))
```

In Extract (14), the solicitude leads to minimal movement out of closings, but in Extract (15), it leads to opening up of the closing. Wong's (2007) textbook analysis revealed that solicitudes were used in only three cases.

Task 6

Solicitudes are a particularly useful preclosing sequence type to teach because of their formulaic nature. Make a list of solicitudes that are typically used in preclosings.

Reason-for-the Call Sequence

In the **reason-for-the call sequence**, the caller restates why s/he called. Wong's (2007) ESL/EFL textbook dialog corpus did not contain this type of preclosing sequence. Grant and Starks (2001) also comment that ESL/EFL textbook dialog closings do not teach learners about how to re-introduce the reason for the call.

> **Reason-for-the call sequence** is a preclosing sequence in which the caller restating why s/he called.

(16) [Button, 1990, p. 121—modified]
```
01   John:           I'll see you over the weekend then.
02   Steve:          Good thing.
03   John:      →    Okay, and I'm glad I ra:ng now an sorted things
04                   out.
05   Steve:     →    Yeah me too.
06   John:           Okay then.
07   Steve:          Oka:y,
08   John:           B[ye.
09   Steve:          [Bye.
```

(17) [Button, 1990, p. 122—modified]
```
01   Vicky:          Good.
02   Vicky:     →    Okay well I just ca:lled to (0.4) the:: (.) ask,=
03   Karen:     →    =thanks [a lo:t,
```

```
04   Vicky:   →                    [although of course I knew [the answer
05                      would be no:
06   Karen:   →                                           [really
07                      Yeah. ((continues))
```

In Extract (16) above, the reason for the call (lines 03–04) leads to a closing. However, in Extract (17) above, the reason for the call (lines 02 and 04–05) leads to drastic movement from closing.

Back-reference Sequence

In the **back-reference sequence**, something that was addressed in the prior talk is talked about again. Wong's (2007) ESL/EFL textbook dialog closings did not contain any examples of the back-reference sequence.

Back-reference sequence is a preclosing sequence in which participants talk about something discussed earlier in the conversation.

In Extract (18) below, Mark refers back to their discussion on Thanksgiving (not shown here). In Extract (19), David refers back to their earlier mention of "the baby" (not shown here).

```
(18)   [Button, 1990, p. 96—modified]
       01   Bob:          Alright [Mark.=
       02   Mark:                 [Well=
       03   Bob:          =       [Hm?
       04   Mark:   →     =       [What are you doing for Thanksgiving.
       05   Bob:          Oh I'm :: visiting my parents. ((continues))
```

```
(19)   [Button, 1987, p. 106—modified]
       01   Robin:        Alright David.
       02   David:   →    So what did the baby say.
       03   Robin:        Oh he asked for you. He slept with me two nights
       04                 this wee:k he asked for you in the morning . . .
                          ((continues))
```

In both cases, the other party collaborates in keeping the conversation open, and the back-reference leads to drastic movement out of the closings.

In-conversation Object Sequence

With an **in-conversation object**, a first speaker displays to a second that s/he is available to continue the conversation. Again, Wong's (2007) textbook data did not reveal instances of this kind.

> **In-conversation object sequence** is a preclosing sequence in which participants use utterances such as *mm hmm, um, yeah,* or the like to display their availability for further talk without making any substantive contribution to that talk.

The in-conversation object can either lead to a quick closing or engender further talk:

(20)   [Liddicoat, 2007, p. 274—modified]
```
01   Kylie:           Call me when you get in won't you?
02   Norm:            Yeah.
03   Kylie:           Okay then, Norm.
04   Norm:            Okay.
05   Kylie:      →    Uh:m,
06              →    (0.4)
07   Kylie:           So have a safe trip.
08   Norm:            Yeah.
09   Kylie:           And a good time.
10   Norm:            Sure will
11   Kylie:           Right.
12   Norm:            Alright.
13   Kylie:           Bye bye.
14   Norm:            Bye
```

(21)   [Button, 1987, p. 117—modified]
```
01   Geri:            Oka:y
02   Shirley:         Alright?
03   Geri:       →    Mm-h[m?
04   Shirley:    →          [Did you talk to Dana this week?
05   Geri:            hh yeah . . .
```

In Extract (20), after Kylie's in-conversation object "Uh:m" at line 05, Norm does not talk further at line 06, and the conversation comes to a close soon afterwards with a solicitude sequence and a terminal exchange. By contrast, in Extract (21), after Geri's in-conversation object "Mm-hm?," Shirley proceeds to open up the conversation with a new topic at line 04 ("Did you talk to Dana this week?"). Thus, the in-conversation object contributes to moving drastically out of the closing.

Topic-initial Elicitor Sequence

Similar to back-reference and in-conversation object, a **topic-initial elicitor** signals the availability of a participant to continue the conversation (also see

Chapter 4). Wong's (2007) textbook dialog analysis did not reveal any cases of **topic-initial elicitor**.

> **Topic-initial elicitor sequence** is a preclosing sequence in which participants solicit a new but non-specific topic for discussion.

Topic-initial elicitors provide space for participants to bring up a new topic if they wish:

(22) [Liddicoat, 2007, p. 272—modified]
    01 Tracy: . . . but it's okay now=
    02 David: =Yeah (.) °yeah. °
    03 Tracy: →   **Anything else?**
    04 David: →   **No, nothing's happening.**
    05   Ok:ay.
    06 David: Okay.
    07 Tracy: Bye.
    08 David: Bye.

(23) [Liddicoat, 2007, p. 272—modified]
    01 Diane: =Okay.
    02   (0.2)
    03 Helen: →   **Anything else happening,**
    04 Diane: →   **Oh yeah=I saw Grace the other day.**
    05 Helen: Yea:h, how is she.
    06 Diane: She's fine she looks a bit tired still but she's fine.
    07 Helen: She's good.

In Extract (22) above, Tracy's topic initial elicitor receives David's "No, nothing's happening." The conversation comes to a close. However, in Extract (23), Helen's topic initial elicitor is taken up by Diane with "Oh yeah=I saw Grace the other day." This leads to drastic movement out of the closing.

Announced Closing Sequence

If participants want to avoid the risk of a new topic developing, they may produce an **announced closing sequence**.

> **Announced closing sequence** is a preclosing sequence in which participants overtly state that the conversation should close and/or give a reason for ending the conversation.

In Extract (24) below, Geri's announced closing at line 03 is accepted by Shirley at line 04, and the conversation proceeds to a closure (not shown here):

```
(24)   [Button, 1987, p. 120—modified]
       01   Shirley:      I can [hear it from this [side
       02   Shiloh:            [ragh!    rugh  [ragh!
       03   Geri:    →                         [Okay well let me get o:ff,
       04   Shirley: →   Yeah go do your work,
```

Schegloff and Sacks (1973) refer to utterance such as *Let me get off, The baby is crying, I gotta go, my dinner is burning* as "caller techniques," which makes reference to the caller's interest (p. 311). "Called techniques," on the other hand, include expressions such as *This is costing you a lot money*, which makes reference to the called party's interest (Schegloff & Sacks, 1973, p. 310). In the extract below, a "called technique" is used:

```
(25)   [Schegloff & Sacks, 1973, p. 310—modified]
       01   A:       Uhm livers and gizzards and stuff like that makes
       02            it real yummy. Makes it too rich for me but: makes
       03       →    it yummy. Well I'll let you go. I don't want to tie
       04            up your phone.
```

Announced closings can also lead to drastic movement out of the closing:

```
(26)   [Button, 1990, p. 121—modified]
       01   Ronald:      Well it's a political cartoo:n.
       02   Maggie:      Oh, Okay sweetie.
       03   Ronald:      [Okay-
       04   Maggie:  →   [Well I'll let you go. I'm in the middle of
       05                cleaning up this mess.
       06   Ronald:  →   .hh What are you- what's the mess. Some[thing-
       07   Maggie:                                            [Oh
       08                we- no no we change the clothes around.
       09                ((continues))
```

Maggie's announced closing at lines 04–05 piqued Ronald's interest in what the mess is, and with that, the conversation remains open.

Moral or Lesson Sequence

In moral or lesson preclosings, a participant offers a final summary typically with an idiomatic utterance (also see Chapter 4 on topic termination). Wong's (2007) textbook corpus did not contain any examples of this type.

> **Moral or lesson sequence** is a preclosing sequence in which participants use a moral or lesson to summarize the topic so far.

In the extract below, Theresa summarizes the topic with "Things always work out for the best" (lines 02–03), to which Dorrine agrees at line 04 ("Oh certainly"):

(27) [Schegloff & Sacks, 1973, p. 307—modified]
    01 Dorrine: Uh- you know, it's just like bringing the- blood up.
    02 Theresa: →   **Yeah well, THINGS UH ALWAYS WORK OUT**
    03   **FOR THE BEST.**
    04 Dorrine: →   **Oh certainly. Alright Tess.**
    05 Theresa: Uh huh, Okay,
    06 Dorrine: Goodbye.
    07 Theresa: Goodnight.

After the agreement, Dorrine initiates closure with a preclosing signal "Alright," and the conversation proceeds to a closure. (The reader may listen to the example above by going to Schegloff's webpage online and clicking on "soundclips" for his 1973 paper, "Opening Up Closings".) Table 6.2 summarizes the preclosing sequences.

Some of these sequences are more likely to lead to minimal movement out of the closing (Button, 1990):

(1) announced closing;
(2) appreciation;
(3) arrangement;
(4) reason-for-the-call;
(5) solicitude.

Table 6.2 Types of Preclosing Sequences

Preclosing Sequences	Examples
1. Arrangement	I'll see you in the morning.
2. Appreciation	Thank you.
3. Solicitude	Take care.
4. Reason-for-the call	I just called to find out if you're going.
5. Back-reference	So what are you doing for Thanksgiving?
6. In-conversation object	Mm hmm?
7. Topic-initial elicitor	Anything else to report?
8. Announced closing	OK, let me get back to work.
	OK, I'll let you go.
9. Moral or lesson	Yeah well, things always work out for the best.

Others are more likely to lead to drastic movement out of the closing (Button, 1990):

(1) back reference;
(2) in-conversation object;
(3) topic-initial elicitor;
(4) moral or lesson.

Task 7

Consider the following extracts. What type of preclosing sequence(s) are used in each extract?

(1) [Button, 1987, p. 121—modified]
01   John: I'll see you over the weekend then.
02   Steve: Good thing.
03   John: Okay, and I'm glad I ra:ng now an sorted things out.
04   Steve: Yeh me too.
05   John: Okay then,
06   Steve: Oka:y,
07   John: B[ye.
08   Steve: [Bye.

(2) [Schegloff, 2007, p. 258—modified]
01   Deb: And that's- that's the only thing I'm
02   saying, anyway, I gotta get going, 'cause
03   I'm at work.
04   Mar: ° okay. ° ((whisper voice))
05   Deb: So: I'll talk to you later.
06   Deb: Okay.
07   Deb: Bye.
08   Mar: Bye.

(3) [Liddicoat, 2007, p. 274—modified]
01   Kylie: Call me when you get in won't you?
02   Norm: Yeah.
03   Kylie: Okay then, Norm.
04   Norm: Okay.
05   Kylie: Uh:m,
06   (0.4)
07   Kylie: So have a safe trip.
08   Norm: Yeah.
09   Kylie: And a good time.
10   Norm: Sure will.
11   Kylie: Right.

```
12   Norm:   Alright.
13   Kylie:   Bye bye.
```

(4) [Schegloff, 2007, p. 261—modified]
```
01   Reb:   =Listen I've gotta go 'cause I'm gonna go to dance
02          class:
03   Art:   =Okay:=
04   Reb:   =But um (.) I'll be home- What're you doing this
05          evening.
06   Art:   Uh: nothing, (.) What do you do- do something?
07   Reb:   Uh sure I was just thinking we could talk (0.2)
08   Art:   Okay.=
09   Reb:   =some mo:re or: (.) or maybe we could go out to
10          movie or something.
11   Art:   Oh okay
12   Reb:   °(    )°=
13   Art:   =Sure.
14   Reb:   [So- ]
15   Art:   [I'm-] I'm going over to Laurie's right now.
```

Wong (2007) reveals that a major gap in her textbook dialog closings was that learners are not shown how closings can be opened up. The preclosing sequence types used in scripted dialogs are quite restricted, relying largely on arrangement and appreciation sequences. Other studies on closings in ESL/EFL textbook dialogs also report an overall lack of authenticity even to the extent of not treating closings at all (Bardovi et al., 1991; Grant & Starks, 2001; Wong, 2007). Leave-taking or saying *goodbye* is not as easy as it appears, especially in a second or foreign language context. The seemingly simple or formulaic utterances characteristic of conversation closings should not be taken for granted. CA insights on closings can help ESL/EFL teachers and learners appreciate the subtleties and coordinated efforts involved in negotiating conversational closure.

Teaching Conversation Closings

In this section, we describe a few activities that are inspired by the CA findings on closings as an initial attempt to address current gaps in second language instruction in this area. Teachers are encouraged to adapt these activities to their own needs and to use authentic talk whenever possible.

Preclosing Signals

Awareness-raising Activity: *How do I Know this is the End?*

(1) Begin by finding out learners' knowledge of closings in their native language(s) and in the target language:

    (a) How do you close a conversation on the telephone or in face-to-face interaction?

    (b) Can you list some examples of typical words and expressions used in closings?

    (c) Do you ever find closings awkward? For example, is it hard to shut down a conversation with someone? Is it hard to keep someone interested in talking?

    (d) Have you ever felt taken aback or offended by the abruptness of someone's conversation closure? If so, why?

    (e) Have you ever misinterpreted someone's closing signal(s)? If so, describe the circumstances and the language that was used.

    (f) What other issues can you think of relating to conversation closings?

(2) Give learners sample closings below and ask them to answer the following question for each example: what is the first indication that someone is about to close the conversation?

    (a) [Schegloff & Sacks, 1973, p. 317—modified]

01	A:	O.K.
02	B:	O.K.
03	A:	Bye Bye.
04	B:	Bye.

    (b) [Button, 1990, pp. 97–98—modified]

01	Emma:	um sleep well tonight sweetie,
02	Lottie:	Okay well I'll see you in the morning.
03	Emma:	Alright,
04	Lottie:	Alright,
05	Emma:	Bye bye dear.
06	Lottie:	Bye bye.

    (c) [Button, 1990, p. 101—modified]

01	Marian:	And you call me at nine tomorrow morning.
02	Emma:	Alright darling I appreciate it.
03	Marian:	Okay,
04	Emma:	Bye bye.
05	Marian:	Bye bye.

    (d) [Button, 1990, p. 101—modified]

| 01 | Sam: | Nice talking to you honey maybe I'll see |

```
02                    you Thursday.
03      Marge:        uh Oh alright love to see you. .hh And uh
04                    tell your little girlfriend over there little
05                    girlfriend hello and everything like that.
06      Sam:          I will dear.
07      Marge:        Okay.
08      Sam:          Thank you,
09      Marge:        Bye bye,
```

```
(e)     [Button, 1990, p. 121]
01      John:         I'll see you over the weekend then.
02      Steve:        Good thing.
03      John:         Okay, and I'm glad I rang now and sorted
04                    things out.
05      Steve:        Yeah me too.
06      John:         Okay then.
207     Steve:        Okay,
08      John:         B[ye.
09      Steve:         [Bye.
```

(3) Have learners compare their answers with each other and then discuss as a class.
(4) Present the list of preclosing signals shown earlier in this chapter.
(5) Consider cross-cultural variations in the use of preclosing signals.

Variation

Ask learners to listen for preclosing signals in their native languages and English and bring the examples to the next class for discussion.

Practicing Activity: *The Right Signal?*

(1) Use Examples (a)–(e) above to create a fill-in-the-blank exercise by taking out all the preclosing signals.
(2) Have learners work in pairs to complete the exercise.
(3) Have learners practice role-playing the dialogs based on their answers.
(4) For each example, have each pair perform in front of the class as the rest of the class takes notes on the appropriateness of the closing signals.
(5) After all the role-plays for each example have been completed, decide as a class what is the most appropriate signal for that example.
(6) Show the actual preclosing signals used in the examples.
(7) Discuss the issues that arise from the discrepancies between the learners' choice of preclosing signals and the ones used in the examples.

Variations

(i) Give choices for what could go in the blanks.
(ii) Use more examples from the suggested readings or your own recordings.

Preclosing Sequences

Awareness-raising Activity: *Sorting Closings*

(1) Give learners a collection of closings, some taken from real conversations (e.g., from this chapter and the suggested readings) and others from ESL/EFL scripted dialogs. See Bardovi-Harlig et al. (1991), Grant and Starks (2001), and Wong (2007) for samples of textbook dialog closings.
(2) Mix up the examples and ask learners to sort through them and make two piles: (1) real closings and (2) made-up closings.
(3) Ask learners to compare their sorting with one another and explain their decisions.
(4) Build on the discussion by asking learners to make a list of the expressions used in the following conversation closings:

<blockquote>

(a) [Button, 1990, pp. 97–98—modified]
01 Emma: um sleep well tonight sweetie,
02 Lottie: Okay well I'll see you in the morning.
03 Emma: Alright,
04 Lottie: Alright,
05 Emma: Bye bye dear.
06 Lottie: Bye bye.

(b) [Button, 1990, p. 121—modified]
01 John: I'll see you over the weekend then.
02 Steve: Good thing.
03 John: Okay, and I'm glad I rang now and sorted
04 things out.
05 Steve: Yeah me too.
06 John: Okay then.
07 Steve: Okay,
08 John: B[ye.
08 Steve: [Bye.

(c) [Button, 1990, p. 105—modified]
01 Alfred: Well, we'll see what happens.
02 Lila: Okay,
03 Alfred: Thank you very much Mrs. Asch,
04 Lila: Thanks for calling,
05 Alfred: Goodbye,

</blockquote>

```
06   Lila:      Bye bye,
```

(d) [Button, 1990, p. 104—modified]
```
01   Marge:    Tell your girlfriend I said hello.
02   Sam:      I will dear.
03   Marge:    Okay.
04   Sam:      Thank you,
05   Marge:    Bye bye,
06   Sam:      Bye bye.
```

(5) Introduce the notion of preclosing sequence types such as arrangement, appreciation, solicitude, and announced closing, using terminology suitable for your learners.
(6) Discuss cross-cultural variations.
(7) Wrap up the discussion by addressing any remaining concerns about preclosing sequences.

Variations

(i) Have learners match sequence types such as "arrangement" or "appreciation" with the specific lines in the examples above.
(ii) Have learners collect examples of preclosing sequences from the media or their daily interaction.

Practicing Activity: *Cocktail Party*

(1) Ask learners to mill about the classroom as if they were at a cocktail party (for younger learners, use another party venue aside from cocktail party). To make this more fun, give learners something to drink and some snacks to munch on while talking at this feigned cocktail party.
(2) Learners are to make small talk with one another for a specified length of time (e.g., 2–3 minutes) until they hear you give a 1-minute warning (e.g., with a bell). During this 1-minute span, they are to bring the current conversation to a close. When the time is up, they have to move on to have another conversation with another person.
(3) Give learners cue cards so that when they close the conversation, they are required to use preclosing sequences such as arrangements, announced closing, solicitude, etc. They are to use a different preclosing sequence type for each conversation that they engage in. The teacher decides when the party ends.
(4) Solicit learners' feedback about the activity. Address any questions that arise.

Variations

(i)   Give learners cue cards that ask one person to close down the conversation and the other to keep it open.

(ii) Have learners make some real phone calls, using the preclosing sequences to exit the conversations. Ideally, these phone calls should be tape-recorded (with permission), and the recordings can be brought to class for discussion.

(iii) Have learners role-play the following sample scenarios:

    (a) A person has applied for a job and has gone for an interview. The interviewer and interviewee talk about various aspects of the job and the interviewee's qualifications. Then, it is time to close the conversation.

    (b) Two people who are good friends haven't seen one another in two years. They run into each other on the street and chat about this and that in catching up with their lives. Suddenly, one realizes that s/he is late for an appointment.

(iv) Give learners textbook closings and real closings to act out. Some receive textbook closings; others receive real ones. Pairs of learners perform the closings one "act" at a time, while the rest of the class guesses whether the closing is from a textbook dialog or is an authentic one. Learners give reasons to support their guess.

Chapter Summary

Along with openings, another critical component in overall structuring practices is closings. The ability to close a conversation is just as much of a basic survival skill in social interaction. Openings and closings go hand in hand. CA research reveals that speakers rely on a variety of preclosing signals, sequences and terminal exchanges in bringing a conversation to a close. Sometimes, these interactional practices lead to minimal or drastic movement out of the closings. However, the complex nature of closings is often missing or watered down in ESL/EFL textbook dialogs. Thus, for the language instructor, a deep understanding of the complexities of closings based on examination of real ones is essential. Armed with the information provided in this chapter, an instructor may hone in on ways of teaching learners to communicate in more authentic ways, ones that take into consideration the nature of real interaction and how people do language in the real world on a turn-by-turn basis.

Key Concepts

- **Announced closing sequence:** A preclosing sequence in which participants overtly state that the conversation should close and/or give a reason for ending the conversation.

- **Appreciation sequence:** A preclosing sequence in which participants express or repeat thanks to one another.
- **Arrangement sequence:** A preclosing sequence in which participants make or restate plans to contact one another or get together.
- **Back-reference sequence:** A preclosing sequence in which participants talk about something discussed earlier in the conversation.
- **In-conversation object sequence:** A preclosing sequence in which participants use utterances such as *mm hmm, um, yeah*, or the like to display their availability for further talk without making any substantive contribution to that talk.
- **Mentionable:** A "last topic" that a participant raises at or near the end of a conversation.
- **Moral or lesson sequence:** A preclosing sequence in which participants use a moral or lesson to summarize the topic so far.
- **Overall structuring practices:** Ways of organizing a conversation as a whole, as in openings and closings.
- **Preclosing sequence:** One or more adjacency pairs where participants initiate closure before the terminal exchange.
- **Preclosing signal:** A lexical item such as *OK, OK then, alright, alright then, well, so, anyway, yes, yah*, or the like, which neither adds anything new to a current topic nor raises a new one.
- **Reason-for-the call sequence:** A preclosing sequence in which the caller restates why s/he called.
- **Solicitude sequence:** A preclosing sequence in which participants express concerns, well-wishes, regards to third parties, holiday greetings, or the like.
- **Terminal exchange:** An adjacency pair where participants exchange *goodbye* and end a conversation.
- **Topic-initial elicitor sequence:** A preclosing sequence in which participants solicit a new but non-specific topic for discussion.

Post-reading Questions

1. Describe the basic closing components in English conversation.
2. List the various kinds of preclosing sequences. Which ones are more likely to lead to closure of the conversation? Which ones are more likely to lead to expansion of the conversation?
3. Can you think of other preclosing sequence types that were not discussed in this chapter?
4. If you were to teach (English) language learners about closings, how would you go about it?
5. Having read this chapter, what questions or concerns still remain about the teaching or learning of closings?
6. Select one of the suggested readings listed below and present a summary and critique of the article in class.

Suggested Readings

Button, G. (1987). Moving out of closings. In G. Button & J. Lee (Eds.), *Talk and social organization* (pp. 101–151). Clevedon/Philadelphia: Multilingual Matters.

Button, G. (1990). On varieties of closings. In G. Psathas (Ed.), *Interaction competence* (pp. 93–148). Washington, D.C.: International Institute of Ethnomethodology and Conversation Analysis and University Press of America.

Griswold, O. (2003). How do you say good-bye? In K. Bardovi-Harlig & R. Mahan-Taylor (Eds.), *Teaching pragmatics*. Washington, D.C.: Department of State (http://exchanges.state.gov/media/oelp/teaching-pragmatics/griswold.pdf).

Luke, K. K., & Pavlidou, T.-S. (Eds.) (2002). *Telephone calls: Unity and diversity in conversational structure across languages and cultures*. Amsterdam: John Benjamins.

Pavlidou, T.-S. (2008). Interactional work in Greek and German telephone conversation. In H. Spencer-Oatey (Ed.), *Culturally speaking* (2nd edition) (pp. 118–137). New York: Continuum.

Placencia, M. E. (1997). Opening up closings—the Ecuadorian way. *Text 17*(1), 53–81.

Schegloff, E., & Sacks, H. (1973). Opening up closings. *Semiotica, 8*(4), 289–327.

Wong, J. (2007). Answering my call: A look at telephone closings. In H. Bowles & P. Seedhouse (Eds.), *Conversation analysis and language for specific purposes* (pp. 271–304). Bern: Peter Lang.

Wong, J. (forthcoming b). Telephone talk: Closings. In N. Houck & D. Tatsuki (Eds.), *Pragmatics from theory to practice: New directions*. Volume 2. Alexandria, VA: TESOL Publications.

Chapter 7

Repair Practices and Language Teaching

Pre-reading Questions

1. What is your sense of how much you self-correct your talk in ordinary conversation?
2. What comes to mind when you think of correcting the talk of another speaker? For example, does it seem difficult or easy? Is it something that you do regularly?
3. Do you know of someone who says *uh*, *um*, *er*, or *eh* a lot when speaking? If so, do you think it is a speech flaw that should be corrected?
4. Do you think second language learners can be taught how to monitor and correct their own talk and how to seek correction from others when engaged in ordinary conversation? If so, what would you suggest?

Chapter Overview

This chapter discusses the practices of repair in talk-in-interaction (e.g., Schegloff et al., 1977). In ordinary conversation, repair is not symptomatic of a disfluent or incompetent speaker but an important component of one's interactional competence. The recurring practices of repair remain, for the most part, not widely known by language teachers, at least not at the level of explicit knowledge (McCarthy, 1998; Nakamura, 2008). Language instructors need to develop a solid understanding of these practices in order to reach out to learners in a variety of ways. We discuss the concept of repair by considering dichotomies such as repair initiation vs. repair outcome and self-repair vs. other repair. We also describe the different types of repair: self-initiated self-repair, self-initiated other-repair, other-initiated self-repair, and other-initiated other-repair. We use naturally occurring talk for illustration. Pedagogical relevance is noted throughout the chapter. We conclude with suggested awareness-raising and practicing activities that teachers can use to help learners develop the ability to address problems of speaking, hearing, or understanding in real conversation.

Repair Practices

As stated in Chapter 1, **repair practices** are an important component in our model of interactional practices.

> **Repair practices** are ways of addressing problems in speaking, hearing, or understanding of the talk.

Our everyday conversations are full of errors, imperfections, clarifications, mishearings, Freudian slips, and so on, but there is a set of systematic inter-actional practices that help us reach and maintain mutual understanding. The organization of repair is regarded as the "self-righting mechanism" in social interaction (Schegloff et al., 1977, p. 381). Of the differing practices of talk-in-interaction that we discuss, repair bears the closest connection with language pedagogy because teachers do correction and help students with misunderstandings (Kasper & Kim, 2007; Nakamura, 2008) (see Chapter 8 on pedagogical repair). Second language acquisition researchers of the interac-tionist persuasion are likewise concerned with aspects of repair (Kurhila, 2001; Hosoda, 2006; Kasper & Kim, 2007; Wong, 2000a, 2000b). CA insights on repair practices offer those in second language pedagogy and second language acquisition research more tools for the trade.

Researchers in second language acquisition have emphasized that language learners need to hold their own in a conversation and to keep the talk going smoothly (Gass & Selinker, 2008; Nakamura, 2008; Scarcella, 1988). The repair system is key to those efforts, occupying a central place in teachers' understanding of interactional competence (Celce-Murcia, 2007). Scarcella (1988) stated two decades ago, "[t]he ability to carry out self-repair and to elicit repair from one's conversational partner is an essential skill for a second or foreign language learner" (p. 76). Twenty years later, Gass and Selinker (2008) have noted that researchers may examine learners' self-corrections to gain insights into oral language proficiency. No doubt, then, it is important for ESL/EFL teachers to have some basic knowledge about repair and its system-atic patterns.

In what follows, we explore the concept of repair by considering a related set of dichotomies. We then discuss the different types of repair.

Concept of Repair

If face-to-face conversation is the "cradle of language acquisition" (Clark, 1996, p. 9), repair is responsible for keeping the cradle rocking. Repair nour-ishes talk-in-interaction in myriad ways, sometimes latent and sometimes blatant.

Author's story (JW): My son Nathan was two years old. One day, I said to him: "Nathan, Mommy is wearing her UCLA shirt. Would you like to wear your UCLA shirt, too?" Nathan replied: "NO! MY-CLA!" I took Nathan's reply as an unequivocal *yes*. ["UCLA" stands for "University of California at Los Angeles."]

Nathan located an error in his mother's just prior turn and did a correction of her "problematic" utterance (i.e., replacing "U" with "my"). Indeed, Nathan's talk displayed an emerging understanding of the possessive pronoun and its use in context. As Clark (1996) writes, "language is rarely used as an end in itself" (p. 387). In examining what a language learner notices as in need of repair, one gains access into his/her developing awareness of the language system (Clark, 1978).

Task 1

How do you correct your own talk as you are speaking? What do you say or do to let the other speaker know that you are self-correcting? How do you seek repair if you did not hear or understand someone? What do you say or do?

In order for repair to be relevant for participants, there must be something that is the object of repair, i.e., **trouble-source**.

Trouble-source is a word, phrase, or utterance treated as problematic by the participants.

A trouble-source is also referred to as a problem, repairable or trouble spot. It is important to emphasize that a trouble-source is something that participants *treat as* troublesome or problematic. Errors are not always treated as trouble-sources (see complete transcription key at the beginning of the book):

(1) [Schegloff, 1979a, p. 265—modified]
      01 A: →   **Fridays is** a funny day, most of the people
      02   in schoo:l .hh that's why I only have classes
      03   on Tuesday and Fri:day .hh (0.3) one cla:ss,
      04   because most of them have o:ff those days . . .

The plural form of "Friday" is not treated by the speaker as a trouble-source. On the other hand, not all repairs involve errors:

(2)   [Fox & Jasperson, 1995, p. 80]
    01   M: →   I don't kno:w but **it's-** it's gonna cost quite a
                bit.

M's cut-off "it's-" is not a discernible error, but he treats it as something to be repaired. Thus, the concepts of repair and trouble-source are umbrella terms: repair subsumes correction and trouble-source subsumes errors. We now describe two sets of dichotomies that can help us better understand the concept of repair: (1) initiation vs. outcome; (2) self vs. other (Schegloff et al., 1977).

Repair Initiation vs. Repair Outcome

Key to understanding the concept of repair is that it is an interactional process that involves an initiation and outcome. Whatever was being talked about prior to the **repair initiation** is momentarily stopped until the completion of the repair although some repairs do not lead to completion.

Repair initiation refers to the practice of signaling or targeting a trouble-source.

Repair outcome refers to the solution to the trouble-source or abandonment of the problem.

A repair can be initiated and completed in the same turn or across turns. In the example below, the cut-off on "Thur" initiates the repair, which is completed in the same turn with "Tuesday":

(3)   [Liddicoat, 2007, p. 175]
    01   Anna: →   oh so then he is coming back on **Thur-** on
    02   **Tuesday**.

In the next example (Extract [2] reproduced), M initiates repair at the cut-off "it's" and repeats "it's" in the repair outcome ("it's gonna cost quite a bit"):

(4)   [Fox & Jasperson, 1995, p. 80]
    01   M: →   I don't kno:w but **it's-** it's gonna cost quite a bit.

In this case, it is not obvious what the trouble-source is except perhaps for the fact that M is having some difficulty speaking. In the next example, B initiates repair at line 04 on A's trouble-source at line 01 ("selling cigarettes"), and the repair is completed by A at line 05:

(5)   [Schegloff et al., 1977, p. 370]
      01   A: Hey the first time they stopped me from selling
      02   cigarettes was this morning.
      03   (1.0)
      04   B: →   **From selling cigarettes**
      05   A: →   **From buying cigarettes**. They said uh . . .

Since repair is composed of points of initiation and completion, one can think of it as a process with stages, i.e., **repair segment** (Schegloff, 1979a).

Repair segment is the interactional space extending from repair initiation to repair completion.

In Extract (3) above, the repair segment extends from "Thur-" to "Tuesday." In Extract (5) above, the repair segment begins at "From" at line 04 and ends at "cigarettes" at line 05. Like an elastic band, a repair segment expands to allow more than one try at fixing a trouble-source (Schegloff, 1979a). A repair can also be initiated on a repair itself.

Task 2

Consider the following examples. What is the trouble-source? What is the repair initiation? What is the repair outcome (i.e., solution to the trouble-source)?

(1)   [Fox & Jasperson, 1995, p. 89]
01   G: .hhh There are at least two sh- what they call shells.

(2)   [Schegloff et al., 1977, p. 366—modified]
01   N: But could we- could I stay up?

(3)   [Schegloff, 1979a, p. 279—modified]
01   Bee: . . . the school- school uh (1.0) bookstore doesn't carry
02   anything anymore

(4)   [Wong phone data]
01   Irene: but um how's- how's the summer school class going?

Self- vs. Other-repair

Another important dichotomy in understanding the concept of repair is self vs. other. Repair can be initiated and completed by the speaker of the trouble-source him/herself or by another participant. In the following extract, Hannah offers a repair at line 03 of her trouble-source at line 01:

(6)   [Schegloff et al., 1977, p. 366]
```
01   Hannah:   →   And he's going to make his own
                   paintings.
02   Bea:          Mm hmm,
03   Hannah:   →   And- or I mean his own frames.
04   Bea:          Yeah,
```

By contrast, in the extract below, Bee treats Ava's "playing around" at line 07 as a trouble-source and offers a repair at line 08:

(7)   [Schegloff et al., 1977, p. 365—modified]
```
01   Bee:    Where did you play basketball?
02   Ava:    (The) gy:m.
03   Bee:    In the gy:m?
04   Ava:    Yea:h. Like group therapy. You know=
05   Bee:    [Oh:::.
06   Ava:    [half the group that we had la:st term was there and
07       →   we just playing arou:nd.
08   Bee: → Uh- fooling around.
```

Self-repair and other-repair are ordered in a certain way: there is a preference for self-repair over other-repair in ordinary conversation.

Preference for self-repair refers to the phenomenon in ordinary conversation where one often gets and takes the first opportunity to fix his/her own trouble-source while other-repair tends to be held off or mitigated.

This preference may be understood in three ways. First, self-initiation opportunities come earlier, are taken earlier, and often lead to successful self-repair in the same turn, as shown in Extract (3) above. Second, other initiated repairs often yield self-repair:

(8)   [Schegloff et al., 1977, p. 377—modified]
```
01   Ken:       He likes that waiter over there,
02   Al:    →   Waiter?
03   Ken:   →   Waitress, sorry.
04   Al:        That's better,
```

At line 02, Al initiates repair on Ken's trouble-source "waiter" at line 01, which leads to Ken's self-repair at line 03. Third, other corrections are often mitigated, e.g., done with uncertainty markers such as "You mean" in the example below:

(9) [Schegloff et al., 1977, p. 378—modified]
```
01  Lori:    →   But y' know single beds are awfully thin to
02                sleep on.
03  Sam:          What?
04  Lori:         Single beds. [They're-
05  Ellen:   →                 [You mean narrow?
06  Lori:         They're awfully narrow yeah.
```

With respect to second language talk, we still do not know whether the preference for self-repair operates in the same way (Gardner & Wagner, 2004). There is some work, however, that shows slight modifications of this preference in second language conversations (Gaskill, 1980; Hellermann, 2009; Kasper & Kim, 2007; Wong, 2000c).

Types of Repair

As stated above, repair initiations and completions may be accomplished by the same speaker of the trouble-source or by different speakers across turns. This gives rise to four types of repair:

(1) self-initiated self-repair;
(2) self-initiated other-repair;
(3) other-initiated self-repair;
(4) other-initiated other-repair.

Self-initiated Self-repair

We now take a closer look at repairs that are initiated and completed by the same speaker of the trouble-source. We consider four types of self-initiated self-repair (see Schegloff, 1992b for "fourth-position repair"):

(1) same-turn repair;
(2) transition-space repair;
(3) third-turn repair;
(4) third-position repair.

SAME-TURN REPAIR

The majority of repairs in ordinary conversation are **same-turn repairs**.

> **Same-turn repair** refers to an attempt by the speaker of the trouble-source to address the trouble-source within the current turn.

There can be multiple same-turn repairs within a single turn in part because a repair can be initiated on a repair itself. Same-turn repairs should be of particular interest to language teachers because self-corrections are the signs of oral language development (Gass & Selinker, 2008). There are five types of repair initiators used in same-turn repair:

(1) cut-off of an utterance or sound (e.g., "Thur-");
(2) sound stretch (e.g., "O:::h");
(3) pause (e.g., (0.3));
(4) non-lexical perturbation (e.g., "uh");
(5) repetition (e.g., "school- school").

It is important to point out that when a language learner produces a pause, cut-off, sound stretch, *uh*, *um*, or the like, it is not necessarily a sign of disfluency but may be indicative of a competent speaker using these same-turn repair initiators. Relatedly, as Ochs and Schieffelin (1983) note, repetition is one of the most misunderstood areas of study. Some researchers regard repetition as signs of a disfluent speaker (Shimanoff & Brunak, 1977). CA research shows that both native and nonnative participants use repetition in interaction (Carroll, 2004; Goodwin, 1981; Olsher, 2004; Schegloff, 1987b; Wong, 2000c). The five types of same-turn repair initiators are often used in a **word search**.

> **Word search** refers to a speaker grasping for a word that is temporarily unavailable or on the tip of his/her tongue.

In the case below, Beth initiates a word search at line 01 with "um" and a (0.4)-second pause:

(10) [Wong phone data]
```
01  Beth:  →   .h you sort of want- this is thee um (0.4)
02  Lin:        final week?
03  Beth:       Well not quite-we had finals hh um (0.4) about
04              thee sixteenth I guess it is (let's see) (0.2)
05              seventeenth and nineteenth and then I have to::
06              ge- gr- get grades in by the twenty third.
```

At line 02, Lin offers a solution to the search ("final week"), which turns out to be not quite right, as evident in Beth's next turn.

There are four methods for doing same-turn repair (Schegloff, 1979a):

(1) insertion;
(2) deletion;
(3) replacement;
(4) abandonment.

Insertion

> **Insertion** is a same-turn repair method of fixing the trouble-source by inserting an item immediately after the repair initiator, which is often a cut-off, before continuing with the utterance underway.

The method of **insertion** is exemplified below:

(11)   [Schegloff, 1979a, p. 270—modified]
```
01   Bee:   →   hh Hey do you see V- (0.3) fat old Vivian
02                 anymore?
03   Ava:          No, hardly, and if we do: y'know, I just say
04                 hello quick and y'know just pass each other
05                 in the [hallway. still hanging
06   Bee:               [Is she
07   Ava:          around (with) Bo:nny?
```

Bee begins with an interrogative ("Hey do you see"). She then initiates repair with the cut-off ("V-") and the (0.3)-second silence, after which two adjectives ("fat old") are inserted before "Vivian."

Deletion   Another same-turn repair method is **deletion**.

> **Deletion** is a same-turn repair method of fixing a trouble-source by deleting an item immediately prior to the repair initiator, which is often a cut-off, before continuing with the utterance underway.

In Extract (12) below, Shelley deletes the item "just":

(12)   [CA ASI 2004 data—modified]
```
01   Shelley:   alright well I talked to him earlier and I told
02                  him I didn't know what the scoop was and
03       →         now: I don't know .hh if I should jus- if I
04                  should blow off u:m tha:t stupid trial thing
05                  or what I mea:n (.) I don't know.
```

At line 03, Shelley initiates repair with a cut-off ("jus-") and proceeds to delete the cut-off word ("just"). To show that "just" has been deleted, Shelley repeats what comes before the deleted item (i.e., pre-frames it).

Replacement   A third same-turn repair method is **replacement**.

> **Replacement** is a same-turn repair method of fixing a trouble-source by replacing it with another item before continuing with the utterance underway.

In the case below, "We" is replaced with "I":

(13)   [Schegloff, 1979a, p. 274—modified]
```
01   A:   →   We went to the one uh- I went to the one uh-
02               Thursday on uh (0.9) up there by Knoxberry
                 Farm.
```

Because A initiates repair a few words after the trouble-source "We," she repeats what comes after the trouble-source (i.e., post-frames it) to precisely locate what is being replaced.

Abandonment   The final method of same-turn repair is **abandonment**.

> **Abandonment** is a same-turn repair method of aborting an already started repair attempt, after which the speaker starts afresh.

An example of aborted attempt is given below:

(14)   [Fox & Jasperson, 1995, p. 80—modified]
```
01   H:   →   And I hav- (.) my class starts at two:.
```

H initiates repair with a cut-off on "have," but instead of using insertion, deletion, or replacement, he completely abandons the trouble-source and starts anew.

> **Author's story (JW):** When I was studying first-year Mandarin-Chinese, I struggled to understand my beloved Chinese professor, who always spoke at a fast clip (He was known as "little frog"). I couldn't entirely follow him. It didn't occur to me until someone pointed out, "Sometimes he doesn't finish his sentences. He just goes on to say something else." That helped me to see why I wasn't understanding him.

It is important for teachers to avoid overcorrecting because all speakers use self-repairs, which include repetitions, restarts, non-lexical perturbations (e.g., *uh*, *um*, *er*), insertions, deletions, and so on. How many times have teachers told students to speak in complete sentences or to start over so as to clean up any repetitions, hitches, or self-repairs? But this is not how natural conversation works. Repetition, for example, is not a sign of disfluency. It is used as an important technique to pre-frame or post-frame a trouble-source as in Extracts (12) and (13) above.

Task 3

Identify the same-turn repair methods in the following examples:

(1) [Schegloff, 2007, p. 276]
01   Bee: . . . and he put- they <u>put</u> us in this gi<u>gan</u>tic lecture
02   hall.

(2) [Wong phone data]
01   Li: Uh he come- he (.) usually comes back in the
02   morning .h and then he:: (h) goe::s to be::d you see=

(3) [Wong, 2000b, p. 46—modified]
01   Chen: Yes uh:: his uh:: secretary told me that .h he would
02   be working at the off- in the office from two to
03   four.

(4) [Schegloff, 1993, p. 33—modified]
01   Bee: You have any cla- you have a class with Billy?

(5) [Wong, 2000b, p. 47—modified]
01   Irene: Okay what- just um:: so I know what (.) what
02   classroom do you meet in.

(6) [Wong phone data]
01   Beth: At the end of Labor Day people start (0.2) aren't
02   traveling as much.

(7) [Schegloff, 2007, p. 278—modified]
01   Bee: Because I als- I tried Barnes and Nobles and, (0.6)
02   they didn't have anything they don' have any art
03   books she told me.

Wong (2000b) reports that some ESL speakers whose native language is Mandarin use the token *yeah* in a repair segment at a stage just after initiating repair but before completing the repair:

(15)   [Wong, 2000b, p. 48—modified]
01   Li: →   Uh he come- **yeah** he (.) usually comes back in the
02   morning .h and then he:: (h) goe::s to be::d you
                    see=

Li initiates repair at the cut off "come-" and produces the token "yeah" before completing the repair. This use of *yeah* functions as an indicator that the speaker is "attentive and aware" throughout the repair process (i.e., I've got it now) (Wong, 2000b, p. 60). This does not appear to be a regular practice of proficient speakers of English in Wong's data.

TRANSITION-SPACE REPAIR

The next type of self-initiated self-repair is **transition-space repair**.

> **Transition-space repair** refers to an attempt to fix the trouble-source by its speaker just after the first possible completion point of the turn-constructional unit that includes the trouble-source.

In the following example, Clara's transition-space repair targets "green light" at line 01 as the trouble-source:

(16)   [Jefferson, 2007, p. 446]
01   Clara: I thought you weren't going to stop at that green
02   light.
03   ((pause))
04   Clara: →   **I mean red light.**
05   Bess: Red light. Tha::t's right,

Notice that the trouble-source is in turn-final position, which is a regular place for this type of repair. After a slight pause, Clara initiates and completes the repair with "I mean red light," now emphasizing "red."

> **Author's story (HW):** As a language learner, I remember obsessing with composing complete sentences before opening my mouth, and that was one of the reasons I had such a difficult time joining in any conversation or class discussion. Knowing that proficient speakers self-edit throughout their talk and do so in orderly ways would have been liberating.

THIRD-TURN REPAIR

A third type of self-initiated self-repair is **third-turn repair**.

Third-turn repair refers to an attempt to fix the trouble-source by its speaker in the third turn relative to the trouble-source turn although an intervening turn produced by another does not display a problem with that prior turn.

Third-turn repairs resemble transitional space repairs in that they are both initiated and completed by the speaker of the trouble-source; however, as the name suggests, they are done in the third turn of a sequence:

A: Turn 01
B: Turn 02
A: →   Turn 03 (Turn 01 now targeted as problematic)

Like transition-space repairs, third-turn repairs typically target a trouble-source that is at or near the turn-final position in the trouble-source speaker's just prior turn (Schegloff, 1996):

(17)   [Jefferson, 2007, p. 450—modified]
    01   Bess: →   . . . her money isn't **finite**,
    02   Gail: Uh huh
    03   Bess: →   **I mean _infinite_.**
    04   Gail: Oh <u>right</u> right!

Gail's continuer "uh huh" at line 02 displays that she does not have a problem with Bess's just prior talk at line 01. However, Bess initiates repair in her next turn, now saying that the money is not "finite" but "infinite."

Task 4

What kind of self-initiated self-repair is involved in the examples below (i.e., same-turn, transition-space, or third-turn)? What is the trouble-source? What is the repair initiation? What is the repair outcome? If it is same-turn repair, what is the repair technique used (e.g., insertion, deletion, etc.)?

(1)   [Schegloff & Lerner, 2009, p. 110—modified]
    01   Louise: I read a very interesting story today.
    02   Mom: Uhm what's that.
    03:   Louise: Well not today, maybe yesterday, aw who knows
    04   when who- it's called _Dragon Stew_

(2)   [Schegloff et al., 1979a, p. 270—modified]
01   Bee: hh But it's not too bad.
02   Ava: That's goo[d ((very quiet))
03   Bee: [Did you have any- cl-
04   You have a class with Billy this te:rm?
05   Ava: Yeah he's in my abnormal class.

(3)   [Schegloff, 2007, p. 281—modified]
01   Bee: You have a class with Billy this te:rm?
02   Ava: Yeah, he's in my abnormal class.
03   Bee: Oh yeah, [how
04   Ava: [Abnormal Psych,

(4)   [Schegloff et al., 1977, p. 370—modified]
01   J: Is it going to be at your house?
02   B: Yeah.=
03   J: =Your apartment?=
04   B: =My place.

(5)   [Schegloff, 1997b, p. 523—modified]
01   Curt: He- he's about the only regular he's about the only
02   good regular out there is Keegan still go out?

(6)   [Schegloff et al., 1977, p. 370—modified]
01   B: then more people will show up. because they
02   won't feel obligated to sell. to buy.

THIRD-POSITION REPAIR

The final type of self-initiated self-repair we discuss is **third-position repair** (Schegloff, 1992b).

> **Third-position repair** is an attempt to fix the trouble-source by its speaker based on the next speaker's response, which displays a possible misunderstanding of the trouble-source turn.

One of the most widely touted strands in second language acquisition research is the interactionist perspective, which emphasizes that negotiation of meaning plays a critical role in providing input and interaction for second language learners (Gass, 2003). Third-position repair is precisely one such resource for doing meaning negotiation.

Unlike third-turn repair, in which the intervening turn by the next speaker is usually short (e.g., continuer) and does not display any problem of hearing or understanding, third-position repair is triggered by the intervening turn:

A: Turn 01
B: Turn 02 (displays problem with Turn 01)
A: →   Turn 03 (Turn 01 now targeted as trouble-source)

In the following example, it becomes clear by line 03 to speaker H that speaker C misunderstood "everybody" at line 01, and H proceeds to clarify at line 04:

(18)   [Schegloff class handout]
        01   H: →   Let me tell you. **Everybody** really had an
        02   evening last night.
        03   C: →   Oh really. **Where did everybody go.**
        04   H: →   **Well I mean everybody that went anywhere.**
        05   C: Oh.

Third-position repairs are aimed at avoiding, averting, or correcting mis-understanding. They generally deal with two kinds of problems (Schegloff 1987b, 1992b):

(1) incorrect reference;
(2) incorrect relevant next action.

Extract (18) above is an example of incorrect reference, where H's reference to "everybody" is misunderstood by C. In the case of incorrect relevant next action, a complaint would be taken erroneously as a joke or vice versa. In the next example, B's preclosing of the conversation "I'll probably see you one of these day:s" at lines 01–02 is treated by A as a complaint (see Chapter 6 on preclosing):

(19)   [Schegloff, 1987b, pp. 208–209—modified]
        01   B: →   Well, honey? **I'll probably see you one of these**
        02   **day:s,**
        03   A: Oh:: God yeah,
        04   B: [Uhh huh!
        05   A: [We-
        06   A: →   **But I c- I just [couldn't get down [there.**
        07   B: →   **[Oh-   [Oh I know,**
        08   **I'm not asking [you to [come down-**
        09   A: [Jesus   [I mean I just I didn't have
        10   five minutes yesterday.

Speaker A treats lines 01–02 as a complaint by offering an excuse at line 06 ("I just couldn't get down there."), which is continued at lines 09–10 ("I just didn't have five minutes yesterday."). At lines 07–08, B initiates a third-position repair, denying that she was complaining ("Oh- Oh I know, I'm not asking you to come down").

The format for doing third-position repair involves four components. When they are all present, they usually occur in the order of (a)–(d), as shown below (Schegloff, 1992b, pp. 1304–1308):

(a)   Repair-initiating component (optional)
     e.g., *no; no no; no, no, no; oh; oh no; oh yeah; well.*
(b)   Acceptance/agreement (most optional)
     e.g., *yeah, I know, I realize that too, that's OK, Oh I know.*
(c)   Rejection of misunderstanding (optional)
     e.g., *I don't mean that, I'm not X-ing,* That's *not what I mean.*
(d)   Repair proper (most likely to be present)
     e.g., *I mean Y.*

In Extract (18) above, the third-position repair includes the components of (a) and (d). In Extract (19), the third-position repair includes (a)–(c). Extract (20) below shows (a), (b), and (d) used in a third-position repair:

(20)   [Schegloff, 1992b, p. 1306—modified]
```
       01   Bonnie:     Because I'm not even sure if we're going to have it
       02               yet because a bunch of people say [maybe, maybe,
       03   Jim:                                          [Yeah
       04   Bonnie:     it's bugging me.
       05               (1.5)
       06   Jim:        Oh uhh hh I'm sorry, .hh
       07   Bonnie:  →  No, that's okay, I mean y'know I can understand
       08               because- this was just a late idea that me and
       09               Barb had.
```

Understanding third-position repairs is important for researchers and teachers, because one can examine whether and how learners go back and repair their own utterances to address a misunderstanding. One could also inspect how a nonnative speaker, during native–nonnative conversations, comprehends a prior turn and whether that leads to a native speaker's third-position repair, and if so, how.

Research involving American university students learning German shows that native speakers of German use "covert" third-position repairs so as not to shine the spotlight on the trouble-source in a direct manner (Kasper & Kim, 2007, p. 26). That is, they minimize learners' misunderstanding by not using the typical format of third-position repair (i.e., *No + I don't mean X + I mean Y*). Extract (21) below illustrates a case of covert third-position repair. Speaker D, a German facilitator of a conversation-for-learning session, is talking informally with speaker E, an American university student learning German:

(21)   [Kasper & Kim, 2007, p. 26—modified]
    01   D: And do you live with your parents?
                      Und wohnst du bei deinen eltern?
    02   E: Yeah.
                      ja.
    03   D: yeah?
                      ja?
    04   E: heh heh [heh
    05   D: →   [**and how do you get to school in**
    06   **the morning?**
                      [*und wie kommst du morgens zur*
                      uni?
    07   E: →   **Yeah.**
                      ja.
    08   D: →   **Do you go by car?**
                      Fahrst du mit dem auto?
    09   E: no bus.
                      nein bus.

At line 07, the learner responds to the facilitator's *wh*-question as if it were a *yes/no* question. This leads to the facilitator redoing the trouble-source turn of lines 05–06 with "do you go by car?" at line 08. The facilitator's third-position repair is covert in the sense that he did not use the *No, I don't mean X + I mean Y* format; the misunderstanding is handled tacitly with the native speaker recalibrating his own talk rather than directly zooming in on the learner's incorrect utterance (Kasper & Kim, 2007).

Another way for native speakers to accommodate to nonnative speaker talk is the use of delay in third-position repairs. In the following extract, Liz has not spoken with Wang for a while:

(22)   [Wong phone data]
    01   Liz: →   **Are you in Theater Arts now?**
    02   Wang: →   **Yes uh no. This is uh the place I live.**
    03   Liz: yeah.
    04   Wang: **with American family.**
    05   Liz: yeah.
    06   Wang: **Um, this is ne- near UCLA in Brentwood.**
    07   Liz: →   **No, but I mean are you still in the Theater Arts**
    08   **department?**
    09   Wang: yes.
    10   Liz: yeah.
    11   Wang: yes.
    12   Liz: yeah.

At line 02, Wang misinterprets Liz's question, thinking she was asking whether he is physically at the Theater Arts department at this moment. A precursor to

Wang's misunderstanding is his equivocal reply "Yes uh no." Wang tells Liz that he is now at home ("This is uh the place I live") with further specification at lines 04 and 06. Liz could have intervened earlier (i.e., at lines 03 and 05). However, she delays her third-position repair till lines 07–08, which in effect allows Wang more interactional space for self-correcting although he does not. Research has revealed that in native–nonnative conversations, proficient speakers often sidestep learners' errors without overtly focusing on them; they focus on the larger goal of moving the conversation forward instead (Firth, 1996; Kurhila, 2001; Wong, 2005). Similarly, research on conversations between the hearing and the hearing-impaired has shown that the hearing partner can prevent face-threatening situations by letting trouble-sources pass uncorrected or smoothing things over in other ways (Skelt, 2007). This tendency to avoid overt corrections applies to aphasic conversation as well (Perkins, 2003).

Self-initiated Other-repair

Repair can be initiated by *self* but completed by *other*. In the next example, speaker B initiates repair when he tries to think of the first name of "Watts." In the next turn, A offers a solution to the trouble-source by offering with "Dan Watts":

```
(23)   [Schegloff et al., 1977, p. 364—modified]
       01   B:   →   He had this uh Mister W- whatever k- I can't
       02                think of his first name, Watt on, the one that
       03                wrote [that piece.
       04   A:   →            [Dan Watts.
```

Self-initiated other-repair often involves a word search, as shown in Extract (10) above, reproduced below:

```
(24)   [Wong phone data]
       01   Beth:   →   .h you sort of want- this is thee um (0.4)
       02   Lin:    →   final week?
       03   Beth:       Well not quite=we had finals hh um (0.4) about
       04                thee sixteenth I guess it is (let's see) (0.2)
       05                seventeenth and nineteenth and then I have to::
       06                ge- gr- get grades in by the twenty third.
```

Beth's self-initiation of repair at line 01 is completed by Lin at line 02 (although Lin's repair is rejected by Beth in the next turn).

Other-initiated Self-repair

Repair can be initiated by *other* and completed by *self.* In other-initiated self-repair, Turn 02 initiates repair on a trouble-source in Turn 01, and the repair is completed in Turn 03 by the trouble-source speaker (also see Chapter 3 on other-initiated repair done as insertion sequences):

A: Turn 01
B: Turn 02 (initiates repair)
A: Turn 03 (completes repair)

Data used to highlight the importance of negotiation of meaning in second language acquisition research are typically instances of other-initiated self-repair (Gass, 2003; Gass & Selinker, 2008):

(25)   [Gass & Selinker, 2008, p. 308]
       01   NNS: How have increasing food costs changed your
       02   eating habits?
       03   NS: Oh, rising costs we've cut back on the more
       04   expensive things, GONE to cheaper foods.
       05   NNS: →   **Pardon me?**
       06   NS: →   **WE'VE GONE to cheaper foods.**

(26)   [Gass & Selinker, 2008, p. 329]
       01   NNS: What happen for the boat?
       02   NS: →   **What?**
       03   NNS: →   **What's wrong with the boat?**

Instances like those above are viewed as crucial in second language acquisition, providing learners with opportunities to negotiate meaning. However, whether and how these sequences are distinctive to language learning remain an empirical issue (Firth & Wagner, 2007; Hosoda, 2006; Kasper, 2006; Wong, 2000a, 2000b). In what follows, we consider how proficient speakers do other-initiated self-repair. As will be shown, this particular type of repair exhibits orderliness, coordination, and a range of complexities.

   If a trouble-source is not self-repaired in the current turn or transition space, the first opportunity for repair initiation is in the next turn by another speaker. Just as same-turn repairs have a set of specific repair initiators, other-initiated self-repairs use a different set of initiation techniques, and these techniques are ordered in terms of their power to shine the spotlight on the trouble-source, ranging from weakest to the strongest (Schegloff et al., 1977):

(1)   Open class repair initiators: *Huh?, Pardon?, Sorry?, What?, Excuse me?*
(2)   *Wh*-interrogatives: *who, when, where*
(3)   Partial repetition of the trouble-source + *wh*-interrogative
(4)   Partial repetition of the trouble-source
(5)   *You mean* + understanding check

The stronger the spotlight, the firmer is the grasp of the one who does the repair initiation of what the prior speaker possibly means.

Task 5

> Look again at the set of five weak to strong repair initiators Are there
> ones that you tend to use in the classroom (more than others)? Are
> there ones that your students tend to use more than others? Can you
> think of ways in which to help learners use these five types of repair
> initiators in ordinary conversation?

OPEN CLASS REPAIR INITIATORS

The weakest set of initiators is also referred to as "open class" repair initiators
because they do not specify what the trouble-source is or the nature of the
problem (i.e., hearing, understanding, or both) (Drew, 1997). It is up to the
recipient of *Huh?*, *What?*, or the like to figure out exactly what the trouble-
source is and how to fix it:

(27) [Schegloff et al., 1977, p. 367—modified]
      01   D: Well did he ever get married or anything?
      02   C: →   **Hu:h?**
      03   D: Did he ever get married?
      04   C: I have no idea.

(28) [Schegloff, 1997b, p. 515—modified]
      01   Bonnie: A:nd (3.0) okay do you think you could come?
      02   Pretty much for sure?
      03   Marina: →   **What?**
      04   Bonnie: Do you think you could come pretty much for
                                 sure?
      05   Marina: Sure.

In both extracts, the repair initiators do not specify the nature of the problem.
In Extract (27), D treats the turn-initial "well" and the turn-final "or anything" at line 01 as the trouble-source and fixes it at line 03 by omitting both
items. In Extract (28), Bonnie treats as the trouble-source the turn-initial
items "A:nd (3.0) okay" at line 01 and produces a more fluent and compact
version of the question at line 04 ("Do you think you could come pretty much
for sure?").

Open class initiators are sometimes used to signal disagreement, rejection,
challenge, or topical misalignment (Drew, 1997; Schegloff, 1997b). For
example, in Extract (29) below, Gordon's repair initiator ("Pardon?") targets
Norm's sudden topic change from ride sharing to "Caught me in the ba:th
again" at line 10:

(29)   [Drew, 1997, p. 75—modified]
01   Gordon: <u>Hi</u> No:rm,
02:    Norm: <u>Hi</u> Gordy.
03:    Gordon: <u>Eh</u>:m (0.4) are you <u>going</u> tonight,
04:    Norm: <u>M</u>m.
05:    Gordon: .hhh (0.2) W<u>ou</u>ld yo<u>u</u> mind giving me a l<u>i</u>f[t.
06:    Norm: [No
07:                    Th<u>a</u>t's alr<u>i</u>ght,
08:    Gordon: .hhh (0.3) <u>V</u>ery kind of you.
09:                    (.)
10:    Norm: C<u>a</u>ught me in the b<u>a</u>:th a[gain.
11:    Gordon: →   [**.hhhh Pardon?**=
12:    Norm: =heh C<u>au</u>gh[t me in the b<u>a</u>:th
13:    Gordon: [.hh .hh Oh(hh) I'm sorr(h)y Oh well
14:                    I should l<u>e</u>t yo<u>u</u> get b<u>a</u>ck to <u>i</u>t.

In the next example, the open class repair initiator is a precursor to rejection:

(30)   [Schegloff, 2007, p. 105—modified]
01   A: How would you like to go to a movie later
02   on tonight?
03   B: →   **Huh?**
04   A: A movie you know like a flick?
05   B: Yeah I uh know what a movie is (0.8) It's
06   just that=you don't know me well enough?

When B initiates repair at line 03, A treats "movie" at line 01 as the trouble-source by explaining it as "a flick" (line 04). At lines 04–05, B's response to the repair ("Yeah I uh know what a movie is. It's just that you don't know me well enough?") is in fact a rejection of A's invitation. In other words, "Huh?" foreshadows this rejection. This is a beautiful exemplar of repair as a co-constructed activity replete with dire interactional consequences.

Japanese EFL students sometimes do "gesturally-enhanced repeats" in response to open class repair initiators (*What? Huh?*) (Olsher, 2008, p. 110). The use of gestures functions to "explain or enhance the meaning of the repeated language" in the trouble-source turn (Olsher, 2008, pp. 125–126). In other words, gestures in the environment of other-initiated repair add to the semantic meaning and serve as invaluable input for language learning (Lazaraton, 2004).

Understanding how repair initiators such as *huh?* are used in English can sometimes help avert cross-cultural misunderstandings.

Author's story (HW): In my recent Intercultural Communication class, a Japanese woman said that she always feels a little offended when native speakers of English use *huh?* in response to her talk. When I asked why, she said the same response is considered a bit rude in Japanese.

WH-INTERROGATIVES

Wh-interrogatives are *wh*-questions used as repair initiators to locate the trouble-source, as shown below:

(31)   [Schegloff, 1997b, p. 511—modified]
```
01   Freda:           This is nice did you make this?
02   Kathy:           No Samu made that.
03   Freda:    →      Who?
04   Kathy:           Samu.
```

(32)   [Sacks & Jefferson, 1977, p. 368—modified]
```
01   B:               By the way, I have to go to Lila's.
02   A:       →       Where?
03   B:               Lila's to get (   )
```

Another form of interrogative includes expressions such as *What do you mean*, *What do you mean by that*, or *What do you mean* + [element of prior turn] (Schegloff, 1997b). These utterances may perform two actions: repair initiation and challenge (Schegloff, 1997b; Schegloff & Lerner, 2009). In the following extract, the participants are discussing automobile racing. At line 06, Gary uses the format of *What do you mean* + [element of prior turn] as a repair initiator to challenge Curt's assertion that "Keegan is one of the only good regulars":

(33)   [Schegloff, 1997b, p. 523—modified]
```
01   Curt:            He- he's about the only regular <he's about the only
02                    good regular out there is Keegan still go out?
03   Mike:            Keegan's, out there he's, he run,
04                    (0.5)
05   Mike:            E:[r he's uh::
06   Gary:    →          [What do you mean my:, my [brother in law's
07                       out there,
08   Mike:                                        [doing real good
09                    this year and Gilton's doing real good this year.
```

In this type of repair initiation, the spotlight becomes a bit stronger in the sense that it specifies exactly which part of the prior turn needs to be redone (e.g., person referent). Partial repetition of the trouble source appears to be a frequently used technique in the language classroom to address learner errors (also see "designedly incomplete utterance" in Chapter 8).

PARTIAL REPETITION OF THE TROUBLE-SOURCE + *WH*-INTERROGATIVE

The third technique of other initiation of repair is a partial repetition of the trouble-source followed by a *wh*-interrogative, as shown in the examples below:

(34) [Schegloff, 2007, p. 105—modified]
      01   Bet: Was last time the first time you met Mrs.
      02   Kelly?
      03   (0.2)
      04   Mar: →   **Met whom?**
      05   Bet: Mrs. Kelly.
      06   Mar: Yes.

(35) [Drew, 1997, p. 70—modified]
      01   G: Have <u>you</u> dr<u>o</u>pped some bi<u>o</u>logy notes.
      02   (0.4)
      03   D: →   **Have I wha[t them.**
      04   G: [.hh.hhh D<u>ro</u>pped theh- them. L<u>o</u>s:t.

With this type of repair initiation, the spotlight on the trouble-source becomes even stronger: the speaker is able to repeat one or more words surrounding the *wh*-question word.

PARTIAL REPETITION OF THE TROUBLE-SOURCE

The fourth technique of other initiation of repair is partial repetition of the trouble-source, typically done in rising intonation conveying uncertainty, which serves to invite the speaker of the trouble-source to complete the repair (Schegloff et al., 1977):

(36) [Wong phone data]
      01   Irene: I'm um .h thinking (.) about (.) moving (.) to
      02   Boston.
      03   Han:→   **Boston?**
      04   Irene: (h)u(h) .h Yeah::: I'm at- I'm thinking about
                       <u>that</u>.

In the extract below, the conversation is between two adults and a child who is a first language learner. The child is given two opportunities to do self-repair (lines 02 and 04), and he succeeds on the second try (line 05):

(37)   [Schegloff et al., 1977, p. 373]
    01   Steve: One, two, three, four five six, eleven eight nine ten.
    02   Susan: →   **Eleven? Eight, nine, ten.**
    03   Steve: Eleven, eight, nine, ten.
    04   Nancy: →   **Eleven?**
    05   Steve: **Seven, eight, nine, ten.**
    06   Susan: That's better.

The partial repetition not only makes known precisely which part of the prior turn needs fixing but also repeats the particular part. In that sense, the spotlight on the trouble-source is stronger than partial repetition + *wh-*interrogative.

YOU MEAN + UNDERSTANDING CHECK

The fifth technique for other initiation of repair involves an understanding check often prefaced with *You mean.* This is the strongest form of next turn repair initiator:

(38)   [Wong phone data]
    01   Beth: Well not <u>quite</u>=we had finals hh um (0.4) about thee
    02   sixteenth I guess it is (let's see) (0.2) seventeenth
    03   and nineteenth and then (0.2) I have to:: ge- gr- get
    04   grades in by the twenty third hh.
    05   (0.4)
    06   Lin: →   **You mean n- June?**
    07   Beth: =Yes.
    08   Lin: Oh::

Unlike an open class initiator which leaves unspecified what the trouble-source is, "in the next example," B's repair initiation at line 03 shines the spotlight on A's "just till uh Monday" in the prior turn as the trouble-source, and it is the strongest form of spotlight in the sense that it offers the firmest grasp of what "just till uh Monday" means ("a week from tomorrow"). There is a preference for using stronger over weaker initiators in other-initiation of repair in that weaker ones can get interrupted or be replaced by stronger ones (Schegloff et al., 1977, p. 369). B begins with a partial repetition of "Till" but stops to replace it with *you mean* + understanding check.

(39)   [Schegloff et al., 1977, p. 369—modified]
    01   B: How long you gonna be here?
    02   A: Uh- not too long. Uh just till uh Monday.
    03   B: →   **Till- oh you mean like a week from tomorrow.**
    04   A: Yah.

For teachers, sometimes purposely using the *weakest* repair initiator (e.g., *huh?* or *what?*) can give the students more opportunities to produce longer stretches of talk. This is equivalent to the "minimal grasp strategy" used by caretakers in Samoa: the caretaker uses various strategies to "elicit from the child a reformulation of all or part of the unclear utterance" (Ochs, 1988, p. 331). For students, on the other hand, learning how to use the strongest repair initiator possible is important. In other words, do not let students mainly rely on saying *What?* or *Huh?* when they have partial understanding. Encourage them to use other techniques, such as partial repetitions or partial repetition + *wh*-question, to accentuate what they do hear or understand, as proficient speakers do. Teaching learners the "maximal grasp strategy" can enhance their flexibility in managing meaning negotiations.

Task 6

In the textbook *Speaking Naturally*, the following continuum is presented in teaching learners how to get someone to repeat or slow down. Discuss the accuracy and usefulness of this information in light of what you have read so far about other-initiated self-repair.

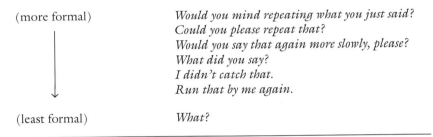

(more formal)

Would you mind repeating what you just said?
Could you please repeat that?
Would you say that again more slowly, please?
What did you say?
I didn't catch that.
Run that by me again.

(least formal)   *What?*

An important part of understanding other-initiation of repair is that it can be used to convey or foreshadow disagreement, doubt, rejection, challenge, or misalignment (Schegloff, 1997b; Waring, 2005c). The segment below is an example of repair initiation used to indicate implicit disagreement. Prior to the segment, Jack has indicated that even though he was able to become a fluent reader in his native language English through extensive reading, he was not able to do the same in learning Chinese:

(40) [Waring, 2005c, p. 170]
      01   Tamar: W- you don't have much [input from Chinese as=
      02   Libby: [input.
      03   =you would have from English.=
      04   Jack: =B- there's a lot of materials [I mean-
      05   Libby: [different age too.

```
06                  Right? Jack?
07    Jack:         Mm
08                  (0.9)
09    Jack:   →     How do you mean [different age?
10    Libby:                        [You're older now.=
11    Jack:         old-
12    Prof:         heh heh [heh heh heh
13    Tamar:                [heh heh heh
14    Jack:         It should be easier. I'm brighter.
```

At lines 05–06, Libby attributes Jack's difficulty to age, i.e., he was older when he was learning to read in Chinese, and Jack initiates repair on that attribution at line 09. Jack's repair initiation conveys implicit disagreement. A number of sequential details support this analysis: his lack of immediate uptake at line 06, the ambiguous "mm" at line 07, and the long (0.9) second gap at line 08 combine to suggest that a dispreferred response is coming up. While Jack's actual disagreement emerges at line 14, where he argues that older is better for becoming a fluent reader, that disagreement is foreshadowed by his repair initiation at line 09. ESL/EFL learners may not catch on to these nuances of other-initiation of repair without explicit instruction.

There is some interesting contrast in the use of other-initiation of repair between native and nonnative speakers (Hosoda, 2006; Wong, 2000c). In the first example below, Lin uses the initiator of partial repetition of the trouble-source, but he does not do so in the next turn, which is by far where the vast majority of other-initiation of repairs occurs (Schegloff, 2000) (the first arrow indicates the trouble-source):

(41) [Wong, 2000c, p. 249]
```
      01    Beth:   →     So they were gonna go all the way to Montreal in
      02                  nine days.
      03    Lin:          Oh::
      04                  (0.2)
      05    Lin:    →     Nine days?
      06    Beth:         Yeah
```

Lin initially receipts the trouble-source talk with "Oh::", giving the sense that the just prior talk was not problematic. But then, he initiates repair later at line 04 after a pause. Thus, although second language learners may produce the initiator of partial repetition of the trouble-source, sometimes they are not yet able to place it immediately after the trouble-source turn.

In the next example, Chen's repair initiator is delayed even more:

(42) [Wong, 2000c, p. 251]
```
      01    Joan:         I- j- I just talked to Li Hua?
      02    Chen:         Oh::
      03    Joan:   →     An::d that's how I got your number.
```

04		(0.2)
05	Chen:	Oh.
06	Joan:	An::d she [was-
07	Chen: →	**[Oh:: you- you got my number from Li**
08		**Hua.**
09	Joan:	Yeah.
10	Chen:	But just uh:: two hours (0.2) two hours ago I went
11		to the office of Harry . . .

ESL/EFL teachers need to be aware that when learners produce response tokens such as *yeah*, *uh huh*, *mm hmm*, or even assessments (e.g., *wow*, *good*), they do not necessarily display understanding, as shown in the above two examples. Shining the spotlight on the trouble-source by using the strongest technique possible and in the "strongest" sequential position (i.e., the immediate next turn) may be problematic for ESL/EFL learners. Indeed, having maximal grasp of the talk is precisely what is at stake for language learners. Understanding how other-initiation of repair is done by proficient speakers gives teachers the resources to help learners master a wide range of techniques in meaning negotiations.

Author's story (JW): When my daughter Monica taught adult ESL in Boston's Chinatown, the following exchange took place in the class:

Monica:	How many times have you been married?
Li:	((muttering to self)) how many, how many how many . . . 26!
Monica:	((shocked)) 26 times!
Li:	((also puzzled)) Once again!
Monica:	How many times have you been married?
Li:	how many <u>times</u> . . . ah, yeah, yeah . . . one time.
Monica:	O::h!

Li's repair initiation "Once again!" is clearly not the proper technique, especially when it is addressed to a teacher (He meant to say, "Would you please repeat that?" or "Pardon me?"). The ability to ask for assistance in the classroom is one of the important language objectives in ESL teaching (Vogt & Echevarria, 2005). In the SIOP (sheltered instruction observational protocol) model, the following utterances are listed as key phrases for learners to master in order to solicit support from the teacher or from another student (Vogt & Echevarria, 2005):

- *I don't understand.*
- *Would you please explain that to me?*
- *Would you please model that for me?*
- *Would you please demonstrate that for me?*

The above CA findings on other-initiators of repair can be used to expand this list, thereby invigorating the repertoire of learner resources for soliciting support in the classroom.

Other-initiated Other-repair

In other-initiated self-repair, the repair is initiated by another but fixed by the speaker of the trouble-source. Rarely is repair both initiated and completed by another speaker (Schegloff et al., 1977). When it is, we may speak of other-initiated other-repair, which may take two forms: exposed correction versus embedded correction (Jefferson, 1987).

EXPOSED CORRECTION

In **exposed correction**, correction is done overtly and becomes the object of the talk itself.

> **Exposed correction** refers to stopping the trajectory of talk to overtly address a trouble-source.

In the following extract, Jan's pronunciation of the word "ki:l" ("kiln") at line 02 is treated as the trouble-source by Ron, who does an overt correction, "exposing" her mispronunciation at line 05:

```
(43)   [Jefferson, 1987, p. 88—modified]
       01   Jan:         I guess they paid two-twenty thousand for the house
       02                and two thousand for the ki:l.
       03   Beth:        Mm::,
       04   Jan:         Technically,
       05   Ron:    →    (It's a) kil:n.
       06   Jan:         Kil:n, I don't know how to say it,
       07   Ron:         You always say kil.
       08   Jan:         I don't know I thought that's righ[t.
       09   Beth:                                          [Yeah.
       10   Ron:                                          [It's like-
       11   Ron:         Is that right? You say kil?
       12   Beth:        Kil:n, I don't know I've heard both . . .
```

In her subsequent turn at line 06, Jan accepts Ron's correction, now repeating "kil:n" correctly and acknowledging the error ("I don't know how to say it"). Thus, correction becomes the interactional business (Jefferson, 1987, p. 95).

In contrast to the case above, in the extract below, the recipient of the exposed correction rejects it at line 18 by repeating his original pronunciation of "made" as "madid":

(44)   [Jefferson, 1987, p. 89—modified]
```
01    Meg:              It came from England Loren,
02                      (0.4)
03    Loren:            Ah-ah:::,
04                      Ah-ah it's stamped on the botto:m,
05                      (3.5)
06                      I:ndia:.
07                      (4.0)
08            →         Madid in India.
09                      (0.9)
10    Meg:    →         °Ma:de. In India not madid,°
11    Loren:            .hh
12    Meg:              °in India,°
13                      (1.2)
14    Loren:            (you said) m:madid.
15                      (1.0)
16    Meg:              You: shouldn't say madid.
17                      (0.5)
18    Loren:  →         Madid in En:gland.
19                      (0.4)
20                      Da-uh-i-in In:dia. .hh
21                      (0.4)
22                      °England .hh°
```

Exposed corrections such as the above often reveal lapses in competence or conduct, which typically leads to talk in which participants apologize, joke, explain, ridicule, or the like (Jefferson, 1987).

EMBEDDED CORRECTION

Aside from doing other-initiated other-repair blatantly as in exposed correction, there are ways of doing so latently, i.e., **embedded correction** (Jefferson, 1987).

Embedded correction refers to slipping in a correction in passing, without stopping the ongoing trajectory of the talk.

In the example below, the phrase "the police" at line 01 is the trouble-source:

(45)   [Jefferson, 1987, p. 93—modified]
```
01    Ken:    →         Well- if you're gonna race, the police have said
                        this
02                      to us.
```

03	Roger:		That makes it even better. The challenge of running
04		→	from **the <u>cops</u>!**
05	Ken:	→	**The cops** say if you wanna race, uh go out at four
06			or five in the morning on the freeway . . .

Roger treats Ken's saying of "the police" as problematic by embedding a replacement in his own turn (i.e., "the cops" with added stress at line 04). Ken accepts the embedded correction by incorporating "The cops" in his next turn at line 05.

Just as an exposed correction may be rejected by a co-participant, so can an embedded correction:

(46) [Jefferson, 1987, p. 94—modified]

01	Emma:		That Pa:t isn't she a do:[:ll?
02	Penny:	→	[Yeh isn't she **pretty**,
03	Emma:	→	Oh: she's a **beautiful** girl.=
04	Penny:	→	=Yeh I think she's a **pretty** girl . . .

At line 02, Penny refers to Pat as "pretty," but Emma upgrades the assessment to "beautiful" in the next turn. Penny rejects Emma's upgrade, preserving her downgraded assessment "pretty" at line 04. In short, participants have an interactional option, so to speak, of accepting or rejecting the correction.

Embedded correction resembles recasts or reformulations discussed in the SLA literature, which are found to be inherently ambiguous as correction techniques. Han (2002), for example, details four conditions under which recasts can be effective: (1) individualized attention, (2) consistent focus, (3) developmental readiness, and (4) intensity. In the absence of these conditions, the learner may have no idea that a correction has taken place.

Author's story (JW): This conversation took place between my son Nathan and me when he was three years old. He was intrigued that a motorcycle was parked at a funny angle in front of the house.

Nathan:	Mom, whobody parked the motorcycle?
Jean:	What?
Nathan:	Whobody parked the motorcycle?
Jean:	Who parked the motorcycle?
Nathan:	Yeah, whobody parked the motorcycle?

Task 7

For each example below, answer the following questions:

(1) What is the trouble-source? (There may be more than one.)

(2) Where does the repair segment begin and where does it end?

(3) Who initiates the repair and who completes it?

(4) How is the repair initiated and completed?

(1) [Wong phone data]
```
01   A:   .h well:: the school is alr- alright (h) (h) not that goo::d but
02        it's alright.
03   B:   Is it what you think it wou- thought it would be?
04   A:   .h .h NO::: NOT AT ALL(h)(h) hih-hih-hih-hih-hih-hih-hih
05        you know the school work is really busy . . .
```

(2) [Liddicoat, 2007, p. 188—modified]
```
01   A:   Isn't it next week we're out of school?
02   B:   Yeah next week. No not next week, the week after.
```

(3) [Wong phone data]
```
01   A:   . . . yeah (0.2) that's nice (0.2) but uh we will miss you hih-
02        hih
03   B:   Oh:: I'm- I:: I will miss you too:: I mean I- (h)u(h) .h. I
04        love all of you so much.
05   A:   Uh huh.
```

(4) [Liddicoat, 2007, p. 190—modified]
```
01   A:   So I guess I'll see you this afternoon.
02   B:   When?
03   A:   Oh I'm coming to the planning meeting=Roger can't
04        make it.
```

(5) [Fox & Jasperson, 1995, p. 86]
```
01   A:   Now, I want to simp- I want to break it down further than
02        that, right?
```

(6) [Schegloff, 2007, p. 103—modified]
```
01   A:   =(now) you taught her how to dance, didn't you?
02   B:   Huh?
03   A:   Weren't you teaching her some new steps the other day?
04   B:   Yeah.
```

(7) [Wong phone data]
01 A: So when are you going to (.) Boston.
02 B: .h I'm going to go:: the last uh:: two weeks (0.2) of July.
03 A: Uh huh
04 B: .h so::
05 A: Oh: so you mean just stay there for two weeks?
06 B: .h Y-eah so that I can uh: get a job first before I move back
07   there.

(8) [Wong phone data]
01 A: Oh by the way did you get the tapes?
02   (0.4)
03 B: Oh yeah I did
04 A: You di::d and did you get the- the stuff I sent you like
05   uh (.) some release
06   (1.4)
07   the- the film release the xerox co::py
08 B: Oh:: yeah:: yeah:: yeah that's really neat I haven't seen that
09   (.) for such a long time.

Schegloff remarked ten years ago:

> The talk that language learners are going to have to do when they're not
> in the hothouse of the classroom is situated in the real world where they
> have real things to do, and that's the talk that people ideally should be
> recording and studying if they want to understand what the real world
> problems are for those who are speaking a language that is not their native
> language.
>
> (Wong & Olsher, 2000, p. 122)

By paying close attention to repair practices, teachers can become privy to
precisely where learner language needs fine-tuning.

Author's story (JW): My daughter Monica and her friend from China
were discussing the health benefits of eating oatmeal daily.

Monica: It's [oatmeal] good for you.
Lu: It's good for everybody!

In the anecdote above, Lu did not yet understand that *you* may be used as a
general reference.

For second language learners, one of the real-life problems is understanding
the talk of other speakers and making themselves understood. Even though

ESL/EFL students may use repair practices in their native languages, learning how to do so in a target language requires explicit instruction and focused practice. Teachers should provide learners with the range and complexity of repair practices to help them become fully interactionally competent. Given the critical role of self-corrections and negotiation of meaning in second language acquisition, understanding the interactional practices of repair can only sharpen teachers' ability to fully engage learners in participating in conversation.

Teaching Repair Practices

The teaching of repair has traditionally been limited to seeking clarifications. The full range of repair practices has typically not been a focus of pedagogical materials and classroom instruction in ESL/EFL teaching (see Barraja-Rohan & Pritchard, 1997; Olsher, forthcoming for exceptions). Here we suggest some activities that may be used to help raise learners' awareness of repair and enhance their ability to incorporate repair in their everyday conversation.

Same-turn Repair

Awareness-raising Activity: *Correct Yourself*

(1) Begin by finding out what your learners know about repair in their native language and/or English:

    (a) Do you correct your own talk? If so, how much do you think you do it and when do you do it?

    (b) How important do you think it is to know how to self-correct?

    (c) Does any specific strategy or vocabulary come to mind? If so, please list them.

    (d) What concerns do you have about self-correcting in conversation?

(2) Show learners the following segments of naturally occurring self-repair and ask them to answer the following questions for each example: What is the error or problem, and how is it fixed?

    (a) [Wong, 2000b, p. 48—modified] (insertion)

```
01   A:   Uh he come- he usually comes back in the
02        morning.
```

    (b) [Wong phone data] (insertion)

```
01   A:   uh:: so do you (.) what (.) do you need me to bring?
```

    (c) [Wong, 2000b, p. 47—modified] (insertion)

```
01   A:   Okay what- just um:: so I know what (.)
02        what classroom do you meet in?
```

    (d) [Schegloff et al., 1977, p. 365—modified] (insertion)

```
01   A:   His teacher was this uh Mr. W- I can't think
02        of his first name Watts, the one who got sick.
```
(e)   [Wong, phone data] (replacement)
```
01   A:   . . . I have to- I need to type two papers.
```
(f)   [Schegloff et al., 1977, p. 364] (replacement)
```
01   A:   She was telling me all the people who were
02        gone this year I mean this spring.
```
(g)   [Schegloff, 1979a, p. 284—modified] (replacement)
```
01   A:   . . . this fellow I have- fellow this ma:n . . . who
02        I have for linguistics is really too much . . .
```
(h)   [Wong phone data] (deletion)
```
01   A:   . . . at the end of Labor Day people start (0.2)
02   aren't traveling as much.
```
(i)   [Wong phone data] (deletion)
```
01   A:   Did he tell you I was- I tried to call you last
02        night?
```
(j)   [Fox & Jasperson, 1995, p. 80—modified] (abandonment)
```
01   A:   And I have- (.) my class starts at two.
```
(k)   [Schegloff, 1979a, p. 284—modified] (abandonment)
```
01   A:   Yeah I bet they got rid of all the one:: well
02   one I had in the first term there, she died.
```
(l)   [Wong phone data] (abandonment)
```
01   A:   they- they live (.) in uh they only have one
02        room.
```

(3) Have learners share their answers in class discussion and introduce techniques for initiating self-repair (e.g., cut-off, sound stretch, pause, etc.). As a general teaching strategy, listen very carefully to your learners' talk. When they incorporate self-repairs, praise them. For example, if an ESL/EFL learner were to say *Is that what you th- think- thought would happen*, praise him/her for self-repairing the talk, emphasizing that s/he is employing interactional practices that proficient speakers use.

(4) Discuss possible cross-cultural variations.

Practicing Activity: *Matching Game*

Put the examples (a)–(l) in item 2 above on separate strips. Put labels (i.e., insertion, deletion, etc.) on separate cards or on the board. Learners pick up a same-turn repair strip and say it aloud. Then, they are to match it with one of the cards. For more advanced learners, use more labels than there are strips so that learners are more challenged to know the correct answer.

Variations

(i)   One learner reads each strip with the same-turn repair aloud while others chime in, stating which technique is used (e.g., insertion, deletion, etc.).

(ii) Put the same-turn repair on one side of the card and the name of the technique on the other side. Learners read aloud the same-turn repair, state the repair initiator technique, and turn the card over to reveal the answer.

(iii) Learners make their own cards, writing one example for each repair-initiator.

Other-initiated Repair

Awareness-raising Activity: *Say that Again?*

(1) Begin a discussion by finding out what learners know about other-initiated repair in English and/or their native languages:

(a) When you do not hear or understand what someone has said, what do you usually say?

(b) When someone says *What? Huh?* or *Sorry?*, is it always clear to us what the problem is?

(c) Do you know of any ways of asking someone to repeat if you did not hear or understand it? If so, what are they?

(d) What questions or problems do you have about how to ask others to repeat, clarify, confirm, or correct an utterance?

(2) Provide learners with the following list of repair initiators in context and ask them to consider: What differences exist among the various initiators? When is each used in what context? Are these techniques mutually interchangeable?

(a) *Huh? Pardon? Sorry? What? Excuse me?*
[Schegloff, 1997b, p. 515—modified]
01 A: And okay do you think you could come?
02   Pretty much for sure?
03 B: What?
04 A: Do you think you could come pretty much for sure?
05 B: Sure.

(b) *Wh*-questions: *who, when, where*
[Schegloff, Sacks, and Jefferson, 1977, p. 368—modified]
01 B: By the way, I have to go to Lila's.
02 A: Where?
03 B: Lila's to get my books.

(c) Partial repetition + *wh*-question
[Sacks, 1992a, p. 8]
01 A: Okay, uh I was saying my name is Smith and I'm
02   with the Emergency Psychiatric Center.
03 B: Your name is what?
04 A: Smith.

```
05  B:   Smith?
06  A:   Yes.
```

(d) Partial repetition
[Wong phone data]
```
01  B:   Wa- I was wondering if you were gonna be home
02       tomorrow afternoon I could maybe come over after
03       summer school.
04       (0.4)
05  A:   Um:: I'll be at my mother's tomorrow afternoon.
06  B:   Oh::=
07  A:   No I'm just sitting there waiting for an oil burner
08       man=you can come over then.
09  B:   You're sitting there waiting for an oil burner?
10  A:   Yeah(h)(h) .h heh:: No:: you know you have to
11       (h)(h)huh-hih I
12       think I am=I'm not sure (0.2) um:: you know you
13       have to get the burner cleaned or something for the
14       summer?
```

(e) *You mean* + understanding check
[Schegloff et al., 1977, p. 369—modified]
```
01  B:   How long are you going to be here?
02  A:   Uh not too long uh just till uh Monday.
03  B:   Oh you mean like a week from tomorrow.
04  A:   Yeah.
```

(3) Have learners share their answers in class discussion and introduce the idea of weak to strong initiation in terms that your learners would understand. As a general teaching strategy, listen very carefully to your learners' talk. When they incorporate any of the above initiators, praise them.

(4) Discuss possible cross-cultural variations.

Variation

Ask learners to collect examples of repair initiators from their own language and bring to class discussion.

Practicing Activity: *The Power to Repair*

(1) Makes sets of six cards, one with the statement below, and the other five each containing one of the repair initiators:
     Zoe will drop by to pick up the toy after school at 3 o'clock.

     (a) *What? Huh? Pardon? Sorry?*
     (b) *Who, Where, When,* etc.

(c) Partial repetition + *who, where, when,* etc.
(d) Partial repetition
(e) *You mean* + understanding check

(2) Place learners into groups of six. One reads the card with the statement. Other learners take turns to pick up one card each, responding to the utterance using the repair initiator on that card. Everyone else guesses which initiator is used.

Variations

(i) The teacher models the activity first by reading the statement and showing the possible (a)–(e) responses.
(ii) Change or use more than one statement.
(iii) Give each group more than one set of cards so that learners get more than one turn.

Third-position Repair

Awareness-raising Activity: *That's Not What I Meant!*

(1) Begin by asking the following question: Have you ever been involved in misunderstandings in English or in your native language (e.g., misinterpreting another's joke as serious, question as complaint, offer as criticism)?

(2) Give learners the following example and ask: What is the misunderstanding, how is it resolved, and what specific language is used to resolve it?

> [Schegloff, 1987b, pp. 208–209—modified]
> 01   A: Well, honey? I'll probably see you one of
> 02   these days,
> 03   B: Oh yeah, but I just couldn't get down there.
> 04   A: Oh I know, I'm not asking you to come
> 05   down.

(3) Have learners share their answers in class. Explain the four components of third-position repairs. Use terminology suitable for your learners.

(a) Repair-initiating component (optional)
    e.g., *no; no no; no, no, no; oh; oh no; oh yeah; well.*
(b) Acceptance/agreement (most optional)
    e.g., *yeah, I know, I realize that too, that's OK, Oh I know.*
(c) Rejection of misunderstanding (optional)
    e.g., *I don't mean that, I'm not X-ing, That's not what I mean.*
(d) Repair proper (most likely to be present)
    e.g., *I mean Y.*

(4) Discuss possible cross-cultural variations.

Variation

Make up your own examples using the four components in various combinations.

Practicing Activity: *Misunderstanding Script*

(1) Solicit from learners some situations in which misunderstandings actually happened to them or someone they know (e.g., a joke was taken seriously, an offer was heard as a complaint, a question was heard as a criticism, and so on). These real-life misunderstanding scripts form the basis for practicing third-position repairs.

(2) Put learners in pairs. Ask them to write down what they remember from the conversation and compose the hypothetical misunderstanding script using third-position repairs.

(3) Ask learners to role-play the conversation. Audio- or video-record the role-plays.

(4) Playback the recordings and ask learners to identify the components of third-position repair in each script.

(5) Learners vote on the best script, and the teacher gives a prize.

Variations

(i) Give pairs of learners one scenario each in which one speaker misunderstands another. Make up these scenarios on index cards. For example, one gets the card to tell a joke, and the other is instructed to take the joke seriously. The pairs are to resolve any misunderstanding using third-position repair.

(ii) Instead of recording the role-play, ask learners to take notes on the components of third-position repair used in each script.

Chapter Summary

Repair practices are an integral component of interactional competence. They are more nuanced, detailed, and orderly than we may realize. Repair subsumes correction. It is an umbrella term for practices addressed to problems in speaking, hearing, or understanding of the talk. There are four types of repair: (1) self-initiated self-repair; (2) self-initiated other-repair; (3) other-initiated self-repair; (4) other-initiated other-repair. Self-initiated self-repair includes same-turn repair, transition-space repair, third-turn repair, and third-position repair. Third-position repair focuses on dealing with misunderstandings. Other-initiated self-repair utilizes a range of initiation techniques, as does same-turn repair. Other-initiated other-repair takes the forms of exposed correction and embedded correction. Knowledge of these repair practices not only forms the basis for helping learners better manage the negotiation of meaning but also provides teachers with a new lens for appreciating the orderliness of self-correction even in learner language. For learners, realizing that repairs are common in native-speaker talk can be liberating and empowering. Awareness-raising and practicing activities were suggested.

Key Concepts

- **Abandonment:** A same-turn repair method of aborting an already started repair attempt, after which the speaker starts afresh.
- **Deletion:** A same-turn repair method of fixing a trouble-source by deleting an item immediately prior to the repair initiator, which is often a cut-off, before continuing with the utterance underway.
- **Embedded correction:** Slipping in a correction in passing without stopping the ongoing trajectory of the talk.
- **Exposed correction:** Stopping the trajectory of talk to overtly address a trouble-source.
- **Insertion:** A same-turn repair method of fixing the trouble-source by inserting an item immediately after the repair initiator, which is often a cut-off, before continuing with the utterance underway.
- **Preference for self-repair:** The phenomenon in ordinary conversation where one often gets and takes the first opportunity to fix his/her own trouble-source while other-repair tends to be held off or mitigated.
- **Repair initiation:** The practice of signaling or targeting a trouble-source.
- **Repair outcome:** The solution to the trouble-source or abandonment of the problem.
- **Repair practices:** Ways of addressing problems in speaking, hearing, or understanding of the talk.
- **Repair segment:** The interactional space extending from repair initiation to repair completion.
- **Replacement:** A same-turn repair method of fixing a trouble-source by replacing it with another item before continuing with the utterance underway.
- **Same-turn repair:** An attempt by the speaker of the trouble-source to address the trouble-source within the current turn.
- **Third-position repair:** An attempt to fix the trouble-source by its speaker based on the next speaker's response, which displays a possible misunderstanding of the trouble-source turn.
- **Third-turn repair:** An attempt to fix the trouble-source by its speaker in the third turn relative to the trouble-source turn although an intervening turn produced by another does not display a problem with that prior turn.
- **Transition-space repair:** An attempt to fix the trouble-source by its speaker just after the first possible completion point of the turn-constructional unit that includes the trouble-source.
- **Trouble-source:** A word, phrase, or utterance treated as problematic by the participants.
- **Word search:** A speaker grasping for a word that is temporarily unavailable or on the tip of his/her tongue.

Post-reading Questions

1. What is a repair segment? What is repair initiation? What is repair outcome?
2. What initiators are used in same-turn repair? What techniques are used to do other initiation?
3. Use a graphic organizer to depict as many types of repair as you can and their relationships.
4. Explain preference for self-repair.
5. Why is the information on repair practices useful to language teachers?
6. How can transcripts of repair practices be used in language teaching?
7. What questions about repair remain after reading this chapter?
8. Select one of the suggested readings below, and provide a summary and critique.

Suggested Readings

Fox, B., & Jasperson, R. (1995). A syntactic exploration of repair in English conversation. In P. W. Davis (Ed.), *Descriptive and theoretical modes in the alternative linguistics* (pp. 77–134). Amsterdam: John Benjamins.

Kasper, K., & Kim, Y. (2007). Handling sequentially inapposite responses. In Z. Hua, P. Seedhouse, L. Wei, & V. Cook (Eds.), *Language learning and teaching as social inter-action* (pp. 22–41). Basingstoke: Palgrave Macmillan.

Nakamura, I. (2008). Understanding how teacher and student talk with each other: An exploration of how "repair" displays the co-management of talk-in-interaction. *Language Teaching Research, 12*(2), 265–283.

Olsher, D. (2004). Talk and gesture: the embodied completion of sequential actions in spoken interaction. In R. Gardner & J. Wagner (Eds.), *Second language conversations* (p. 221–245). New York: Continuum.

Schegloff, E. (1979a). The relevance of repair to syntax-for-conversation. In T. Givón (Ed.), *Syntax and semantics 12: Discourse and syntax* (pp. 261–286). New York: Academic Press.

Schegloff, E. (1987b). Some sources of misunderstanding in talk-in-interaction. *Linguistics 25*(1), 201–218.

Schegloff, E. (1992b). Repair after next turn: The last structurally provided defense of intersubjectivity in conversation. *American Journal of Sociology, 97*(5), 1295–1345.

Schegloff, E., Jefferson, G., & Sacks, H. (1977). The preference for self-correction in the organization of repair in conversation. *Language, 53*(2), 361–382.

Waring, H. (2005c). The unofficial businesses of repair initiation: Vehicles for affiliation and disaffiliation. In A. Tyler, M. Takada, Y. Kim, & D. Marinova (Eds.), *Language in use: Cognitive and discourse perspectives on language and language learning* (p. 163–175). Washington, D.C.: Georgetown University Press.

Wong, J. (2000c). Delayed next turn repair initiation in native/non-native speaker English conversation. *Applied Linguistics, 21*(1), 244–267.

Chapter 8

Conversation Analysis and Instructional Practices

Pre-reading Questions

1. What are some features of teacher talk in the language classroom?
2. What kinds of feedback strategies do you use in the language classroom? What are their advantages and disadvantages?
3. What are some of the problems you face in designing and implementing activities in the language classroom?
4. Have you heard of IRF/IRE (initiation–response–feedback/evaluation)? If yes, what is your opinion of its value to learning?

Chapter Overview

CA not only enriches our knowledge of *what* to teach, it also sharpens our understanding of *how* to teach. CA findings can enhance our overall sensitivity to the complexities of classroom talk (Mori, 2004). They can also specify how various interactional practices create or inhibit opportunities for participation and, by extension, opportunities for learning. This chapter reviews CA findings on three areas of instructional practices in language classrooms and tutorial settings: (1) pedagogical repair; (2) task design; (3) management of participation. We conclude with suggestions on how these findings may be translated into instructional policies in the language classroom.

Instructional Practices

In the previous chapters, we have described how interactional practices are encapsulated in conversation as a system. We offered detailed accounts of turn-taking practices, sequencing practices, overall structuring practices, and repair practices. These practices are the stuff that conversation is made of and what participants themselves orient to. Knowledge of these practices enriches the existing curriculum for the teaching of conversation in previously unexplored ways. For example, turn-taking is considered an important part of interactional competence (Celce-Murcia, 2007), but the very detailed ways in which turn-taking works are typically not available to teachers as foundational knowledge. Sequencing (e.g., request, compliment, complaint) is often presented to learners as isolated utterances, for example, on a continuum of formality, without the rich interactional context in which each utterance occurs as revealed by CA findings. Overall structuring practices such as openings and closings are sometimes underrepresented, misrepresented, or limited in terms of range and depth in ESL/EFL textbooks. Repair is one of the most important aspects of interactional competence, but it is not yet a regular component of ESL/EFL texts beyond strategies for seeking clarification. Just as teachers need to know grammar, phonology, and sociolinguistics as part of their foundational knowledge, they also need a thorough understanding of interactional practices as a basis for teaching conversation. These interactional practices are indispensable to understanding how language works.

Besides offering the details of interactional practices that enhance the existing curriculum in the teaching of conversation, CA findings also shed light upon teachers' instructional practices in classrooms and tutorial settings. By focusing on instructional practices, we bypass the important body of literature using CA to answer questions of learning. Interested readers should consult the 1997 and 2007 *Modern Language Journal* (*MLJ*) issues as well as Kasper (2009) for excellent overviews of "CA for SLA." The amount of CA work on instructional practices is still limited. We discuss a few of these practices in the next sections: pedagogical repair, task design, and management of participation.

Pedagogical Repair

A major focus of mainstream second language acquisition research is corrective feedback, which can be situated on a continuum from explicit to implicit, the latter including recasts and various negotiation moves (Gass & Mackey, 2006). Within the CA framework, the notion of corrective feedback falls under the umbrella of repair, i.e., practices for addressing problems in speaking, hearing or understanding, and applied linguists have examined how such repair is embodied in pedagogical contexts (see Chapter 7 for repair).

Pedagogical repair refers to repair practices that address problems of comprehension and production in learning contexts.

Pedagogical repair is other-initiated by the teacher or peers in instructional contexts. It targets learners' specific comprehension and production problems including linguistic errors. The goal is to facilitate the learning task. Pedagogical repair departs from repair in ordinary conversation in a number of ways. The three features of pedagogical repair are:

(1) learner turns as the location for trouble-sources;
(2) *other* comprising both teachers and peers;
(3) varying repair trajectories by pedagogical contexts.

In what follows, we consider the context-dependent nature of pedagogical repair and the specific practices of pedagogical repair.

Context-dependent Repair

Repair types vary by whether the pedagogical context is **form-focused** or **meaning-focused** (Seedhouse, 2004).

> **Form-focused context** is a context in which attention is drawn to language forms either implicitly or explicitly.

> **Meaning-focused context** is a context in which attention is drawn to the content of what is being communicated rather than to form and accuracy.

In form-focused contexts, **delegated repair** appears to dominate (Kasper, 1986).

> **Delegated repair** is a feedback procedure where the teacher initiates the repair but passes its completion onto another learner(s).

The following extract is a case of delegated repair (see complete transcription key at the beginning of the book; T=teacher). The class is doing a fill-in-the-blank exercise that involves putting verbs into the "present perfect" or "present perfect progressive":

```
(1)    [Waring classroom data]
01     Kevin:      ((reading)) The team has (.) performed (.) for kings.
02                 queens. and presidents. as well as school children
03                 since they (.) started playing in 1926. more than (.)
04                 one (.) hundred million people in over
05          →      nine(.) ty: different countries (1.0) have bee:n
06                 seeing them.
07                 (1.6)
08     T:          O:::ka:[:::::::y? ]
09     Kevin:             [°(    )°]
10     T:     →    Let's see, the t- the tea:::m >what do you-
11                 what does everybody else have.<
12                 (0.5)
```

```
13   Sarah:   →   seen.
14   Marie:   →   have been seeing.
15   T:            Oka:y? ((continues))
```

At line 10, the teacher initiates repair on Kevin's trouble-source "have been seeing" at lines 05–06 by partially repeating the trouble-source turn. She then produces a cut-off, abandoning a question directed to Kevin ("what do you-"), and proceeds to seek repair completions from other students, which Sarah and Marie provide at lines 13 and 14.

Similarly, when the trouble-source is related to the aim of the activity, teacher-initiated learner repair is used more often than teacher-initiated teacher repair (van Lier, 1988). In other words, more time is devoted to involving the learner in reaching the correction when the trouble-source is central to the pedagogical goal at the time.

Task 1

What are the pros and cons of using delegated repair? Use the transcript above as a basis for your discussion if necessary.

In meaning-focused contexts, however, self-initiated self-repair appears more often (Kasper, 1986; van Lier, 1988; Jung, 1999):

```
(2)   [Kasper, 1986, p. 35—modified]
      ((T=teacher; L=learner))
      01   T:        They're both trying to help their children in which
      02              way.
      03   L:   →   In they think the way they think are best- is best.
```

At line 03, the learner self-repairs by inserting "the way" before "they think" and then replacing "are best" with "is best." Meaning-focused contexts also tend to feature self-initiated other-repair (Seedhouse, 2004). In the following extract that involves a role-play activity, L2's self-initiation of repair (i.e., a word search) at lines 08–09 is completed simultaneously by the teacher at line 10 and the peers at line 11:

```
(3)   [Jung, 1999, p. 158—modified]
      ((role-play: making a restaurant reservation over the phone;
      LL=multiple learners))
      01              ((phone rings))
      02   L1:       Allo::.
      03   LL:       ((laughs))
      04              (1.0)
```

05	L1:		Hello. E::r Ale- Alexander's hard, hard rock? Hard
06			rock.
07			May I <u>help</u> you?
08	L2:	→	**Yes, e::r can I ma:ke? E::r ((shifts gaze to T))**
09			**what's the::?**
10	T:	→	**Um, [a reservation.**
11	LL:	→	**[A reservation.**
12	L2:		Reservation for the e:r e:r e:r Friday the. The
13			ninth for
14			e:r five people?=
15	LL:		=For five=
16	L1:		=At what time?

In addition, since meaning-focused contexts prioritize the efficiency of communication, the teacher tends to both initiate and complete the repair, as seen in the following extract (Kasper, 1986):

(4) [Kasper, 1986, p. 37]

01	L:		She told me that Elaine was leaving and er
02	T:	→	**yes that she had left yes.**

Instead of prompting or waiting for the learner to self-correct, the teacher quickly embeds the correction "had left" at line 02 without interrupting the flow of the learner's talk. Table 8.1 summarizes the relationship between repair and pedagogical context.

Task 2

Consider the table on repair and pedagogical contexts below. Does it reflect your own teaching practice? Should any changes be made to better facilitate language learning?

Given the separation of repair initiation from both its trouble-source and its solution, it seems integral to a teacher's pedagogical competence to manage the appropriate distance between these items, e.g., making decisions regarding

Table 8.1 Relationship between Repair and Pedagogical Context

Pedagogical Context	Initiation	Completion
Form-focused	teacher	peer
Meaning-focused	learner	learner
	learner	teacher/peer
	teacher	teacher

when to provide an immediate repair and when to work out a repair over multiple turns. In a similar vein, the separation between *self* and *other* presents yet another set of considerations in making pedagogical decisions. The revelation that correction is not the sole responsibility for the teacher is liberating. The very fact that a trouble-source can be self-activated and self-repaired should make us think twice before jumping in to fix a problem (e.g., increasing "wait time" in Echevarria, Vogt, & Short, 2007). It should also make us ponder the pedagogical values of *self* vs. *other* (initiation of) repair as well as the roles of the multiple players (learner, peer, and teacher) in implementing the repair.

Even more critically, the differences between conversational repair and pedagogical repair beg the question of whether it would be beneficial to render classroom repair more conversation-like given the dominant paradigm of communicative language teaching. The question is yet to be answered, but it provides one new direction in which corrective feedback may be explored. Likewise, the context-dependent nature of repair types also raises the question of whether this distribution (see Table 8.1 above) is pedagogically sound or whether it can be altered to facilitate learning. In short, seeing pedagogical repair as a sequential phenomenon opens up a host of possibilities for expanding our instructional repertoire and furthering the investigation into this very important instructional practice.

> **Author's story (JW):** When I studied Chinese at a summer intensive program, I noticed that the professor repeatedly sprinkled the words *jeige* and *neige* into his lectures, and sometimes they came in clusters such as *jeige jeige jeige* or *neige neige neige*. I kept wondering what he was doing since I had learned that *jeige* means "this" and *neige* means "that." I thought it was perhaps his idiosyncrasy. It finally dawned on me that these demonstratives also function as a stalling technique when searching for a word. Now I realize those are initiators for self-repair, but as a Chinese major, I was never taught in any of my classes that *jeige* and *neige* can be used to initiate same-turn repair. In that sense, the professor's use of conversational repair in classroom talk helped me learn this particular technique inductively.

The same feedback practice may also receive different uptakes depending on the pedagogical contexts. According to Jung (1999), learners respond to the teacher's recasts (i.e., other-initiated other-repair) differently depending on the activity types. In role-plays, the teacher's recast is immediately incorporated into the learner's next turn:

(5) [Jung, 1999, p. 165]
     ((Role-play: making a restaurant reservation over the phone))

```
01   L1:          Alright, what's your request?
02   L2:    →     E::r, I need e:r a table for un- a seat for
03                children for two.
04   T:     →     I need a seat for two children=
05   L2:    →     =a seat for two children.
06   L1:          Yes, yes, that's guaranteed.
07   T:           O:h, we guarantee it=
08   L2:          =Yes, we guarantee it.
```

In teacher-fronted activities, on the other hand, the learner sometimes collaboratively finishes the teacher's recasting turn, where the teacher appears to be showing understanding:

(6)   [Jung, 1999, p. 166]
      ((L6 describes to the teacher the process of making ice cream "*araki*" from his country))

```
01   L6:          And, e:r e:r change uh- change the color.
02;               ((makes circles with fingers to show something is
03                being changed))
04   T:     →     And it changes [the color. ] Yeah.=
05   L6:    →                     [The color.]
```

We now move on to describing the specific practices of pedagogical repair based on CA research.

Practices of Pedagogical Repair

By examining the details of actual pedagogical interaction, CA has unearthed certain previously unidentified error correction techniques. Based on a large collection of L2 lessons and lesson segments from 11 different countries, Seedhouse (2004) found that, in the form-and-accuracy context, teachers typically avoid direct correction and use the following eight types of mitigated feedback strategies (pp. 165–168):

(1)   indirectly indicate there is an error (*pardon?*);
(2)   (partially) repeat the error;
(3)   repeat the original question or initiation;
(4)   repeat the error with rising intonation;
(5)   supply a correct version;
(6)   indicate why X is an error without calling it an error;
(7)   accept the incorrect form and then supply the correct form;
(8)   invite other learners to repair.

Task 3

> Give one example of each for the above eight types of mitigated feedback practices. Then, rank-order the practices from the most frequently to the least frequently used based on your experiences as a teacher or a student. If you have not yet started to teach, rank-order based on how you *would like* the practices to be distributed and discuss why.

Another pedagogical repair practice is **designedly incomplete utterance (DIU)** (Koshik, 2002).

Designedly incomplete utterance (DIU) refers to a grammatically incomplete utterance that invites self-correction by stopping just before a potential trouble-source with prosodic features such as slowing, lengthening, or continuing intonation at the end of the utterance.

In the segment below, the teacher's reading at lines 01–05 is grammatically incomplete but recognizable as a completed action, one that invites self-correction:

```
(7)    [Koshik, 2002, p. 287]
       01    T:    →    h: ((reading)) >he died not from injuries.<
       02                (0.5) ((T and S gaze silently at text))
       03                but drowned
       04                (1.2) ((T and S gaze silently at text))
       05                <after he>
       06                (4.5) ((T and S gaze silently at text))
       07    S:          had been?
       08    T:          there ya go.
       09                (4.0) ((T writes on text))
       10                had been left there for thirteen hours
       11                °without any aid.°
       12    S:          um hum.
```

Notice the slower delivery of "after he" as indicated by the outward-pointing arrows at line 05 and the (4.5)-second silence immediately before the potential trouble-source. As a resource in targeting where the error is located, DIUs are "merely one in a series of practices that combine to assist the student in making the correction" (Koshik, 2002, p. 289). DIU is also a technique frequently used by teachers in the Japanese as a foreign language classroom (Geyer, personal communication).

Yet another error correction technique is the use of **alternative-question repair**, where the question exhibits a preference for one alternative over the other (Koshik, 2005, p. 203).

> **Alternative-question repair** refers to a repair practice formulated as an alternative question, where the first alternative targets the trouble-source and the second provides a candidate correction.

In the following segment between a mother and a child, the mother uses an alternative-question repair at line 04:

(8)   [Koshik, 2005, p. 205]
    01   Child: I need some more blue:.
    02   Mom: you need some more blue?
    03   Child: uh huh,
    04   Mom: → **you need some more blue:? or glue:.**
    05   Child: glue.
    06   Mom: glue?
    07   Child: yap.

In the mother's alternative question, the first alternative targets the child's "blue" at line 01 as the trouble-source, and the second alternative "glue" constitutes a possible solution to the problem. At line 05, the child accepts the correction by repeating "glue."

In sum, by unpacking feedback into two discrete segments (i.e., initiation and completion) that involves a constellation of players (i.e., teacher, learner, peer), CA has painted a fine-grained picture of the pedagogical work involved. In addition, by analyzing actual pedagogical interactions, CA has identified some specific feedback practices in classrooms and tutorial settings such as designedly incomplete utterance (DIU), alternative-question repair, and a range of strategies for avoiding direct corrections.

Task 4

The following extract is taken from a 20-question activity, the goal of which is to practice the forms of "present perfect" and "present perfect progressive" in context. Students take turns to give clues to a celebrity (Michael Jackson, in this case) whom the rest of the class is supposed to identify. The students construct the clues from a card with verbs in their appropriate tense and aspect. How would you characterize the feedback practice at each arrowed turn? Would you have done anything differently?

```
     [Waring classroom data]
01   T:                        ((hands card to Sarah)) o↑kay.
02   Sarah:                    ((looks down at card)) He has (0.8) sin-
03                             u:h singing si[nce
04   T:          →                        [He ha:::::s?
05   Sarah:                    He ha:s bee:[n
06   T:                                   [mhm?-((nods))
07   Sarah:                    singing (0.2) uh since (.) he was eight?
08                             ((looks to T, and T looks at Sarah))
09   T:                        ((turns to LL)) a child?
10   Sarah:                    [°a child?°]
11   T:                        [°mhm?°  ] ((nods))
12                             (0.2)
13          →                  a teenager?
14   LL:                       (mhm teenager.)
15   Sarah:                    °right. (0.2) mhm° He's a young boy,
16                             (0.8)
17   T:          →            He::::: <since he wa::s a young boy,
18   Sarah:                    ((nods))
19   T:          →            >He's not a< young boy any more. ((looks to
20                             Sarah and smiles))
21                             (0.2)
22   Sarah:                    Yes. ((smiles))
23   LL:                       [o::::::h   ]
24   T:                        [Oka::y?]
25   Sarah:                    since he was a young boy, he:: (0.2) and (0.8) he
26                             has won (0.2) an Emmy.
```

Task Design

Detailed CA analyses have also provided important insights into **task designs** in the language classroom (Edwards & Willis, 2005). Two issues have become uniquely salient in CA analysis: (1) the sequential aspect of tasks; (2) unplanned and open tasks.

Task design refers to the planning of a language learning activity that involves real language use with a clear outcome.

Sequential Aspects of Tasks

In mainstream SLA, the most effective tasks are believed to be those that promote meaning negotiation (e.g., comprehension check, confirmation check, and clarification request) and target a single convergent outcome (e.g., information gap) (Pica, Kanagy, & Falodun, 1993). The focus is on information transfer, and a great deal of energy goes into what kinds of forms and content are being targeted. Overlooked are the sequential aspects of task completion. Mori (2002) offers an excellent illustration of the consequence of this neglect. In an advanced Japanese language classroom where the topic is fathers' involvement in family matters, the teacher has given the following instructions for a "discussion meeting" task with native speakers of Japanese invited to the class: (1) explain to the guest the content of the video the textbook related to the "father" theme; (2) ask the guest about the kind of person his/her father is and the kind of relationship s/he has with him; and (3) tell the guest the kind of person your father is and the kind of relationship you have with your father. The task is designed to allow for opinions and impressions about the "father" issue without any pre-allocation of turns, and the students were given time to pre-plan the discussion meeting.

The actual interaction, however, mostly turns out to be a structured interview of the native speaker by the language learners, as shown in the extract below, where Oakland is the language learner and Sasaki the native speaker guest:

```
(9)   [Mori, 2002, p. 330—translated into English]
      01    Oakland:    →    The:n as for your father uh:m (0.5)
      02                     did he have we::ll uhm .hh
      03                     (0.5) really we:ll any interest in his
      04                     children?
      05                     (2.5)
      06    Sasaki:          I::: would say so. °yeah .hh (ya-)° =
      07    Oakland:    →    =how many sibli- how many siblings?
      08    Sasaki:          uh:m two siblings.=I have an older
      09                     brother.
      10    Oakland:         older brother.
      11                     (2.3)
      12    Sasaki:          That's right.
      13                     (0.8)
      14    Oakland:    →    then your father we::ll (1.0) uh:m
      15                     he came home for supper every day
      16                     a::nd, after tha:t did he go back to
      17                     work, again?=or- (1.0)
      18                     stayed home?
      19                     (2.0)
      20    Sasaki:          °uh::[m
      21    Oakland:    →        [so you had supper with your
      22                     uhm father-
      23    Sasaki:     →    yeah yeah yeah=
      24    Oakland:    →    =did you eat with him many [times?
      25    Sasaki:                                     [That's right.
```

As can be seen, after each answer is given, Oakland either says nothing or only provides minimal acknowledgment before launching another question–answer sequence, and the first questioner–answerer role switch only occurs when Oakland displays amazement at Sasaki's response., as shown in the following extract:

(10)   [Mori, 2002, p. 333—translated into English]
```
01   Oakland:          The:n when your father uhm cried-
02                     uh:m did you uhm see it?
03                     (1.3)
04   Sasaki:           uWA:::: (0.8) we:::::ll maybe not
05                     [I think.
06   Yamada:           [°no.°
07   Oakland:     →    wow amazing. Ha hahaha °hahahaha°
08                     (1.5)
09   Sasaki:      →    Have you?
```

In understanding the problem, Mori (2002) notes that in following the instructions, the learners were only able to plan the form and content of what they are going to say in the format of sequence-initiating actions (in the case of items 1 and 2 of the instructions). They were unprepared, on the other hand, for the contingent development of the talk, including offering appropriate assessments to further a topic.

Thus, an integral part of task design should address the sequential organization of talk and specific procedures for accomplishing certain social actions (i.e., initiating a telling), not just what kinds of grammar or vocabulary items are to be used or what kinds of information are to be transferred.

> **Author's story (HW):** In my own teacher-training classes, we would work on specifying the purpose and procedures of an activity. Not until I read Mori (2002) did I realize that there had been a gap in our way of approaching task design that can be detrimental. That is, we tend to focus on macro-levels such as pre-, during-, and post-task planning, at the expense of specific sequential resources learners would need to support the back and forth of any particular interaction.

Unplanned and Open Tasks

CA analysis of classroom interaction has also broadened our understanding of what makes a task productive. One revelation is that, despite great efforts to create authentic tasks in the language classroom, the most authentic tasks often turn out to be off-task talk. We can call this the **paradox of task authenticity**.

> **Paradox of task authenticity** refers to the irony that in the language classroom the most authentic task is sometimes found in off-task talk.

Through a detailed analysis of learners' pre-task planning for the above-mentioned "discussion meeting," Mori (2002) shows that some learners did recognize the potential problem of fulfilling the third item of the instruction (i.e., talking about their own fathers), which cannot be brought off easily via a sequence-initiating action without sounding sudden, and in their pre-task planning they did come up with the strategy of asking about American fathers in general, which in turn makes relevant talking about Japanese fathers in general. But this strategy only finds its way into the talk after the role switch occasioned by Oakland's display of amazement. In the end, the attempt to engage learners in an authentic discussion with native speakers produces contrived interactions, whereas learners' pre-task planning for the discussion affords a more natural site for real-life discussions.

Mori (2004) offers additional evidence for this paradox of task authenticity. In her analysis of a single episode in a Japanese as a foreign language classroom, pair work was intermittently treated as an individual task or an interactive task by different participants at different junctures of interaction. The particular pair work in question is a role-play that involves argument and counter-argument using key expressions. Mori (2004) found that by not looking at each other but checking what is on the board, the learners treat the "argument" task not as an interactive task but as individual processes of constructing texts. In addition, in order to complete the role-play task, members of the pair moved in and out of a word-search side sequence, where they switched to their first language, and again, the side sequence turns out to be more interactive than the supposedly interactive argument role-play.

Based on an analysis of a 50-minute intermediate undergraduate ESL class that was engaged in task-based small group work (discussing articles on the topic of German unification), Markee (2005) also shows how two learners engaged in off-task invitation talk during a topic boundary where the teacher did not frame the next topic (p. 210). Markee (2005) asks, "if the goal of task-based instruction is to engage learners in meaning-focused talk, does it matter whether what they actually talk about is on- or off-task?" (p. 212). He argues that "off-task interaction may be closer to learners' real-life interactional needs than on-task interaction" (Markee, 2005, p. 212).

In other words, the most authentic tasks may not be "designed," after all. Rather, they occur when learners engage in solving real-life classroom problems in the authentic context of a classroom (e.g., figuring out instructions, doing pre-task planning, etc.). It may be worthwhile, then, to describe and explicate what exactly is enabling those unplanned tasks to be truly authentic. We are not advocating abolishing tasks. It may be beneficial, however, for teachers to see the usefulness of off-task talk.

Kahn (2008) proposes an **open task** design framework that departs from the exchange of predetermined information to arrive at a predetermined outcome.

Open task refers to a task designed to unfold in emergent directions as teacher and learners jointly work through exploratory problems.

Based on a detailed analysis of 20 hours of interaction in a beginning-level adult ESL class, Kahn (2008) shows how, in an open task framework, the teacher works to draw out the learners' personal voices in exploring problems such as how to give directions, tell stories, and make appointments in English. The following five task types were identified by Kahn (2008, p. 68):

(1) Predicting Task: make predictions about the target speech
(2) Listening Task: listen to English speaking expert(s) produce speech event
(3) Analyzing Task: examine language choices made by expert speaker(s)
(4) Speaking Task: produce speech event independently and/or collaboratively
(5) Reflecting Task: reflect upon task participation experience(s).

One important feature of an open task is emerging foci, which allows learners to spontaneously attend to lexical, grammatical, and discourse structures of their second language. In the following segment, the class has been doing a Reflecting Task about direction-giving designed to solve a real-life problem. The site for this English class has just been moved. To start the lesson, the teacher began with a Speaking Task, where the learners were asked to exchange directions for getting to one another's homes from this new location. The teacher is now leading an open discussion to reflect on this pair work. During this reflection on the Speaking Task, at line 01, Leo mentions that to get to his partner Antonio's house he has to take the bus to Queens:

(11)　[Kahn, 2008, pp. 80–81]
```
      01   Leo:          I-I nee-[I     need     take] the bus to Queens.
      02   Teresa:               [>Where you live.<]
      03   T:    →       <Where do you live.>
      04   Antonio:      <Whe:re do you li:ve.>
      05   T:            (°um hm,°) don't forget your do.
      06                 ((writing "where do you live" on board))
((five lines omitted))
      11   T:            Where ↑do:: you live. >o[kay,< NO::W]
      12   Leo:                                 [where do you] [live].
      13   Antoni;                               [where do you] [live].
      14   Juana:        Where  [do
      15   Coco:                [where do (   )
```

```
16   Leo:          <where whe:re> do you live.
17                 ((LL mumbling quietly))
18   T:            mm[mmmmm ((approvingly))
19   Antonio:         [where do you live.
20   T:            Question you need that [do (.) Don't forget it.
21   Leo:                                 [yah
22                 Where do you live.
23   T:            Uh[hu:h,
24   Teresa:          [°where do you live.°
25   T:            Good. >Okay<=
26   Leo:          =↑Where do you work.
```

At line 02, Teresa asks Leo where he lives but without using the auxiliary verb *do*, and that emerges as the pedagogical focus within the open task framework.

Task 5

The above transcript shows a snippet of interaction on giving directions situated in an open task framework that included a Speaking Task and a Reflecting Task. Contrast it with a closed task targeting the same skill in direction-giving, where pairs of students are asked to complete an information gap activity with jigsaw maps. What are the advantages and disadvantages of each?

Management of Participation

Within the framework of sociocultural theory, learning is conceptualized as increasing participation (e.g., Young & Miller, 2004). In this regard, classroom-based CA studies have made visible specific instructional practices that promote or block such participation.

Promote Participation

The practices that promote participation can include:

(1) using unfinished turn-constructional units (TCUs);
(2) working with IRF (Initiation-Response-Feedback);
(3) engaging in identity shift.

USING UNFINISHED TCUs

Based on data from a bilingual third grade class, Lerner (1995) describes ways in which teachers can design their turns to engage learner participation with two kinds of incomplete turn-constructional units (TCUs): (1) TCUs without the last item and (2) TCUs designed as lists (also see He, 2004). In the following segment, the teacher's elicitation question is followed with an unfinished TCU that stops at the stressed preposition "in," and that succeeds in generating the class' chorus response of "New York":

(12)   [Lerner, 1995, p. 117]
    01   T: Where w<u>a</u>s this book pub- published?
    02   (2.0)
    03   →   **Macmillan publishing company <u>in</u>?**
    04   (.)
    05   LL: New York ((mostly in unison))
    06   T: Okay.

Teachers can also use unfinished lists to promote student participation:

(13)   [Lerner, 1995, p. 118]
    01   T: This "to" has an extra "o" (.) so that's a plus plus
    02   plus (.)
    03   →   plus plus plus (.) **like too::: <u>big</u>, (0.2) too::: <u>many</u>,**
    04   **(0.2)**
    05   L: too [:: small]
    06   T: [too::far]

Both types of unfinished TCUs not only invite student participation, but also scaffold and guide such participation in very specific directions (cf. "designedly incomplete utterance" discussed above).

WORKING WITH IRF

A central concept in classroom discourse is the **initiation–response–feedback (IRF)** sequence (Sinclair & Coulthard, 1975). It has also been referred to as IRE, where "E" stands for evaluation (Mehan, 1979).

Initiation–response–feedback (IRF) is a three-part sequence where a teacher's directive is followed by a student's response, which in turn receives the teacher's feedback.

In the following extract, Yuka responds to the teacher's nomination (I) with her answer (R), which is then positively assessed (F) by the teacher:

(14)   [Waring, 2008, p. 582]
    01 T: →   I   °Good.° **Number six, Yuka?**
    02   (0.8)

```
03   Yuka:   →   R   ((reading)) >oh< come o::::n. You really play
04                      the saxophone.
05                      (0.5)
06                      How lo:ng (.) have you been playing the sa-
07                      the saxophone.=
08   T:      →   F   =The ↓saxophone.↓Very good. °very good.°
09                      Number seven?
10                      Miyuki?
```

Task 6

Do you use IRF (initiation–response–feedback) in your classroom?
What are the benefits or drawbacks of IRF?

Criticisms of IRF tend to focus on the amount of talk the teacher does (i.e., two-thirds of the time) and use that as a basis for inferring teacher domination. Only by looking at what teachers do in the IRF sequence (as opposed to simply counting the number of turns) are we able to appreciate the fine pedagogical work that can be carried out through IRF. One value of IRF lies in its potential to engage learner interest in specific pedagogical activities such as quiz games (Hellermann, 2005). The quiz game is an activity used for review purposes, during which students from different teams compete to answer questions. Teacher elicitation in the quiz game is slower than usual, which heightens the tension of the game, as shown in this extract taken from a ninth-grade science class:

(15)   [Hellermann, 2005, p. 928]
      01   T: →   what a:re, (1.5) the four pigments.

Teacher evaluations in quiz games are done in a faster pace, lower pitch, and falling intonation regardless of the correctness of the student response:

(16)   [Hellermann, 2005, p. 935]
```
01   T:      what is a variable. There's two things when
02           you're doing a-
03   L:      a number.
04           (2.0)
05   T:  →   No.
```

Because of this equal treatment of correct and incorrect answers, the evaluative nature of the teacher's feedback move is lessened. Since the goal is to decide on winners in quiz games, the teachers focus on *whether* an answer is correct rather than *why* it is so. Hellermann (2005) notes that learners who normally do not participate would do so in quiz games and that learners are more willing to risk a response in quiz games than in a review-evaluation activity, which may in part be a result of the lessened evaluative nature of the "F" move. In addition, insofar as the competitive tone of the interaction is created by the particular prosodic features of the specific turns within an IRF, it is conceivable that these features may be transferred to other pedagogical contexts to engage learner interest. Momentarily slowing down one's pace in teacher initiation, for example, may be adopted as an attention-getting procedure if necessary.

Teachers can also promote participation by doing specific "steering work" in the "I" of IRF. Based on 36 hours' ESL classroom interactions, Lee (2006b) describes how the teacher guides the students towards the correct answer through a series of contingently and purposefully developed display questions:

```
(17)  [Lee, 2006c, p. 696]
      01  T:   →    Let's try number one, I bought all: my
      02               textboo:ks, (1.0) a time clause.
      03  B:            Yesterday.
      04  T:   →    Let's make it a ti:me clau::se now, (.)
      05               Bernage just said yes::terday=
      06                    [(((pointing to Bernage))]
      07  B:            =The day  [before yesterday.
      08  T:                      [but what is it- hehehe, °no, the day
      09               before doesn't work
      10       →    either° what is a clause, what do you have to have,
      11               to have a clause?=
      12  J:            =Subject [and verb-
      13  T:                     [(  ) °too fast I didn't understand° uh a
      14               subject—(.) plus verb, °so that yesterday is just° and
      15               then:: so you can you make a
      16               clause, I bought all my textbooks?
```

At lines 10–11, the teacher moves from her original question of "time clause" (lines 01–02 and 04–05) to the question of what constitutes a "clause" (lines 10–11), and this reformulation is occasioned by B's response in the prior turn at line 07. By reformulating the question, the teacher calls attention to what is problematic with B's response and provides a clue to solving the problem, thereby does teaching in an entirely contingent way.

Author's story (HW): One of the most difficult skills for novice teachers based on my observations is asking fine-tuned elicitation questions. Without attending to learners' emerging understandings, the questions often move further away from the targeted answers, and that leads to frustration for both the teacher and the learners.

Teachers may also conduct other sorts of work at the feedback (F) position to promote participation. By withholding the third turn in the IRF sequence, for example, "opportunity for student participation continues under the aegis of the teacher's question" (Lerner, 1995, p. 116). The feedback (F) position is also a place for doing parsing (i.e., breaking one item into smaller pieces) or intimating an answer (Lee, 2007). The following is a parsing example, where the teacher successively breaks down her original question into smaller units as a result of closely monitoring the learners' response turns:

```
(18)  [Lee, 2007, p. 1214]
      01   T:         All right, what about the next one, "respect for
      02              classics as
      03              opposed to vernacular forms"?
      04              (2.0)
      05   T:   →     What are the classics?
      06              (2.0)
      07   T:   →     She talks about classics, what are the classics?
      08   L1:        Uh::
      09              (3.0)
      10   L6         °It's like uh::: [classical°
      11   T:                          [Eddie, ( ) you, you are talking (.) to
      12              yourself?
      13   L1:        Old style::
      14   T:         What Jungkim?
      15   L1:        Old style.
      16   T:   →     Old styles, so are they respected?
      17   L1:        Yeah.
      18   T:         Yeah, OK, we say classics (.) respected, now do
      19              you think about Ameri- in American classrooms?
```

To address the (2.0)-second silence at line 04, the teacher highlights one specific component of her original question at line 05. When the learner silence persists at line 06, she reformulates her question into one that directs the learners to the text at line 07. When learner responses finally begin to emerge, she acknowledges "old styles" at line 16 and proceeds to tie her inquiry back to another component of the original question that concerns "respect for classics." In other words, the teacher's third turns attend **contingently** to what transpired in the learners' second turns.

Contingency is a quality of interaction where the design of each turn is thoroughly dependent upon and responsive to its prior turn.

Note that this notion of contingency is different from what is referred to as "contingency" in lesson planning (e.g., backup plans). Contingency is an important concept to keep in mind, since novice teachers tend to focus on bringing off their agendas without being able to remain responsive to learners' emerging needs. Experienced teachers, on the other hand, are able to capitalize on teachable moments by closely monitoring learner contributions.

> **Author's story (HW):** Novice teachers seem particularly uncomfortable dealing with problematic learner responses. In a recent ESL class I observed, a learner produced an answer that was clearly incomprehensible to everyone in the room, in response to which the teacher goes on to offer a range of correct responses herself, and the learner's problematic response was left untreated. Working contingently with problematic learner responses remains a challenge for many of my teachers-in-training.

ENGAGING IN IDENTIFY SHIFT

Identity shift also plays an important role in promoting learner participation and making "conversation" in the classroom possible (Richards, 2006). There are three types of identities (Zimmerman, 1998):

(1) discourse identities (e.g., answerer, complainer, or invitee);
(2) situated identities (e.g., teacher or student);
(3) transportable identities (e.g., nature lover or workaholic).

These identities are not mutually exclusive. Certain situated identities would come with certain discourse identities. The situated identity of a television interviewer, for example, would come with the discourse identity of question asker. The default identities in the classroom are usually the situated identities of teacher and student (Richards, 2006). Opportunities for learner participation open up, however, when learners are propelled to take on discourse identities not typically associated with their situated identities. In the segment below, the teacher asks a genuine question about the meaning of *klong*:

(19) [Richards, 2006, p. 64—modified]
      01 L1:   We discharge into the *klong*.
      02 T: →   **what is a *klong*.**
      03 L1:   →   **a *klong* is typical Thai.**
      04 T: OK because I:: don't know ((laughs))
      05   this word.=
      06 L1:   →   **=its erm**
      07 L2:   →   **it's a small canal.**
      08 T: OK yes thank you.
      09 L1:   →   **a small canal for garbage.**
      10 T: OK like an open sewer?

11	L1:	→	yes yes it is not possible to take a bath.
12			((laughs))
13	T:		no:: ((chuckles)) no.
14	L1:	→	in Bangkok there are many *klongs* it's a
15			quadrillage.
16	T:		yeah quadrillage would be a GRID SYSTEM.
17	L1:	→	this is a grid system of canal.
18	T:		OK And they use it for sewage and er:::
19	L1:	→	yes and rain water but er:: waste water
20			too.

Learners 1 and 2 are put in the position to give new information unknown to the teacher rather than reply to known-answer questions. This shift in discourse identity results in a great deal of unsolicited participation from the learners. Note that the teacher identity remains with her use of "OK yes thank you" (line 08). In the following extract, both discourse and situational identities shift:

(20)   [Richards, 2006, pp. 65–66—modified]

01	T:		. . . do you know the expression IT'S
02			NO USE CRYING OVER SPILT MILK?
03	L2:		yes.=
04	L1:		=ah yes I've heard.=
05	T:		=you have heard this?=
06	L1:		=yes we have (0.5) a similar saying in Japan.=
07	T:	→	=aah what is it in Japanese?
09	L1:	→	er
10			((The Japanese students say it in
11			Japanese with T attempting to repeat))
12	T:	→	and how does that-
13	L1:	→	it's no it's no use it's no point- it's no
14			use (1.0) aah=
15	L3:	→	=the water which spilt over.

Here the teacher not only seeks new information from the learner but also attempts to repeat the answer, as a learner would do. The ensuing interaction blossoms into a highly involved discussion marked by latches and overlaps (not shown here), where participants jointly explore the meanings of associated sayings in their respective cultures.

Introducing transportable identities such as "nature lover" or "supporter of the English cricket team" have the potential to create a more conversation-like classroom (Richards, 2006, pp. 71–72). In considering whether this means teachers should engage in "self-revelation," however, Richards (2006) raises a range of practical concerns such as discipline (e.g., self-revelation undercuts discipline) or teachers' moral beliefs of what it means to be a teacher (e.g., maintaining boundaries).

Author's story (JW): In one of my TESL graduate courses, an assignment I give is to have students learn 50 words and 7 expressions in a foreign language. They have the entire semester to complete the task. Many of them asked their ESL students to teach them the words and expressions (e.g., in Spanish, Polish, Tagalog, etc.). My students reported that their ESL students felt happy and empowered, seeing their teacher struggle to learn their native languages. Some noted that the ESL students opened up more, while others commented that the rest of the class became eager to participate in learning these words and expressions too.

Task 7

The following extract is taken from an adult ESL class where the students were asked to read different articles about inventors and create a timeline together afterwards by stating the year and the major invention for each inventor. The particular inventor in question is Thomas Edison. What do you make of the teacher's turn at line 05? Would you have said anything different? Why or why not?

[Waring classroom data]
```
01   Betty:          ((to T)) he was living in New York?
02   Carol:          Not n-[he:: he born in Ohio, e:::h and then, he=
03   Betty:               [((turns to Carol))
04   Carol:          =moved to Michigan, and e::h he got a job as a:::
05   T:        →     yeah thank you but I want to make the story short?
06   Carol:          ah okay.
```

Block Participation

Detailed analyses of classroom interaction have also uncovered instructional practices that restrict participation:

(1) counter-question;
(2) bypassing topic initiation;
(3) explicit positive assessment (EPA);
(4) chained IRFs.

Markee (1995) shows that counter-questions used by teachers during group work can turn communication-oriented tasks into teacher-fronted activities:

(21) [Markee, 1995, p. 74—modified]
```
01   L6:           there is a problem here she [doesn't ]
02   L15:                                      [(huh h)]
03   L6:           understand
04   L7:           (huh)
05   L6:           and we don't understand what
06                 [what means exactly this]
07   L15:          [why we can't get Aus   ] [witf] (.) oh
08   L6:           we cannot get by Ausch   [v   ] itz
09   T:       →    ok (.) what d'you think it might mean.
10   L15          (uh huh) (.) (uh   [huh)]
11   L6:                             [it   ] might mean (.) probably
12                 u::h we:::: (.) cannot have another Ausch[v]itz again
13                 if uh Germany unites or may be
14   T:       →    Does it mean that?
```

At line 09, instead of answering L6's question, the teacher asks a counter-question that puts L6 in the position of having to respond to a known-answer question. Even after L6 makes an attempt to explain the word at lines 11–13, the teacher asks yet another counter-question at line 14. By asking these counter-questions, the teacher makes it difficult for the learners to engage in genuine meaning negotiation.

Teachers can also block participation by bypassing learners' topic initiations. In the following instance from a Chinese heritage language classroom, the teacher bypasses the learner's topic initiations regarding the types of bridges and persists in bringing off her "read aloud" pedagogical agenda (He, 2004):

(22) [He, 2004, p. 570—translated from Chinese—modified]
```
01   T:     Okay now let's look at "bridge."
02          (0.4)
03   B2:    I know I know wood bridges.
04          (0.2)
05   B2:    Are there are there iron bridges?
06   T:     Bridge ah q-i-ao qiao read after me.
07          ((class read q-i-ao, meaning "bridge" in Chinese in
                unison))
```

As He (2004) writes, "By not providing an answer to B2's question, the teacher in effect interactionally deletes the student's initiation of topic" (p. 570).

Task 8

The following extract is taken from a check-homework activity. Kevin is responding to the fill-in-the-blank item below. If you were the teacher, what would you say to an ESL student at line 04 and why? Discuss your answers in groups.

Wow, I didn't know you were married.
How long _____?

(Purpura & Pinkley, 2000, p. 73)

[Waring classroom data]
```
01   Kevin:     Wow. I didn't know (.) you were married.
02              (0.8)
03              Ho:::w lo:ng have you::::: (.) been married.
04   Teacher:   _____
```

Another teacher practice that can potentially block participation is **explicit positive assessment (EPA)** such as *very good* (Waring, 2008). In particular, EPA specifically delivers the news of "case closed," i.e., no further discussion warranted, and this "case closed" hearing is achieved through a variety of resources.

> **Explicit positive assessment (EPA)** refers to teacher responses to student contributions that contain positive assessment terms such as *good, very good, excellent, perfect,* or the like.

First, the prosodic packaging of EPA turns (i.e., decreased volume, lowered pitch, and slower speed) as well as their co-occurring items (e.g., *Thank you*), are typically associated with the closing of an activity (Brazil, 1997; Goldberg, 2004):

(a) =↓Very good. °Tha:nk you.°
(b) "In the world." °Very goo:d. Tha:nk you.°
(c) ="The ↓saxophone."↓(Very good. °very good.°

Second, in the EPA turns, a good amount of interactional laboring is devoted to putting the learner response on a pedestal, so to speak. Observe the nodding, the smiley voice ($ sign) as well as the emphatic delivery shown below:

(d) =Good ((nodding)) > "In fact the team has< won >ninety eight percent of the games< the:::y (1.0) ha:::ve (0.5) pla:yed so:::::: far."
(e) >°Good.° "How long have you been training for the Olympics."<= Excellent.
(f) =$Very good= "how long have you been married."$=Very good.

Third, EPA does more than upholding the linguistic accuracy of the learner response. It embodies an encouraging, congratulating, and rewarding gesture at the finish line, which cements its interpretation as "case closed." It is a bouquet for the podium moment.

(23)   [Waring, 2008, pp. 585–586]
```
01   T:          Oka:y? u::::::h ((looks around the room)) Miyuki.
02                (1.5) ((Miyuki looks up and then down at textbook))
03   Miyuki:     ((reading)) The Harlem Glo- (1.0)—((looks closer at
04                the textbook)) °tera-° [((looks up)) trotter.]
05   T:                                  [t   r   o   t        ] te:rs,
06   Miyuki:     ((looks down)) Globe [trotters,]
07   T:                                [trotters,]
08                °mhm?°
09   Miyuki:     ((continues reading)) Globetrotters are a world-
10                famous comic basketball team. They have been
11                playing basketball since 1926. and they ((looks up))
12   T:          mh:m?
13   Miyuki:     ((looks down and continues reading)) and they have
14                been traveling to different countries of the world for
15                more than forty years.=
16   T:    →     =°↓Very good. Tha:nk you.°
17                (.)
18                K↑evin. We skipped ↑you. >Go ahead.<
```

Throughout this sequence, we observe Miyuki's struggle with pronouncing "Globetrotters" as well as her nonverbal quest (line 11) for the teacher's assurance not only on the linguistic form but also on her floor rights. We also observe the teacher's close monitoring of Miyuki's emerging response via timely assistance and reassurance. What transpired is not a unilateral delivery of a correct answer on Miyuki's part, but a highly coordinated production. The "very good" at line 16 is hearable not only as a positive evaluation on immediately prior linguistic performance but also as a congratulatory applause for the entire journey, and it is this very applauding quality associated with the finish line that generates the understanding of EPA as no further negotiation warranted.

Waring (2008) shows that by treating one learner's correct response as conclusive, exemplary, and beyond challenge, and by lavishing approval for the entire process that the learner has gone through to reach that response, EPA serves to preempt further talk on the issue by implicating the latter as unnecessary. What it does is deprive the learners of any interactional space for questioning, exploring, or simply lingering upon any specific pedagogical point. Its use, therefore, can block rather than promote learning opportunities.

Author's story (HW): During a post-observation meeting with one of my student teachers, I caught myself saying, "That was very nice!" after

> hearing her reflections and moved directly to my comments. It did not turn out to be a very productive meeting. I was struck by the gap between my understanding of EPA as an interactional practice and my actual use of this practice.

Finally, aside from its potential to promote learner participation, IRF can also block such participation. Based on a single case analysis of an adult ESL classroom, Waring (2009) shows that, during a homework review activity, a chain of IRFs gives the impression of unproblematic learning until that chain is broken by one learner-initiated question, which kicks off a whole series of questions raised by multiple learners. These questions reveal all sorts of understanding problems on the learners' part that remained unexpressed during the chained IRFs. For a detailed account of student-initiated participation, see Jacknick (2009).

Reconsidering Instructional Policies in the Language Classroom

In this section, we reiterate the pedagogical relevance of the above CA findings regarding the three aspects considered: pedagogical repair, task design, and management of participation. Since CA research on instructional practices is still in its infancy, any translation of its findings into classroom practice must be viewed as preliminary. Our suggestions below are meant to provoke and broaden teacher thinking in managing the various pedagogical decisions they face.

Broadening Corrective Feedback

With regard to corrective feedback, the main lesson from CA analyses is that training in dealing with learner errors should go beyond a list of feedback strategies such as elicitation, recast or metalinguistic comments to incorporate an understanding of the sequential nature of corrective feedback. In particular, careful considerations should be given to the multiple possibilities afforded by the separation between repair completion and repair initiation as well as the roles of *self* and *other* (i.e., learner, peer, teacher) at each stage of the repair process. For example, once an error or problem surfaces, it is not solely up to the teacher to either identify or fix the problem. The learner can conduct self-initiation, and the peers other-initiation. By the same token, once a problem is identified via repair initiation, the burden of repair does not rest solely upon the teacher. Both *self* and peer repair are legitimate options.

Of course, knowing these options is not the same as knowing when to exercise which. We have learned that repair trajectories vary by activity types or pedagogical contexts. For example, learners are much more prone to self-initiation of repair in pair and group activities, and teacher initiations figure more prominently in teacher-fronted activities or form-focused contexts. We can accept these empirical distributions as a pedagogical recommendation. We can also take these findings on the context-dependency of repair as a point of departure for further deliberating the pedagogical values of different repair practices as we make moment-by-moment decisions in the reality of teaching. We can conduct our own action research, in other words.

Finally, corrective feedback is not a catalog of strategies to be pulled off the shelf and "applied" in the classroom. CA's approach to situating each practice within its sequential context makes it possible to discover a wide range of practices teachers engage in to contingently treat problematic learner contributions.

Rethinking Task Design

Designing pedagogical tasks is a key component of any teacher training program. Our focus has traditionally been placed upon the macro-structure of the task, such as creating an information-gap activity aimed at a single convergent outcome as well as the specific linguistic items needed for accomplishing the task. Learners are typically given a set of instructions on what needs to be done procedurally (e.g., ask each other questions about X, answer questions about Y, etc.) and linguistically (e.g., use the modal verbs in *yes/no* questions). Task planning tends not to take into consideration the sequential resources learners would need to successfully bring off the target interaction. The learners in Mori's (2002) study, for example, were not prepared with the sequential resources for initiating a telling. Neither were they prepared with the sequential resources to respond appropriately to their native speaker guests' telling. As a result, they managed to turn what is supposed to be a discussion into an interview. When it comes to task design then, it is important to plan not just procedurally and linguistically, but also sequentially. This would, of course, require a certain level of familiarity with the sequential requirements related to different tasks and a great deal of thoughtfulness on the part of the teacher.

An even more challenging problem presented by CA analyses with regard to task design, however, is that the most authentic interaction often turns out to be off-task talk. This means two things for language teachers. First, we might need to think twice about our policy towards off-task talk. Is off-task talk to be encouraged given its authenticity? How do we manage the on-task/off-task tension if we were to allow a certain amount of off-task talk? Where do we draw the line? Second, we might need to rethink the notion of "task" in the first place. The "designed-ness" of tasks (e.g., information-gap activity with a single convergent outcome) goes against the dynamic nature of interaction to which learners should ideally be exposed. In other words, we might need to rethink what kinds of tasks truly promote learning. An example of a conceptual shift of "task" can be found in Kahn (2008), where she proposes the idea of "open task"—tasks designed to promote learner contributions to the direction and outcome of their learning activity. In "open tasks," the content is problems for discussion and exploration, the outcome is learner input towards the aim of the activity (e.g., telling life-lesson stories), and the interaction involves all participants in the classroom (learner-learner and teacher-learners).

Linking Practices to Participation

CA studies have shown that the instructional practices are directly linked to the extent to which learners can participate in the learning process. What this means on the macro-level is the pressing need for connecting the dots between each teacher move and its potential impact on learner participation, and by extension, learning opportunities. The conceptual challenge, put otherwise, is for teachers to become highly alert and deeply reflective about the consequences of what we do in the classroom. At the level of turn design, for example, we can construct our turns as unfinished so as to invite learner participation, and we can leave the F slot open in the IRF to allow continuing contributions in response to our original question. In addition, we should take great care not to shut down opportunities for participation with explicit positive assessment items such as *very good* in the F slot. Wong and Waring (2009) suggest a list of alternatives to explicit positive assessments, such as saying *very good* in a non-final intonation, accepting correct responses with less evaluative tokens (e.g., *okay*), problematizing correct responses, asking follow-up questions, or eliciting peer contribution. Finally, creating a productive learning environment also means refraining from turning every opportunity into a testing activity as well as taking risks in making relevant the various identities of both the teacher and the learners. It is important to remember that CA inquiries into instructional practices and learning opportunities have only just begun, and there is a great deal yet to be discovered. The good news is, these discoveries need not be made in CA analyses alone. They are waiting to be made in the very richness of classroom life via teachers' own keen observations and careful reflections.

Task 9

Video-record one of your own or your colleagues' ESL/EFL classes for approximately one hour. Secure permission beforehand. Transcribe a 10-minute segment if possible. Consider the following questions, based on the video:

(1) How was error correction conducted? What specific strategies were used in which contexts?
(2) What kinds of tasks were used? Was there any mismatch between the intended goal and the actual task implementation? Was there any off-task talk? If yes, how was it treated?
(3) Were IRFs used? If yes, how did the initiation and feedback moves promote or block participation?

Chapter Summary

Although the majority of CA findings contribute to our understandings of conversation structures, there is also a growing body of CA research aimed specifically at informing our instructional practices in the ESL/EFL classroom in three domains: pedagogical repair, task design, and management of participation. First, by foregrounding the sequential and situated nature of corrective feedback, CA analysis has made explicit a wider range of instructional options in treating problematic learner contributions, and it has forced us to consider the extent to which each option meets learners' emerging needs as the sequence unfolds. Third, the findings that learners are often unprepared for the sequential demands of classroom tasks and that the most authentic talk is often off-task poses great challenges for classroom instructors. Not only does it seem necessary to incorporate sequential considerations into task design, the very notion of task begs reconsiderations. Finally, the idea that instructional practices can be manipulated to promote or block learner participation offers the very reason for us to be thoughtful about every pedagogical decision we make. In short, CA research into instructional practices has generated more questions than it has provided answers, and greater insights are yet to be unveiled and greater understandings achieved if we are to create "a cost effective and hospitable place" for language learning (van Lier, 1988, p. 212).

Key Concepts

- **Alternative-question repair:** A repair practice formulated as an alternative question, where the first alternative targets the trouble-source and the second provides a candidate correction.
- **Contingency:** A quality of interaction in which the design of each turn is thoroughly dependent upon and responsive to its prior turn.
- **Delegated repair:** A feedback procedure where the teacher initiates the repair but passes its completion onto another learner(s).
- **Designedly incomplete utterance (DIU):** A grammatically incomplete utterance that invites self-correction by stopping just before a potential trouble-source with prosodic features such as slowing, lengthening, or continuing intonation at the end of the utterance.
- **Explicit positive assessment (EPA):** Teacher responses to student contributions that contain positive assessment terms such as *good, very good, excellent, perfect,* or the like.
- **Form-focused context:** A context in which attention is drawn to language forms either implicitly or explicitly.
- **Initiation–response–feedback (IRF):** A three-part sequence where a teacher's directive is followed by a student's response, which in turn receives the teacher's feedback.
- **Meaning-focused context:** A context in which attention is drawn to the content of what is being communicated rather than form and accuracy.

- **Open task:** A task designed to unfold in emergent directions as teacher and learners jointly work through exploratory problems.
- **Paradox of task authenticity:** The irony that in the language classroom the most authentic task is sometimes found in off-task talk.
- **Pedagogical repair:** Repair practices that address problems of comprehension and production in learning contexts.
- **Task design:** The planning of a language learning activity that involves real language use with a clear outcome.

Post-reading Questions

1. What is the difference between pedagogical repair and conversational repair (also see Chapter 7)?
2. In your opinion, what kinds of repairs are more conducive to language learning?
3. Explain IRF and EPA as well as their relevance in teaching.
4. Given the CA findings on IRF and corrective feedback, would you alter your teaching practices in these areas? Why or why not?
5. What are some of the solutions you can think of to address the paradox of task authenticity?
6. Given the CA findings on the management of participation, what are some of the other practices that have the potential to promote or block learning opportunities based on your teaching and learning experiences?
7. Select one of the suggested readings listed below and present the article in class, summarizing the article's key points and offering your comments, questions, and concerns.

Suggested Readings

Hall, J. K. (2007). Redressing the role of correction and repair in research on second and foreign language learning, *Modern Language Journal, 91*(4), 511–526.

Hellermann, J. (2005). The sequential and prosodic co-construction of a "quiz game" activity in classroom talk. *Journal of Pragmatics, 37*(6), 919–944.

Koshik, I. (2002). Designedly incomplete utterances: A pedagogical practice for eliciting knowledge displays in error correction sequences. *Research on Language and Social Interaction, 35*(3), 277–309.

Mori, J. (2002). Task design, plan, and development of talk-in-interaction: An analysis of a small group activity in a Japanese language classroom. *Applied Linguistics, 23*(3), 323–347.

Mori, J., & Zuengler, J. (2008). Conversation analysis and talk-in-interaction in the classroom. In M. Martin-Jones, A. M. de Mejia, & N. H. Hornberger (Eds.), *Encyclopedia of language and education* (2nd edition), Volume 3: *Discourse and education* (pp. 15–27). New York: Springer.

Richards, K. (2006). Being the teacher: Identity and classroom conversation. *Applied Linguistics, 27*(1), 51–77.

Seedhouse, P. (2005b). "Task" as research construct. *Language Learning*, *55*(3), 553–570.

Waring, H. Z. (2008). Using explicit positive assessment in the language classroom: IRF, feedback, and learning opportunities. *Modern Language Journal*, *92*(4), 577–594.

Wong, J., & Waring, H. Z. (2009). "Very good" as a teacher response. *ELT Journal*, *63*(3), 195–203.

References

Antaki, C. (2002). "Lovely": Turn-initial high-grade assessments in telephone closings. *Discourse Studies*, 4(1), 5–24.

Arminen, I., & Leinonen, M. (2006). Mobile phone call openings: tailoring answers to personalized summonses. *Discourse Studies*, 8(3), 339–368.

Atkinson, J. M., & Heritage, J. (Eds.). (1984). *Structures of social interaction: Studies in conversation analysis*. Cambridge: Cambridge University Press.

Bardovi-Harlig, K., Hartford, B. A. S., Mahan-Taylor, R., Morgan, M. J., & Reynolds, D. W. (1991). Developing pragmatic awareness: Closing the conversation. *ELT Journal*, 45(1), 4–14.

Barraja-Rohan, A-M. (2003). How can we make Australian English meaningful to ESL learners? In Bianco J. Lo, & C. Crozet (Eds.), *Teaching invisible culture: Classroom practice and theory* (pp. 101–118). Melbourne: Language Australia.

Barraja-Rohan, A.-M., & Pritchard, C.R. (1997). *Beyond talk: A course in communication and conversation for intermediate adult learners of English*. Melbourne, Australia: Western Melbourne Institute of TAFE (now Victoria University of Technology).

Beach, W. (1993). Transitional regularities for "casual" "okay" usages. *Journal of Pragmatics*, 19, 325–352.

Beebe, L. M., Takahashi, T., & Uliss-Weltz, R. (1990). Pragmatic transfer in ESL refusals. In R. C. Scarcella, E. S. Anderson, & S. D. Krashen (Eds.), *Developing communicative competence in a second language* (pp. 55–73). New York: Newbury House.

Bernsten, S. (2002). Using conversation analysis to examine pre-sequences in invitation, offer and request dialogues in ESL textbooks. Unpublished Master's thesis, University of Illinois at Urbana-Champaign.

Biber, D. & Conrad, S. (2009). *Real grammar*. Upper Saddle River, NJ: Pearson Education ESL.

Blum-Kulka, S., House, J., & Kasper, G. (Eds.). (1989). *Cross-cultural pragmatics: Requests and apologies*. Norwood, NJ: Ablex.

Bolden, G. (2008). Reopening Russian conversations: The discourse particle—*to* and the negotiation of interpersonal accountability in closings. *Human Communication Research*, 34, 99–136.

Bolden, G. (forthcoming). Opening up closings in Russian. In G. Raymond, G. Lerner, & J. Heritage (Eds.), *Enabling human conduct: Naturalistic studies of talk-in-interaction in honor or Emanuel A. Schegloff*. Amsterdam: John Benjamins.

Borowitz, A. (2008). Obama's use of complete sentences stirs controversy. *Huffington Post*, August 19, 2008.

Bowles, H. (2006). Bridging the gap between conversation analysis and ESP: An applied study of the opening sequences of NS and NNS service telephone calls. *English for Specific Purposes, 25,* 332–357.

Bowles, H., & Seedhouse, P. (2007). *Conversation analysis and language for specific purposes.* Bern: Peter Lang.

Boxer, D. (1996). Complaints and troubles-telling: Perspectives from ethnographic interviews. In J. Neu & S. Gass (Eds.), *Speech acts across cultures* (pp. 217–239). The Hague: Mouton.

Boxer, D., & Pickering, L. (1995). The problem of the presentation of speech acts in ELT materials: The case of complaints. *ELT Journal, 49*(1), 44–58.

Boyd, J. R., & Boyd, M. A. (1981). *Connections: Communicative listening and speaking activities.* New York: Regents.

Brazil, D. (1997). *The communicative value of intonation in English.* Cambridge: Cambridge University Press.

Brown, H. D. (2007). *Principles of language learning and teaching* (5th edition). White Plains, NY: Pearson.

Burns, A. (1998). Teaching speaking. *Annual Review of Applied Linguistics, 18,* 102–123.

Button, G. (1987). Moving out of closings. In G. Button & J. R. E. Lee (Eds.), *Talk and social organization* (pp. 101–151). Clevedon/Philadelphia: Multilingual Matters.

Button, G. (1990). On varieties of closings. In G. Psathas (Ed.), *Interaction competence* (pp. 93–148). Washington D.C.: International Institute of Ethnomethodology and Conversation Analysis and University Press of America.

Button, G. (1991). Conversation-in-a-series. In D. Boden & D. H. Zimmerman (Eds.), *Talk and social structure: Studies in ethnomethodology and conversation analysis* (pp. 251–277). Berkeley and Los Angeles: University of California Press.

Button, G., & Casey, N. J. (1984). Generating the topic: The use of topic initial elicitors. In J. M. Atkinson & J. Heritage (Eds.), *Structures of social action: Studies in conversation analysis* (pp. 167–190). Cambridge: Cambridge University Press.

Button, G., & Casey, N. (1985). Topic nomination and pursuit. *Human Studies, 8*(3), 3–55.

Button, G., & Casey, N. (1988/1989). Topic initiation: Business-at-hand. *Research on Language and Social Interaction, 22,* 61–92.

Campion, P., & Langdon, M. (2004). Achieving multiple topic shifts in primary care medical consultations: A conversation analysis study in UK general practice. *Sociology of Health and Illness, 26*(1), 81–101.

Canale, M., & Swain, M. (1980). Theoretical bases of communicative approaches to second language testing and teaching. *Applied Linguistics, 1*(1), 1–47.

Carroll, D. (2004). Restarts in novice turn beginnings: Disfluencies or interactional achievements? In R. Gardner & J. Wagner (Eds.), *Second language conversations* (pp. 201–220). London: Continuum.

Carroll, D. (2005). Vowel-marking as an interactional resource in Japanese novice ESL conversation. In K. Richards & P. Seedhouse (Eds.), *Applying conversation analysis* (pp. 214–234). Basingstoke: Palgrave.

Carroll, D. (forthcoming). Taking turns and talking naturally: Teaching conversational turn-taking. In N. Houck & D. Tatsuki (Eds.), *Pragmatics from theory to practice: New directions.* Volume 2, Alexandria, VA: TESOL Publications.

Carter, R., & McCarthy, M. (1997). *Exploring spoken English.* Cambridge: Cambridge University Press.

Castro, O., & Kimbrough, V. (1980) *In touch*, Book 2. New York: Longman.

Celce-Murcia, M. (2001). Language teaching approaches: An overview. In M. Celce-Murcia (Ed.), *Teaching English as a second or foreign language* (3rd edition) (pp. 3–21). Boston, MA: Heinle & Heinle.

Celce-Murcia, M. (2007). Rethinking the role of communicative competence in language teaching. In E. Alcon Soler & M. P. Safont Jorda (Eds.), *The intercultural language use and language learning* (pp. 41–58). Dordrecht: Springer.

Celce-Murcia, M., & Olshtain, E. (2000). *Discourse and context in language teaching: A guide for language teachers*. Cambridge: Cambridge University Press.

Chavalier, F. H. G. (2008). Unfinished turns in French conversation: How context matters. *Research on Language and Social Interaction, 41*(1), 1–30.

Clancy, P. M., Thompson, S. A., Suzuki, R., & Tao, H. (1996). The conversational use of reactive tokens in English, Japanese, and Mandarin. *Journal of Pragmatics, 26*, 355–387.

Clark, E. (1978). Awareness of language: Some evidence from what children say and do. In A. Sinclair, R. J. Jarvella, & W. J. M. Levelt (Eds.), *The child's conception of language* (pp. 17–43). New York: Springer.

Clark, H. H. (1996). *Using language*. Cambridge: Cambridge University Press.

Clift, R. (2001). Meaning in interaction: the case of "actually". *Language, 77*(2), 245–291.

Comfort, J. (1996). *Effective telephoning*. Oxford: Oxford University Press.

Creider, S. (2007). Pragmatically completed unfinished turns (PCUUs). Unpublished manuscript, Teachers College, Columbia University.

Crow, B. K. (1983). Topic shifts in couples' conversations. In R. T. Craig & K. Tracy (Eds.), *Conversational coherence* (pp. 137–156). Beverly Hills, CA: Sage Publications.

Curl, T. (2006). Offers of assistance: Constraints on syntactic design. *Journal of Pragmatics, 38*, 1257–1280.

Curl, T. S., & Drew, P. (2008). Contingency and action: A comparison of two forms of requesting. *Research on Language and Social Interaction, 41*(2), 129–153.

Davidson, J. (1984). Subsequent versions of invitations, offers, requests, and proposals dealing with potential or actual rejection. In J. M. Atkinson & J. Heritage (Eds.), *Structures of social action: Studies in conversation analysis* (pp. 102–128). Cambridge: Cambridge University Press.

Davidson, J. (1990). Modifications of invitations, offers and rejections. In G. Psathas (Ed.), *Interaction competence* (pp. 149–179). Washington, D.C.: University Press of America.

Dersley, I., & Wootton, A. (2000). Complaint sequences within antagonistic argument. *Research on Language and Social Interaction, 33*(4), 375–406.

Drew, P. (1984). Speakers' reporting in invitation sequences. In J. M. Atkinson & J. Heritage (Eds.), *Structures of social action: Studies in conversation analysis* (pp. 129–151). Cambridge: Cambridge University Press.

Drew, P. (1997). "Open" class repair initiators in response to sequential sources of troubles in conversation. *Journal of Pragmatics, 28*, 69–101.

Drew, P. (1998). Complaints about transgressions and misconduct. *Research on Language and Social Interaction, 31*(3–4), 295–325.

Drew, P. & Heritage, J. (1992). *Talk at work: interaction in institutional settings*. Cambridge: Cambridge University Press.

Drummond, K., & Hopper, R. (1993). Some uses of "yeah." *Research on Language and Social Interaction, 26*, 203–212.

Earle-Carlin, S., & Proctor, S. (1995). *Word of mouth*. Boston, MA: Heinle & Heinle.

Echevarria, J., Vogt, M. E., & Short, D. (2007), *Making content comprehensible for English learners: The SIOP model* (3rd edition). Columbus, OH: Allyn & Bacon.

Edwards, C. & Willis, J. (2005). *Teachers exploring tasks in English language teaching*. Basingstoke: Palgrave.

English Language Center. (1991). *Expeditions into English*. Brigham Young University, English Language Center, UT.

Firth, A. (1996). The discursive accomplishment of normality: On "lingua franca" English and conversation analysis. *Journal of Pragmatics*, 26, 237–259.

Firth, A., & Wagner, J. (2007). Second/foreign language as a social accomplishment: Elaboration on a reconceptualized SLA. *Modern Language Journal*, 91, 798–817.

Ford, C. E. (2004). Contingency and units in interaction. *Discourse Studies*, 6(1), 27–52.

Ford, C. E., & Thompson, S. A. (1996). Interactional units in conversation: Syntactic, intonational, and pragmatic resources for the management of turns. In E. Ochs, E. A. Schegloff, & S. A. Thompson (Eds.), *Interaction and grammar* (pp. 134–184). Cambridge: Cambridge University Press.

Ford, C. E., Fox, B., & Thompson, S. A. (2002). Constituency and the grammar of turn increments. In C. E. Ford, B. A. Fox, & S. A. Thompson (Eds.), *The language of turn and sequence* (pp. 14–38). Oxford: Oxford University Press.

Fox, B. A. (1999). Directions in research: Language and the body. *Research on Language and Social Interaction*, 32(1/2), 51–59.

Fox, B., & Jasperson, R. (1995). A syntactic exploration of repair in English conversation. In P. W. Davis (Ed.), *Descriptive and theoretical modes in the alternative linguistics* (pp. 77–134). Amsterdam: John Benjamins.

Fujii, Y. (2007). Tell me about when you were hitchhiking: The organization of story initiation by Australian and Japanese speakers. *Language in Society*, 36, 183–211.

Gambrell, L., Morrow, L. & Pressley, M. (Eds.) (2007). *Best practices in literacy instruction* (3rd edition). New York: Guilford.

Gardner, R. (2004). On delaying the answer: Question sequences extended after the question. In R. Gardner & J. Wagner (Eds.), *Second language conversations*. London: Continuum.

Gardner, R. (2007a). Broken starts: Bricolage in turn starts in second language talk. In Z. Hua, P. Seedhouse, L. Wei, & V. Cook (Eds.), *Language and learning and teaching as social inter-action* (pp. 58–71). London: Palgrave.

Gardner, R. (2007b). The *Right* connections: Acknowledging epistemic progression in talk. *Language in Society*, 36(3), 319–341.

Gardner, R., & Wagner, J. (Eds.) (2004). *Second language conversations*. London: Continuum.

Gaskill, W. (1980). Correction in native speaker-nonnative speaker conversation. In D. Larsen-Freeman (Ed.), *Discourse analysis in second language research* (pp. 125–137). Rowley, MA: Newbury House.

Gass, S. (2003). Input and interaction. In C. Doughty & M. H. Long (Eds.), *The handbook of second language acquisition* (pp. 224–255). Oxford: Basil Blackwell.

Gass, S., & Mackey, A. (2006). Input, interaction and output: An overview. *AILA*, 19, 3–17.

Gass, S., & Neu, J. (Eds.). (1999). *Speech acts across cultures*. Berlin: Mouton de Gruyter.

Gass, S., & Selinker, L. (2008). *Second language acquisition* (3rd edition). New York: Routledge.

Golato, A. (2002). German compliment response. *Journal of Pragmatics*, *34*(5), 547–571.

Goldberg, J. A. (2004). The amplitude shift mechanism in conversational closing sequences. In G. Lerner (Ed.), *Conversation analysis: Studies from the first generation* (pp. 257–298). Amsterdam: John Benjamins.

Goodwin, C. (1979). The interactive construction of a sentence in natural conversation. In G. Psathas (Ed.), *Everyday language: Studies in ethnomethodology* (pp. 97–121). New York: Irvington.

Goodwin, C. (1981). *Conversational organization: Interaction between speakers and hearers*. New York: Academic Press.

Goodwin, C. (1984). Notes on story structure and the organization of participation. In J. M. Atkinson & J. Heritage (Eds.), *Structures of social action* (pp. 225–246). Cambridge: Cambridge University Press.

Goodwin, C. (1986). Between and within: Alternative treatments of continuers and assessments. *Human Studies*, 9, 205–217.

Goodwin, C. (1996). Transparent vision. In P. Drew & J. Heritage (Eds.), *Talk at work: Interaction in institutional settings* (pp. 370–404). Cambridge: Cambridge University Press.

Grant, L., & Starks, D. (2001). Screening appropriate teaching materials: Closings from textbooks and television soap operas. *International Review of Applied Linguistics*, *39*, 39–50.

Grice, H. P. (1975). Logic and conversation. In P. Cole & J. L. Morgan (Eds.), *Syntax and semantics*, Volume 3, *Speech acts* (pp. 41–58). New York: Academic Press.

Griswold, O. (2003). How do you say good-bye? In K. Bardovi-Harlig & R. Mahan-Taylor (Eds.), *Teaching pragmatics*. Washington, D.C.: Department of State (http://exchanges.state.gov/media/oelp/teaching-pragmatics/griswold.pdf).

Guthrie, A. (1997). On the systematic deployment of okay and mmhmm in academic advising sessions. *Pragmatics*, 7, 397–415.

Hall, J.K. (2007). Redressing the roles of correction and repair in research on second and foreign language teaching. *Modern Language Journal*, *91*(4), 511–526.

Han, Z.-H. (2002). A study of the impact of recasts on tense consistency in L2 output. *TESOL Quarterly*, *36*(4), 543–572.

Hatch, E. M. (1978). Discourse analysis and second language acquisition. In E. M. Hatch (Ed.), *Second language acquisition* (pp. 401–435). Rowley, MA: Newbury House.

Hatch, E. M. (1992). *Discourse and language education*. Cambridge: Cambridge University Press.

He, A. W. (1998). Answering questions in LPIs: A case study. In R. Young & A. W. He (Eds.), *Talking and testing: Discourse approaches to the assessment of oral proficiency* (pp. 101–116). Amsterdam: John Benjamins.

He, A. W. (2004). CA for SLA: Arguments from the Chinese language classroom. *Modern Language Journal*, *88*(4), 568–582.

Hellermann, J. (2005). The sequential and prosodic co-construction of a "quiz game" activity in classroom talk. *Journal of Pragmatics*, *37*(6), 919–944.

Hellermann, J. (2009). Practices for dispreferred response using *no* by a learner of English. *IRAL*, *47*, 95–126.

Herbert, R. K. (1989). The ethnography of English compliments and compliment responses: A contrastive sketch. In W. Oleksy (Ed.), *Contrastive pragmatics* (pp. 3–35), Amsterdam: John Benjamins.

Herbert, R. K. (1990). Sex-based differences in compliment behavior. *Language in Society, 19*, 201–224.

Heritage, J. (1984a). *Garfinkel and ethnomethodology.* Cambridge: Polity Press.

Heritage, J. (1984b). A change-of-state token and aspects of its sequential placement. In J. M. Atkinson & J. Heritage (Eds.), *Structures of social action: Studies in conversation analysis* (pp. 299–345). Cambridge: Cambridge University Press.

Holt, E., & Drew, P. (2005). Figurative pivots: The use of figurative expressions in pivotal topic transitions. *Research on Language and Social Interaction, 38*(1), 35–62.

Hosoda, Y. (2006). Repair and relevance of differential language expertise. *Applied Linguistics, 27*, 1, 25–50.

Houck, N., & Tatsuki, D. (Eds.) (forthcoming). *Pragmatics from theory to practice: New directions.* Alexandria, VA: TESOL Publications.

Houtkoop-Steenstra, H. (1991). Opening sequences in Dutch telephone conversations. In D. Boden & D. Zimmerman (Eds.), *Talk and social structure* (p. 232–250). Berkeley: University of California Press.

Hua, Z., Seedhouse, P. Wei, L. & Cook, V. (Eds.) (2007). *Language learning and teaching as social inter-action.* London: Palgrave.

Hutchby, I., & Barnett, S. (2005). Aspects of the sequential organization of mobile phone conversation. *Discourse Studies, 7*(2), 147–172.

Huth, T. (2006). Negotiating structure and culture: L2 learners' realization of L2 compliment–response sequences in talk-in-interaction. *Journal of Pragmatics, 38*, 2025–2050.

Huth, T, & Taleghani-Nikazm, C. (2006). How can insights from conversation analysis be directly applied to teaching L2 pragmatics. *Language Teaching Research, 10*(1), 53–79.

Hymes, D. (1974). *Foundations in sociolinguistics.* Philadelphia, PA: University of Pennsylvania Press.

Iwasaki, S. (2009). Initiating interactive turn spaces in Japanese conversation: Local projection and collaborative action. *Discourse Processes, 46*(2), 226–246.

Jacknick, C. M. (2009). A conversation-analytic account of student initiated participation in an ESL classroom. Unpublished doctoral dissertation: Teachers College, Columbia University.

Jefferson, G. (1978). Sequential aspects of storytelling in conversation. In J. Schenkein (Ed.), *Studies in the organization of conversational interaction* (pp. 219–248). New York: Academic Press.

Jefferson, G. (1983). Notes on some orderliness of overlap onset. *Tilburg Papers in Language and Literature, 28*, 1–28.

Jefferson, G. (1984). On stepwise transition from talk about a trouble to inappropriately next-positioned matters. In. J. M. Atkinson & J. Heritage (Eds.), *Structures of social action: Studies in conversation analysis* (pp. 191–222). Cambridge: Cambridge University Press.

Jefferson, G. (1985). Notes on systematic deployment of acknowledgment tokens such as "yeah" and "Mm hm." *Tilburg Papers in Language and Literature, 30*, 1–18.

Jefferson, G. (1987). On exposed and embedded correction in conversation. In G. Button & J. R. E. Lee (Eds.), *Talk and social organization* (pp. 86–100). Clevedon: Multilingual Matters.

Jefferson, G. (1988) On the sequential organization of troubles talk in ordinary conversation. *Social Problems, 35*(4), 418–442.

Jefferson, G. (1993). Caveat speaker: Preliminary notes on recipient topic-shift implicature. *Research on Language and Social Interaction, 26*(1), 1–30.

Jefferson, G. (2002). Is "no" an acknowledgment token? Comparing American and British uses of (+)/(−) tokens. *Journal of Pragmatics, 34*, 1345–1383.

Jefferson, E. A. (2004a). Glossary of transcript symbols with an introduction. In G. Lerner (Ed.), *Conversation analysis: Studies from the first generation* (pp. 1–31). Cambridge: Cambridge University Press.

Jefferson, G. (2004b). "At first I thought." In G. Lerner (Ed.), *Conversation analysis: Studies from the first generation* (pp. 131–170). Amsterdam: John Benjamins.

Jefferson, G. (2007). Preliminary notes on abdicated other-correction. *Journal of Pragmatics, 39*, 445–461.

Jung, E.-H. (1999). The organization of second language classroom repair. *Issues in Applied Linguistics, 10*(2), 153–171.

Kahn, G. (2008). The social unfolding of task, discourse, and development in the second language classroom. Unpublished doctoral dissertation, Teachers College, Columbia University.

Kasper, G. (1986). Repair in foreign language teaching. In G. Kasper (Ed.), *Learning, teaching and communication in the foreign language classroom* (pp. 23–41). Aarhus, Denmark: Aarhus University Press.

Kasper, G. (2006a). Beyond repair: Conversation analysis as an approach to SLA. *AILA Review, 19*, 83–99.

Kasper, G. (2006b). Speech acts in interaction: Towards discursive pragmatics. In K. Bardovi-Harlig, C. Félix-Brasdefer, & A. S. Omar (Eds.), *Pragmatics and language learning, 11*, 281–314.

Kasper, G. (2009). Locating cognition in second language interaction and learning: Inside the skull or in public view? *International Review of Applied Linguistics 47*, 11–36.

Kasper, G., & Blum-Kulka, S. (1993). *Interlanguage Pragmatics*. Oxford: Oxford University Press.

Kasper, G., & Kim, Y. (2007). Handling sequentially inapposite responses. In Z. Hua, P. Seedhouse, L. Wei, & V. Cook (Eds.), *Language learning and teaching as social inter-action* (pp. 22–41). Basingstoke: Palgrave Macmillan.

Koshik, I. (2002). Designedly incomplete utterances: A pedagogical practice for eliciting knowledge displays in error correction sequences. *Research on Language and Social Interaction, 35*(3), 277–309.

Koshik, I. (2005). Alternative questions used in conversational repair. *Discourse Studies, 7*(2), 193–211.

Kurhila, S. (2001). Correction in talk between native and non-native speaker. *Journal of Pragmatics, 33*(7), 1083–1110.

Labov, W., & Waletzky, J. (1967). Narrative analysis: Oral versions of personal experience. In J. Helm (Ed.), *Proceedings of the 1966 Annual Spring Meeting of the American Ethnological Society* (pp. 12–44). Seattle and London: University of Washington Press.

Lazaraton, A. (1997). Preference organization in oral proficiency interviews: The case of language ability assessment. *Research on Language and Social Interaction, 30*(1), 53–72.

Lazaraton, A. (2001). Teaching oral skills. In M. Celce-Murcia (Ed.), *Teaching English as a second or foreign language* (3rd edition) (pp. 103–115). Boston, MA: Heinle & Heinle.

Lazaraton, A. (2004). Gesture and speech in the vocabulary explanations of one ESL teacher: A microanalytic inquiry. *Language Learning, 54*(1), 79–117.

LeBaron, C., & Jones, S. (2002). Closing up closings: Showing the relevance of the social and material surround to the completion of interaction. *Journal of Communication, 52*(3), 542–565.

Lee, S-H. (2006a). Second summoning in Korean telephone conversation openings, *Language in Society, 35*, 261–283.

Lee, Y-A. (2006b). Towards respecification of communicative competence: Conditions of L2 instruction or its objective? *Applied Linguistics, 27*(3), 349–376.

Lee, Y-A. (2006c). Respecifying display questions: Interactional resources for language teaching. *TESOL Quarterly, 40*(4), 691–713.

Lee, Y-A. (2007). Third turn position in teacher talk: Contingency and the work of teaching. *Journal of Pragmatics, 39*, 1204–1230.

Lerner, G. H. (1991). On the syntax of sentences-in-progress. *Language in Society, 20*(3), 441–458.

Lerner, G. H. (1992). Assisted storytelling: Deploying shared knowledge as a practical matter. *Qualitative Sociology, 15*, 247–271.

Lerner, G. H. (1995). Turn design and the organization of participation in instructional activities. *Discourse Processes, 19*, 111–131.

Lerner, G. H. (1996). On the "semi-permeable" character of grammatical units in conversation: Conditional entry into the turn space of another speaker. In E. Ochs, E. A. Schegloff, & S. Thompson (Eds.), *Interaction and grammar* (pp. 238–276). Cambridge: Cambridge University Press.

Lerner, G. H. (2003). Selecting next speaker: The context-sensitive operation of a context-free organization. *Language in Society, 32*(2), 177–201.

Levinson, S. C. (1983). *Pragmatics.* Cambridge: Cambridge University Press.

Liddicoat, A. J. (2000). Telephone openings in Samoan. *Australian Review of Applied Linguistics, 23*(1), 95–107.

Liddicoat, A. J. (2007). *An introduction to conversation analysis.* New York: Continuum.

Lindstrom, A. (1994). Identification and recognition in Swedish telephone conversation openings. *Language in Society, 23*, 231–252.

Local, J., & Kelly, J. (1986). Projection and "silences": Notes on phonetic and conversational structure. *Human Studies, 9*, 185–204.

Local, J., & Walker, G. (2004). Abrupt-joins as a resource for the production of multi-unit, multi-action turns. *Journal of Pragmatics, 36*, 1375–1403.

Luke, K. K. (2002). The initiation and introduction of first topics in Hong Kong telephone calls. In K. K. Luke & T.-S. Pavlidou (Eds.), *Telephone calls: Unity and diversity in conversational structures across languages and cultures* (pp. 171–200). Amsterdam: John Benjamins.

Luke, K. K., & Pavlidou T.-S. (Eds.) (2002). *Telephone calls: Unity and diversity in conversational structures across languages and cultures.* Amsterdam: John Benjamins.

McCarthy, M. (1991). *Discourse analysis for language teachers.* Cambridge: Cambridge University Press.

McCarthy, M. (1998). *Spoken language and applied linguistics.* Cambridge: Cambridge University Press.

McCarthy, M., McCarten, J., & Sandiford, H. (2006). *Touchstone, student's book 4.* Cambridge: Cambridge University Press.

Mandelbaum, J. (1987). Couples sharing stories. *Communication Quarterly, 35*(2), 144–170.

Mandelbaum, J. (1989). Interpersonal activities in conversational storytelling. *Western Journal of Speech Communication, 53*, 114–126.

Mandelbaum, J. (1991/1992). Beyond mundane reason: Conversation analysis and context. *Research on Language and Social Interaction, 24,* 333–350.

Markee, N. (1995). Teachers' answers to students' questions: Problematizing the issue of making meaning. *Issues in Applied Linguistics, 6,* 63–92.

Markee, N. (2000). *Conversation analysis.* Mahwah, NJ: Lawrence Erlbaum.

Markee, N. (2005). The organization of off-task classroom talk in second language classrooms. In K. Richards & P. Seedhouse (Eds.), *Applying conversation analysis* (pp. 197–213). Basingstoke, UK: Palgrave Macmillan.

Maynard, D. W. (1980). Placement of topic changes in conversation. *Semiotica, 3/4,* 263–290.

Maynard, D. W. (2003). *Bad news, good news: Conversational order in everyday talk and clinical settings.* Chicago: University of Chicago Press.

Maynard, D., & Zimmerman, D. (1984). Topical talk, ritual and the social organization of relationships. *Social Psychology Quarterly, 47*(4), 301–316.

Mehan, H. (1979). *Learning lessons: Social organization in the classroom.* Cambridge, MA: Harvard University Press.

Messee, J., & Kranich, R. (1982). *English spoken here.* New York: Cambridge University Press.

Mondada, L. (2007). Multimodal resources for turn-taking: pointing and the emergence of possible next speakers. *Discourse Studies, 9*(2), 194–225.

Mori, J. (2002). Task design, plan, and development of talk-in-interaction: An analysis of a small group activity in a Japanese language classroom. *Applied Linguistics, 23*(3), 323–347.

Mori, J. (2004). Negotiating sequential boundaries and learning opportunities: A case from a Japanese language classroom. *Modern Language Journal, 88*(4), 536–550.

Mori, J., & Zuengler, J. (2008). Conversation analysis and talk-in-interaction in the classroom. M. Martin-Jones, A. M. de Mejia, & N. H. Hornberger (Eds.), *Encyclopedia of Language and Education* (2nd edition), Volume 3, *Discourse and education* (pp. 15–27). New York: Springer.

Morita, E. (2008). Highlighted moves within an action: Segmented talk in Japanese conversation. *Discourse Studies, 10*(4), 517–542.

Mosteller, L., & Paul, B. (1994). *Survival English,* Book 5, Saddle River, NJ: Prentice Hall.

Nakamura, I. (2008). Understanding how teacher and student talk with each other: An exploration of how "repair" displays the co-management of talk-in-interaction. *Language Teaching Research, 12*(2), 265–283.

Ochs, E. (1988). *Culture and language development: language acquisition in a Samoan village.* Cambridge: Cambridge University Press.

Ochs. E., & Schieffelin, B. (1983). *Acquiring conversational competence.* London: Routledge & Kegan Paul.

Oh, S.-Y. (2006). English zero anaphora as an interactional resource II. *Discourse Studies, 8*(6), 817–846.

Olsher, D. (2004). The embodied completion of sequential actions in spoken interaction. In R. Gardner & J. Wagner (Eds.), *Second language conversations.* New York: Continuum.

Olsher, D. (2008). Gesturally-enhanced repeats in the repair turn: Communication strategy or cognitive language-learning tool? In S. G. McCafferty & G. Stam (Eds.), *Gesture: Second language acquisition and classroom research* (pp. 109–132). New York: Routledge.

Olsher, D. (forthcoming). Responders. In N. Houck & D. Tatsuki (Eds.), *Pragmatics from theory to practice: New directions*. Volume 2. Alexandria, VA: TESOL Publications.

Omar, A. (1993). Closing Kiswahili conversations: The performance of native and non-native speakers. *Pragmatics and Language Learning, 4*, 104–125.

Pavlidou, T.-S. (2008). Interactional work in Greek and German telephone conversations. In H. Spencer-Oatey (Ed.), *Culturally speaking* (2nd edition) (pp. 118–137), New York: Continuum.

Perkins, L. (2003). Negotiating repair in aphasic conversation: Interactional issues. In C. Goodwin (Ed.), *Conversation and brain damage* (pp. 147–161), New York: Oxford University Press.

Pica, T., Kanagy, R., & Falodun, J. (1993). Choosing and using communicative tasks for second language instruction and research. In S. Gass & G. Crookes (Eds.), *Tasks and language learning: Integrating theory and practice* (pp. 9–34). Clevedon: Multilingual Matters.

Pike, K. (1967). *Language in relation to a unified theory of the structure of human behavior*. The Hague: Mouton.

Placencia, M. E. (1997). Opening up closings—the Ecuadorian way. *Text 17*(1), 53–81.

Pomerantz, A. (1978). Compliment responses: Notes on the co-operation of multiple constraints. In J. Schenkein (Ed.), *Studies in the organization of conversational interaction* (pp. 79–112). New York: Academic Press.

Pomerantz, A. (1984). Agreeing and disagreeing with assessments: Some features of preferred/dispreferred turn shapes. In M. Atkinson & J. Heritage (Eds.), *Structures of social action: Structures in conversation analysis* (pp. 57–101). Cambridge: Cambridge University Press.

Pomerantz, A., & Fehr, A. (1997). Conversation analysis: An approach to the study of social action as sense making practices. In T. A. van Dijk (Ed.), *Discourse studies: A multidisciplinary introduction*, Volume 2, *Discourse as social interaction* (pp. 64–91). London: Sage.

Psathas, G. (1995). *Conversation analysis: The study of talk-in-interaction*. Thousand Oaks, CA: Sage.

Purpura, J. (2004). *Assessing grammar*. Cambridge: Cambridge University Press.

Purpura, J., & Pinkley, D. (2000). *On target workbook 1*, White Plains, NY: Pearson.

Reinhart, S., & Fisher, I. (2000). *Speaking and social interaction*. Ann Arbor, MI: University of Michigan.

Richards, K. (2006). Being the teacher: Identity and classroom conversation. *Applied Linguistics, 27*(1), 51–77.

Richards, K., & Seedhouse, P. (Eds.). (2005). *Applying conversation analysis*. Basingstoke: Palgrave.

Robinson, J. D. (2001). Closing medical encounters: Two physician practices and their implications for the expression of patients' unstated concerns. *Social Science & Medicine, 53*, 639–656.

Ryave, A. L. (1978). On the achievement of a series of stories. In J. Schenkein (Ed.), *Studies in the organization of conversational interaction* (pp. 113–132). New York: Academic Press.

Sacks, H. (1974). An analysis of the course of a joke's telling in conversation. In R. Bauman & J. Sherzer (Eds.), *Explorations in the ethnography of speaking* (pp. 337–353). Cambridge: Cambridge University Press.

Sacks, H. (1975). Everyone has to lie. In M. Sanches & B. Blount (Eds.), *Sociocultural dimensions of language use* (pp. 57–80), New York: Academic Press.

Sacks, H. (1987). On the preferences for agreement and contiguity in sequences in conversation. In G. Button & J. R. E. Lee (Eds.), *Talk and social organization* (pp. 54–69). Clevedon: Multilingual Matters.

Sacks, H. (1992a). *Lectures on conversation*, Volume I. MA: Blackwell.

Sacks, H. (1992b). *Lectures on conversation*, Volume II. MA: Blackwell.

Sacks, H., Schegloff, E. A., & Jefferson, G. (1974). A simplest systematics for the organization of turn-taking for conversation. *Language, 50*(4), 696–735.

Savignon, S. J. (2001). Communicative language teaching for the twenty-first century. In M. Celce-Murcia (Ed.), *Teaching English as a second or foreign language* (3rd edition) (pp. 13–28). Boston, MA: Heinle & Heinle.

Scarcella, R. (1988). Conversational analysis in L2 acquisition and teaching. *Annual Review of Applied Linguistics, 9*, 72–91.

Schegloff, E. A. (1968). Sequencing in conversational openings. *American Anthropologist, 70*(6), 1075–1095.

Schegloff, E. A. (1979a). The relevance of repair to syntax-for-conversation. In T. Givon (Ed.), *Syntax and semantics 12: Discourse and syntax* (pp. 261–288). New York: Academic Press.

Schegloff, E. A. (1979b). Identification and recognition in telephone conversation openings. In G. Psathas (Ed.), *Everyday language: Studies in ethnomethodology* (pp. 23–78). New York: Irvington Publishers.

Schegloff, E. A. (1980). Preliminaries to preliminaries: "Can I ask you a question?" *Sociological Inquiry, 50*(3–4), 104–152.

Schegloff, E. A. (1982). Discourse as an interactional achievement: Some uses of "uh huh" and other things that come between sentences. In D. Tannen (Ed.), *Analyzing discourse: Text and talk* (pp. 71–93). Washington, D.C.: Georgetown University Press.

Schegloff, E. A. (1984). On some gestures' relation to talk. In M. Atkinson & J. Heritage (Eds.), *Structures of social interaction: Studies in conversation analysis* (pp. 28–52). Cambridge: Cambridge University Press.

Schegloff, E. A. (1986). The routine as achievement. *Human Studies, 9*, 111–151.

Schegloff, E. A. (1987a). Recycled turn beginnings: A precise repair mechanism in conversation's turn-taking organization. In G. Button & J. R. E. Lee (Eds.), *Talk and social organization* (pp. 70–85). Clevedon: Multilingual Matters.

Schegloff, E. A. (1987b). Some sources of misunderstanding in talk-in-interaction. *Linguistics, 25*(1), 201–218.

Schegloff, E. A. (1988a). Goffman and the analysis of conversation. In P. Drew & A. Wootton (Eds.), *Erving Goffman, Exploring the interaction order* (pp. 89–135). Boston: Northeastern University Press.

Schegloff, E. A. (1988b). Presequence and indirection: Applying speech act theory to ordinary conversation. *Journal of Pragmatics, 12*, 55–62.

Schegloff, E. A. (1992a). In another context. In A. Duranti & C. Goodwin (Eds.), *Rethinking Context: Language as an Interactive Phenomenon* (pp. 193–227). Cambridge: Cambridge University Press.

Schegloff, E. A. (1992b). Repair after next turn: The last structurally provided defense of intersubjectivity in conversation. *American Journal of Sociology, 97*(5), 1295–1345.

Schegloff, E. A. (1996). Turn organization: One intersection of grammar and interaction. In E. Ochs, E. A. Schegloff, & S. A. Thompson (Eds.), *Interaction and grammar* (pp. 52–133). Cambridge: Cambridge University Press.

Schegloff, E. A. (1997a). Third turn repair. In G. R. Guy, C. Feagin, D. Schiffrin, & J. Baugh (Eds.), *Toward a social science of language: Papers in honour of William Labov*, Volume 2, (pp. 31–40). Amsterdam: John Benjamins.

Schegloff, E. A. (1997b). Practices and actions: Boundary cases of other-initiated repair. *Discourse Processes, 23*, 499–545.

Schegloff, E. A. (2000). When "others" initiate repair. *Applied Linguistics, 21*(2), 205–243.

Schegloff, E. A. (2002). Reflections on research on telephone conversation: Issues of cross-cultural scope and scholarly exchange, interactional import and consequences. In K. K. Luke & T.-S. Pavlidou (Eds.), *Telephone calls: Unity and diversity in conversational structure across languages and cultures* (pp. 249–281). Amsterdam: John Benjamins.

Schegloff, E. A. (2004). Answering the phone. In G. Lerner (Ed.), *Conversation analysis: Studies from the first generation* (pp. 63–107). Amsterdam: John Benjamins.

Schegloff, E. A. (2005). On integrity in inquiry . . . of the investigated, not the investigator. *Discourse Studies, 7*(4–5), 455–480.

Schegloff, E. A. (2007). *Sequence organization in interaction: A primer in conversation analysis*, Volume 1. Cambridge: Cambridge University Press.

Schegloff, E. A., Jefferson, G., & Sacks, H. (1977). The preference for self-correction in the organization of repair in conversation. *Language, 53*(2), 361–382.

Schegloff, E. A., Koshik, I., Jacoby, S., & Olsher, D. (2002). Conversation analysis and applied linguistics. *Annual Review of Applied Linguistics, 22*, 3–31.

Schegloff, E. A., & Lerner, G. (2009). Beginning to respond: Well-prefaced responses to wh-questions. *Research on Language and Social Interaction, 42*(2), 91–115.

Schegloff, E. A., & Sacks, H. (1973). Opening up closings. *Semiotica, 8*(4), 289–327.

Schulze-Wenck, S. (2005). Form and function of "first verbs" in talk-in-interaction. In A. Hakulinin (Ed.), *Syntax and lexis in conversation* (pp. 319–348). Amsterdam: John Benjamins.

Scotton, C. M., & Bernsten, J. (1988). Natural conversations as a model for textbook dialog. *Applied Linguistics, 9*, 372–384.

Seedhouse, P. (2004). *The interactional architecture of the language classroom: A conversation analysis perspective*. Malden, MA: Blackwell.

Seedhouse, P. (2005a). Conversation analysis and language learning. *Language Teaching, 38*, 165–187.

Seedhouse, P. (2005b). "Task" as research construct. *Language Learning, 55*(3), 553–570.

Shimanoff, S., & Brunak, J. (1977). Repairs in planned and unplanned discourse. In E. Keenan & T. Bennett (Eds.), *Discourse across time and space* (pp. 123–167). Los Angeles: University of Southern California Press.

Sinclair, J., & Coulthard, M. (1975). *Towards an analysis of discourse: The English used by teachers and pupils*. London: Oxford University Press.

Skelt, L. (2007). Damage control: Closing problematic sequences in hearing-impaired interaction. *Australian Review of Applied Linguistic, 30*(3), 1–34.

Stivers, T. (2004). "No no no" and other types of multiple sayings in social interaction. *Human Communication Research, 30*, 260–293.

Stokoe, E. (2009). Doing actions with identity categories: Complaints and denials in neighbor disputes. *Text and Talk, 29*(1), 75–97.

Streeck, J. (1993). Gesture as communication I: Its coordination with gaze and speech. *Communication Monographs, 60,* 275–299.

Streeck, J., & Hartge, U. (1992). Previews: Gestures at the transition place. In P. Auer & A. D. Luzio (Eds.), *The contextualization of language* (pp. 135–157). Amsterdam: John Benjamins.

Takahashi, J. (2009). Constructing multi-unit turns in Japanese: *Te*-form as a TCU-extension resource. Paper presented at the NYSTESOL Applied Linguistics Conference, New York City.

Taleghani-Nikazm, C. (2002). A conversational analytic study of telephone conversation openings between native and nonnative speakers. *Journal of Pragmatics, 34,* 1807–1832.

Tanaka, H. (2001). Adverbials for turn projection in Japanese: Toward a demystification of the "telepathic" mode of communication. *Language in Society, 30*(4), 559–587.

ten Have, P. (2007). *Doing conversation analysis: A practical guide* (2nd edition). London: Sage.

Terasaki, A. K. (2004). Pre-announcement sequences in conversation. In G. Lerner (Ed.), *Conversation analysis: Studies from the first generation* (pp. 171–224). Amsterdam/Philadelphia: John Benjamins.

Thompson, S., & Couper-Kuhlen, E. (2005). The clause as a locus of grammar and interaction. *Discourse Studies, 7*(4–5), 481–506.

Thornbury, S. (2005). *How to teach speaking.* Harlow: Longman.

Thornbury, S., & Slade, D. (2006). *Conversation: From description to pedagogy.* Cambridge: Cambridge University Press.

Trosborg, A. (1995). *Interlanguage pragmatics: Requests, complaints and apologies.* Berlin: Walter de Gruyter.

van Lier, L. (1988). *The classroom and the language learner.* London: Longman.

Vasilopoulou, A. (2005). Greek grammar and interaction: Investigating the projectability of verbs in conversation. Paper presented at the 9th International Pragmatics Conference, Riva del Garda, Italy.

Vogt, M., & Echevarria, J. (2005). *Teaching ideas for implementing the SIOP model.* White Plains, NY: Pearson.

Walker, G. (2007). On the design and use of pivots in everyday English conversation. *Journal of Pragmatics, 39*(12), 2217–2243.

Waring, H. Z. (2001). Balancing the competing interests in seminar discussion: Peer referencing and asserting vulnerability. *Issues in Applied Linguistics, 12*(1), 29–50.

Waring, H. Z. (2005a). Peer tutoring in a graduate writing center: Identity, expertise and advice resisting. *Applied Linguistics, 26,* 141–168.

Waring, H. Z. (2005b). "Yeah yeah yeah" as a state-of-knowledge response. Paper presented at the 9th International Pragmatics Conference: Riva del Garda, Italy.

Waring, H. Z. (2005c). The unofficial businesses of repair initiation: Vehicles for affiliation and disaffiliation. In A. Tyler, M. Takada, Y. Kim, & D. Marinova (Eds.), *Language in use: Cognitive and discourse perspectives on language and language learning* (pp. 163–175). Washington, D.C.: Georgetown University Press.

Waring, H. Z. (2007). The multi-functionality of accounts in advice giving. *Journal of Sociolinguistics. 11*(3), 367–369.

Waring, H. Z. (2008). Using explicit positive assessment in the language classroom: IRF, feedback, and learning opportunities. *Modern Language Journal, 92*(4), 577–594.

Waring, H. Z. (2009). Moving out of IRF: A single case analysis. *Language Learning*, *59*(4), 796–864.

West, C., & Garcia, A. (1988). Conversational shift work: A study of topical transitions between women and men. *Social Problems*, *35*(5), 551–575.

Wolfson, N. (1981). Compliments in cross-cultural perspective. *TESOL Quarterly*, *15*(2), 117–124.

Wolfson, N. (1989). *Perspectives: Sociolinguistics and TESOL*. Boston, MA: Heinle & Heinle.

Wong, J. (1984). Using conversational analysis to evaluate telephone conversations in English as a second language textbooks. Unpublished Master's thesis, University of California, Los Angeles.

Wong, J. (2000a). Repetition in conversation: A look at "first and second sayings." *Research on Language and Social Interaction*, *33*(4), 407–424.

Wong, J. (2000b). The token "yeah" in nonnative speaker English conversation. *Research on Language and Social Interaction*, *33*(1), 39–67.

Wong, J. (2000c). Delayed next turn repair initiation in native/non-native speaker English conversation. *Applied Linguistics*, *21*(1), 244–267.

Wong, J. (2002). "Applying" conversation analysis in applied linguistics: Evaluating English as a second language textbook dialogue. *International Review of Applied Linguistics in Language Teaching* (*IRAL*), *40*, 37–60.

Wong, J. (2004). Some preliminary thoughts on delay as an interactional resource. In R. Gardner & J. Wagner (Eds.), *Second language conversations* (pp. 114–131). London: Continuum.

Wong, J. (2005). Sidestepping grammar. In K. Richards & P. Seedhouse (Eds.), *Applying conversation analysis* (pp. 159–173). Basingstoke: Palgrave.

Wong, J. (2007). Answering my call: A look at telephone closings. In H. Bowles & P. Seedhouse (Eds.), *Conversation analysis and language for specific purposes* (pp. 271–304). Bern: Peter Lang.

Wong, J. (forthcoming a). Telephone talk: Pragmatic competency in conversational openings. In N. Houck & D. Tatsuki (Eds.), *Pragmatics from theory to practice*, Volume 2. Alexandria, VA: TESOL Publications.

Wong, J. (forthcoming b). Telephone talk: Closings. In N. Houck & D. Tatsuki (Eds.), *Pragmatics from theory to practice: New directions*. Volume 2. Alexandria, VA: TESOL Publications.

Wong, J., & Olsher, D. (2000). Reflections on conversation analysis and nonnative speaker talk: An interview with Emanuel A. Schegloff. *Issues in Applied Linguistics*, *11*, 111–128.

Wong, J., & Waring, H. Z. (2009). "Very good" as a teacher response. *ELT Journal*, *63*(3), 195–203.

Wright, M. (2004). The phonetic properties of multi-unit first closing turns in British-English telephone call closing sequences. Colloquium of the British Association of Academic Phoneticians, Cambridge, UK.

Young, R. (2008). *Language and interaction: An advanced resource book*. New York: Routledge.

Young, R. F., & Lee, J. (2004). Identifying units in interaction: Reactive tokens in Korean and English conversations. *Journal of Sociolinguistics*, *8*(3), 380–407.

Young, R. F., & Miller, E. R. (2004). Learning as changing participation: Discourse roles in ESL writing conferences. *Modern Language Journal*, *88*(4), 519–535.

Zimmerman, D. (1998). Identity, context and interaction. In C. Antaki & S. Widdicombe (Eds.), *Identities in talk* (pp. 87–106). London: Sage.

Index

Please note that references to Figures will be in *italic* print